The Trouble With Lawyers

MURRAY TEIGH BLOOM

 SIMON AND SCHUSTER   NEW YORK

In memory of
ANNA TEIGHBLUM
1886–1955

ACKNOWLEDGMENTS

In addition to intensive personal interviewing and research around the country during the past three years, I also employed local researchers for special assignments. These included Jeff Bernstein of the *New York Law Journal;* Paul Dean of the *Arizona Republic;* George Ringwald of the Riverside, California, *Enterprise;* and Anne Tanner of Rochester, New York.

The sources who were particularly helpful are clearly indicated throughout the book. I am most grateful to them. There are others who helped only on condition I not name them. I offer them an appreciative salute and offstage thanks.

I owe gratitude, too, to the Ford Foundation, which provided travel funds for me as a consultant during the gathering of material that is encompassed in the chapter on bar public relations.

There is a continuing debt to the MacDowell Colony of New Hampshire, where most of the book's writing was done, and to my indefatigable typist, Sherley Raices. And, finally, to my wife for enduring with intelligence, good cheer and intuition all the agonies of pre- and post-partum blues accompanying the delivery of a one-pound book after a gestation period of thirty-six months.

CONTENTS

INTRODUCTION

My main purpose is to show how the American middle class is victimized by the American legal profession. This isn't the result of a conspiracy hatched at an American Bar Association convention but an inevitable confluence of events.

The American middle class has become the number one victim and target because it has money and property and lacks, generally, *group* power in state legislatures. As a class it also produces most of our lawyers, so perhaps this might call for lengthy psychoanalytic interpretations involving self-hatred or covert cannibalism. But nothing so hypothetical is involved.

Almost every middle-class legal need is an individual one—accidents, home closings, divorce, wills and estates, or the sale of a business. In each of these instances lawyers have, with the help of the organized bar, made themselves *partners* by fixing their fees as a percentage of the amount of money involved. In his relations with business the legal fee is generally fixed by the amount of time the lawyer expends—at a rate of anywhere from $15 to $100 an hour. But in these basic middle-class needs the percentage arrangement is often the only one the lawyer will accept. The lawyer is supported by his bar association in unilaterally imposed minimum fee agreements. Those expensively balmy words, uttered soothingly to the bewildered widow who suddenly finds that the routine settling of her husband's estate will cost her several thousand dollars, have been heard by millions of us: "It's customary."

The rich can take care of themselves. They can and do hire lawyers on salary as house counsel for their corporation, which means that the lawyer will take care of their personal legal needs

—such as estates, wills, closings and the rest—as part of the job. No extra charge. Unfortunately, most of us can't afford our own salaried lawyer.*

The poor have belated, though commendably increasing access to Legalcare and Legal Aid and OEO neighborhood law offices for their jousts with landlords, installment sellers, the divorce courts or even the criminal courts. How *poor* do you have to be to qualify? Not only is poverty miserable, its perimeters are fuzzy: In New York a family of four would be eligible for Community Action for Legal Services if it didn't earn more than $4,500; under Wisconsin's Judicare it would be $4,160; in Nassau County, New York, Legal Aid would take the same family if its total income didn't exceed $6,000; in Philadelphia the cutoff point for the same family would be just under $5,000.

In general, then, if you earn more than $6,000 a year, or have at least $500 in the bank, you can consider yourself middle class in terms of getting a lawyer. This book is for you. *Us.*

Too poor for permanent house counsel and too prosperous for legal aid, we are the fattest prey. Not only are there more of us, but in many ways we are the most helpless.

This is a somewhat unbalanced book. The modern athletic reader—he who reads on the run and jumps to wrong conclusions —may get the impression that most lawyers are crooks or scoundrels or at best expensive cheats. Not only would such a reader be wrong, he would have missed the whole point. Most of our lawyers *are* fairly honest, more or less upright and, in the main, quite decent men. They can be all that—pillars of the community as well—and still be terribly unfair to the American middle class. The modern legal game is one they have devised. The penalties, forfeits and fees are of their making. Even if they abide by the one-sided rules strictly and ethically, it would be completely impossible for us to ever win their game. We can't even hope for a

---

* An October, 1967, brief filed with the U. S. Supreme Court describes the system thus: "It is well known that many companies offer this service to their executives. In some cases, staff or retained counsel charge the executives a discounted fee or no fee for private services; in others, the fee is the usual fee for the service, but is billed to the corporation."

tie. I suppose in time some of us could learn to be good, perpetual losers. But losing is always damned expensive as well as galling.

It is almost too easy for our lawyers. Given the circumstances I wonder if some candid lawyer hasn't paraphrased—out of client earshot, of course—the honest indignation of Lord Clive. In 1773 before a Parliamentary inquiry on his enormous personal grab in India as Governor of Bengal, Clive exclaimed: "By God, Mr. Chairman, at this moment I stand astonished at my own moderation."

"My way of joking is to tell the truth," said George Bernard Shaw. Joseph H. Choate, a great and wealthy American lawyer, had his own joking truth. Once in a dinner speech before the New York State Chamber of Commerce he had them rolling with this one:

> Every man in the community owes a duty to our profession; somewhere between the cradle and the grave he must acknowledge the liability and pay the debt. . . . It was one of the brightest members of the profession, you remember, who had taken his passage for Europe . . . and failed to go. He said one of his rich clients died and he was afraid if he had gone across the Atlantic, the heirs would have gotten all the property.

Times change and that kind of joking is pretty much out today for lawyers. Fun's fun but truth can be troublesome. We don't seem to have the sense of humor our fathers had, or maybe there are just more spoilsport public relations men around at dinners.

That most influential poor man of our age, Karl Marx, once said that money annuls all human relationships. But money is not the only problem here. There are other fractious conditions in the relationships between Americans and their lawyers that need change—great change. For example, the chapter on client security funds discusses the inadequacy of the existing safeguards for the monies held or collected by lawyers for clients; and the small likelihood of restitution when lawyers steal such funds. The reluctance of the Bar and the courts to investigate, try and punish erring lawyers is described in another chapter. And still another section discusses the surprising problems that arise when stupid, lazy or inept lawyers handle certain matters for trusting clients.

I know that individual lawyers have shown great courage in defending unpopular clients—anarchists in the 1880s; communists in the 1950s and civil rights battlers in the 1960s. I know that lawyers have made great individual contributions to useful legislation, to a sharpened sense of justice for all. They are necessary and useful. In an increasingly complex world middle-class America will need more and more legal help.

Recently, I visited Fred Rodell of the Yale University Law School faculty. Considered one of our most astute students of the U. S. Supreme Court, Professor Rodell is, at sixty, also the most antilawyer lawyer in the country.

In 1939 Professor Rodell, who earned a living as a journalist before turning to law, wrote an explosive little book called *Woe Unto You, Lawyers.* Several law reviews said the professor was just kidding. He wasn't. He grandly advocated the abolition of the legal profession. ("You know, I didn't get a raise for ten years after *that,*" Rodell recalls. "I was passed over like a lefthanded third baseman ten times in a row.") This law professor, who had never practiced law and belonged to no bar association, advocated a world without courts or lawyers, of nonlawyer experts deciding disputes.

Tall, thin, hunched-over Fred Rodell is surely the most informally dressed faculty member on the Yale campus. In his chinos, beat-up plaid shirt, bolo tie and a disreputable furled-over Stetson, he looked like the Marlboro cigarette man grown older. And wiser. Once a more than three-packs-a-day man, Professor Rodell has been tamed into the comparative safety of pipe smoking.

In the 1939 book, Fred Rodell wrote in concluding his preface: "I outlined my ideas about the book, and about the law, to a lawyer who is not only able but also extraordinarily frank and perceptive about his profession. 'Sure,' he said, 'but why give the show away?' "

I asked who it was even though I sensed a name clue. He smiled. "Well, he's dead now so I suppose it's all right. It was

Jerome Frank." Frank, one of the great—and controversial—federal judges of the century, was also a legal philosopher with sharp insights into the law, its pretensions and contradictions.

Another legal authority who liked Rodell's book was his friend, Associate Justice William O. Douglas of the U. S. Supreme Court. In 1957 Justice Douglas, the most peripatetic Supreme Court justice in our history, visited Swat, a principality that is part of Pakistan. The Wali of Swat rules his little country firmly and has his own ideas on lawyers and courts. Justice Douglas reported this conversation:

"How many lawyers do you have in Swat," I asked the Wali.
"None," he said.
"Who represents the defendant in a civil suit, or the accused in a criminal case?"
"The defendant himself," said the Wali. "But the judge, of course, sees that he gets a fair trial."
I asked what would happen if an accused felt that he needed a lawyer.
"None would be appointed. You see, Mr. Justice, up here in Swat we have concluded that a lawyer only makes a lawsuit complicated and confusing."

Fred Rodell still isn't prepared to take back a single line he wrote in 1939. He made his feelings pretty clear in an article he did in 1962 for the *Virginia Law Review:*

. . . while law is supposed to be a device to serve society, a civilized way of helping the wheels go round without too much friction, it is pretty hard to find a group less concerned with serving society and more concerned with serving themselves than the lawyers.

He still believes we should do away with lawyers, even if he no longer is sure just how that could be done.

In some ways it isn't a new idea at all. It has been slumbering restlessly in New England soil for nearly two centuries. In 1786 there were general demands in New Hampshire and Vermont that courts should be abolished and the lawyers suppressed. Lawyers were mobbed in the streets and judges threatened. In Massachusetts, town meetings subscribed to solemn resolutions which warned that without a proper check or restraint "that order of Gentlemen denominated Lawyers" would destroy rather than preserve the Commonwealth.

Two centuries have mellowed most of our lingering antipathies. The utopian idea of doing away with lawyers is not for our time—or our children's time. Since lawyers are going to be with us for a long time, let us now make an overdue examination of what is wrong with the legal profession in its relations with the American middle class.

Exposé books are often blemished by the author's lack of peripheral vision, his dogmatic crankiness, his monomania. I hope I've avoided these shortcomings. It is not easy when the subject calls for partisanship, even stridency on behalf of the victim.

Every few years a book appears—usually from a vanity press—telling, in righteous tones, of somebody's ten- or twenty-year battle with the courts or lawyers or a referee in incompetency hearings. They are usually poorly written, almost impossible to follow and filled with exclamation points. As the eyes clamber over these picket fences you drop more and more of your sympathy for the poor fellow. About halfway through the book you are struck by the fact that the author is not so much the object of a devilish conspiracy, but one of "those victims who invite the crime," in the words of criminologist Hans von Hentig. Yet these sad little books color vaguely with the tincts of truth. Cracked bells may not ring true but they can sound an alarm.

The people and situations I write about in this book are not cranks or armed prophets determined to give the world their own skewed vision. Most of them are fairly ordinary people who, like the rest of us, normally want to avoid trouble and fuss as much as possible. The situations they find themselves in are not extraordinary or rare. Mostly they are trying to overcome the lawyers' unfair advantage. Occasionally they are trapped by their own stupidity or stubborn refusal to take proper action in time. But even this is due mostly to fear of the law in all guises—sheriff's auction, garnishee, foreclosure and, of course, lawyers themselves.

Obviously I do have a bias: I am against the present one-sided relationship of the bar with the middle class. That aside, I can in all candor say I like and admire several lawyers immensely; and to honor the mocking cliché, several *are* friends. In fact, without the assistance of some lawyers who are also critical of much in the relationships of the bar and the public, I could not have gathered much of the material for this book.

Wherever possible I have given the names of my informants or the sources where the material was found. But this is not always possible, particularly when the sources' comments are indiscreet or even dangerous to their professional careers. So from time to time through this book you will find quotations for which I do not provide accompanying names and titles. Inevitably this raises the question of verifiability. Writers have been known to make up particularly apposite quotes when their interviewees didn't have the desire or courage to provide them. I offer in affirmation of the genuineness of the unattributed quotes the reputation of a professional writer of magazine articles for more than twenty-five years. Most magazines today have staffs of researchers who check every fact, every quote in a writer's article. A writer guilty of manufacturing quotes and incidents would not last in the business.

Mostly, I hope the unattributed quotes have their own sounds of truth. Sometimes, insiders will recognize the sources. The ex-investigator for the Midwest bar association will be quickly identified by dozens of knowing lawyers in that region.

But more often the attribution is given fully with names and positions. Fortunately, there are lawyers and judges and state officials who have spoken out quite boldly about the evils and abuses in the legal profession. Upon them and upon an aroused public rests our main hope for changing the incredible laws and unilateral bar association rules that are described in this book.

There is the author. What are his crotchets, prejudices and sad experiences that make him so one-sided in his condemnations? What lawyer bit him?

I have been in court as an involved party three times. The first time I sued a man about a contract. With the help of a most able lawyer and a sympathetic jury, I was awarded everything I asked for. The second time was a libel suit, the only one in my career. The magazine was being sued for an article I had written. The plaintiff, a Florida lawyer, admitted that my facts were correct but alleged that I was motivated by personal malice against him, even though we had never met or had any connection, however remote. The basis of his allegation was so preposterous that the jury and judge were openmouthed as he finished his account. The jury was out fourteen minutes, having spent eight minutes selecting a foreman. They came back with a verdict for the magazine and myself.

The third and most recent occasion was in March, 1968, in Federal District Court in New York City. A judge ruled that an article I had written for *Playboy* had been grossly plagiarized by a writer who had sold an article with a similar theme—and many totally similar paragraphs—to another popular magazine. I received $4500 in damages from the offending publication. Again my attorney was thorough, well-prepared and a pleasure to work with. He took the case on a fair 25% contingency and I felt he fully deserved the $1125 fee.

One final, parenthetical note about me and lawyers. I happen to share the same birthday, May 19, with Honest St. Ives, the patron saint of lawyers. A memorial window to this thirteenth-century lawyer, made possible by contributions from American attorneys, was dedicated in 1936 in the Cathedral of Tréguier in France. Of him it was said in his day that he was "a lawyer but no crook, a thing which astonished the people. . . . He defends the children, the widows, and all friendless people. Not only does he accept their defense, but he seeks them as clients . . . he gives them good counsel and he pleads for them. And for all this he receives his reward from God."

That, of course, was seven centuries ago.

1 CLIENTS' MONEY

Apologists for the profession contend that lawyers are as honest as other men, but this is not very encouraging.
—FERDINAND LUNDBERG

How do you get along at the office? Do you trust each other? Or does each have a separate safe for his money?
—GROUCHO MARX
In a letter to Boston lawyer Joseph Welch, after seeing the long list of attorneys on the firm's stationery

Late on a summer day in 1960 Angelo Cometa, a twenty-eight-year-old attorney working in the Indictment Bureau of the New York District Attorney, was about to leave when one of the office messengers asked if he could speak to him for a minute.

Cometa, who comes from Pittston, Pennsylvania, and went to Fordham University Law School, had been in the office about a year and was then earning $7,000. He is short, slender, has a high forehead and is easy to talk to. José Vasquez, the young Puerto Rican messenger, may have thought that a fellow Latin would listen more readily to his strange story.

José had an uncle, Julio Rodriguez Gonzalez, who had been a Korean War veteran. In 1953 the Army chartered a flight to take thirty-five Korean veterans from Camp Kilmer in New Jersey to Standiford Air Force Base in Louisville, Kentucky, to be mustered out. Approaching the field, the Resort Airlines charter flight crashed. Seventeen men survived; eighteen were killed. José's uncle was one of the lucky ones. He was now living, crippled and facially disfigured, in the hills of central Puerto Rico. For the neighborhood he was a rich man.

His "wealth" had come from the negligence trial award that resulted. The widows and orphans of the dead Puerto Rican soldiers had hired Puerto Rican attorneys. They, in turn, turned to one of the leading negligence attorneys in New York, a specialist in plane crash cases, Jerome Golenbock.

In Federal District Court in New York a jury awarded the widows and orphans of the dead soldiers, and the injured soldiers, a total sum of $1,429,000. It was a great 1957 victory for Golenbock.

José's Uncle Julio was awarded $115,000. Actually, he didn't get all the money. First he paid a third of it—about $38,000—to lawyer Golenbock, who had handled the case on a contingent fee basis. Still, $77,000 could go a long way in central Puerto Rico. But he didn't have that much, either. When José's uncle was in New York the big lawyer, Golenbock, had a talk with him and persuaded him to invest the money in special bonds. Bonds of the Esquire Factors Corporation, which lent money at high interest rates to manufacturers. The bonds would pay 15 percent interest. José's uncle was persuaded and left $52,000 with attorney Golenbock, who assured him "it was a sure thing, the bonds were guaranteed."

For several months the interest payments came through regularly, but now there had been delays and José's uncle wrote the lawyer to get his money back. Lawyer Golenbock wrote soothing letters—without checks. The uncle had now written his nephew, José, a full account. Since he was working for the New York *Fiscal* (prosecutor), perhaps he could find out more about this troubling matter.

Recalling the narration of that summer day, Angelo Cometa says: "It sounded strange to me but I knew it was *too* strange for the uncle or José to have made up. I thought that the uncle made a questionable investment on his own, but still maybe it would be a good idea to have Golenbock in for a private talk."

Cometa had some qualms. Golenbock was one of the city's most respected and ablest negligence lawyers, a man who had won many big cases. The gossip among his fellow lawyers was that he was moving up quickly and before long would be up there among the giants of negligence such as Jacob Fuchsberg and Harry Gair, for whom it was a bad year when each didn't make at least $200,-000 in contingent fees. Golenbock, who had gone to Dartmouth and New York University Law School, wasn't in their class yet, but he was believed to be making at least $100,000 a year in fees and had recently been president of the New York State Association of Plaintiff's Trial Lawyers.

Golenbock, a short fellow in his mid-forties, came in readily. He was quiet, unassuming and "almost timid," Cometa recalls. "He didn't look like anyone's idea of what a successful courtroom lawyer should look like. I told him about the war veteran in Puerto Rico—without letting on where the information came from. And then I said: 'Look, Mr. Golenbock. This is not a criminal situation but it is pretty strange. This bond business could sound bad for you and for the bar.' He agreed and said if the man wanted his money back he'd see to it. He had just tried to be helpful and keep his client from putting his money into wild schemes."

Meanwhile José's uncle had been active in Puerto Rico. He got in touch with other families who had been persuaded to invest in the bonds, and they, too, had been having difficulty getting their money. Word got out and they wrote to Angelo Cometa. There were other, even more disturbing letters. These were from widows of the dead soldiers. They wrote that the money the court awarded their children had been placed in trust but they hadn't seen any of it yet.

In September, 1960, Angelo Cometa had been transferred to the Rackets Bureau of the District Attorney's office. He talked to his boss, Frank Hogan, New York's perennial DA, and asked to be allowed to go to Puerto Rico with a Spanish-speaking detective. Hector Velez, a fine cop, who had been born in Puerto Rico, was chosen. In February, 1961, Cometa and Velez flew down.

"We asked the Police Chief in San Juan for help in finding these people. We were down there three weeks and interviewed twenty families all over the island. Most of these people didn't have phones, and some were pretty hard to find. One of them lived on a mountaintop and at the end of an awful road. Most of their stories were the same: the money for their children had been placed in trust until they were twenty-one, with the parent named as guardian. But none of the mothers had been told where the money had been deposited, and they hadn't heard from lawyer Golenbock. We added it all up and found that $203,940 was involved. All of them gave us signed statements, including Uncle Julio, who was still owed $32,000 by Golenbock."

Back in New York, Cometa called Golenbock in and told him what he had unearthed in Puerto Rico. "I asked him if he could help me 'clarify' the situation."

Golenbock said the money was missing, all right. Some of his staff—he employed twenty-two—had stolen it. He was out of the office most of the time, and he simply had not been able to supervise his staff adequately to prevent the theft.

When he found out the money had been stolen did he call the police? No. He hoped his employes would replace the money. Had they? No.

Golenbock was indicted and now other aspects of his difficulties became clear. Not only was the Puerto Rican children's money gone, but he had improperly withheld "for protracted periods approximately $85,000 out of recoveries in forty other accident cases."

He had invested $700,000 in two upstate New York companies, both of which went bankrupt within six months after he made his investments. He had borrowed $175,000 from a bank, which was now seeking repayment. Belatedly, he discovered his office overhead was much too much. He forged several notes which he attempted to borrow against. Internal Revenue was owed $21,000 on income taxes withheld from his twenty-two employes. And he owed money to other lawyers who had sent him cases. He had also purchased seventy-five personal injury cases from other lawyers for $56,500. None of the injured parties involved had been consulted, a clear violation of legal ethics.

On May 20, 1962, he was suspended from law practice. He

pleaded guilty to felony charges and resigned from the bar. Judge Joseph A. Sarafite, Jr., agreed to postpone sentencing on the plea of Golenbock's attorney that his client was trying desperately to make restitution to the Puerto Rican clients. On April 26, 1963, Judge Sarafite asked what restitution had been made. Golenbock's attorney admitted that nothing had been paid the victims but that his client had signed a promissory note payable to the court-appoined guardians of the children. If he got probation instead of a prison sentence, friends of the Golenbock family in Stamford, Connecticut, where he had been a leader in Cub Scout activities, had agreed to pay $20,000 on his behalf toward restitution. But all the notes and the promises didn't add up to a dime of repayment of his theft, Judge Sarafite pointed out to Golenbock's attorney, who pleaded for a suspended sentence:

> The great fallacy of your argument is that it is premised on the proposition that any defendant who commits a larceny may brazenly steal and then know that so long as he promises to pay back that he can buy his way out of jail.

Unmoved by the fact that Mrs. Golenbock had had a nervous breakdown and there were three Golenbock children, Judge Sarafite sentenced Golenbock to two and a half to five years in Sing Sing. In January, 1964, Golenbock appealed but his sentence was upheld, and soon after he began to serve his time. He served a little less than two years and came out early in 1966. He is now negotiating and insuring corporate loans for manufacturers and suppliers. (In most states a disbarred and once imprisoned lawyer has surprisingly good chances of getting back into law two to five years after his disbarment. In New York it almost never happens.)

Golenbock paid back only $4,500 to his victims and former clients. Since the case involved many widows and orphans, it became the particular concern of Federal Judge Frederick Van Pelt Bryan, in whose court Golenbock had won the original $1,429,000 judgment. Judge Bryan turned to Orison Marden, who was then president of the Association of the Bar of New York—he has since become president of the American Bar Association—and Leo Gottlieb, then vice president of the New York County Lawyers Association, which has 10,000 members in Manhattan and is the largest local bar group in the nation.

Judge Bryan asked them to act as special guardians for the victimized infants and their mothers. In addition he appointed as counsel for them Eugene A. Sherpick, president of the County Bar Association; Harry Gair, a leading negligence attorney; and Harris Steinberg, a prominent defense counsel in white-collar criminal cases.

Gottlieb, who is short, energetic and blue-eyed, doesn't look his age: he is past seventy and a senior partner in the prestigious New York law firm of Cleary, Gottlieb and Steen. He graduated from Yale's Sheffield Scientific School before going to Harvard Law. Recently, he recalled the problem and the work these lawyers had done.

"What we had to do was see how we could get some money for these youngsters and their mothers. The case was a stinking shame, and as leaders of the bar we felt terrible. What we did is go back over the whole case from the beginning. I put a bright lawyer in my office, Herb Scheyer, on it and told him to spare no expense. All of us who had been assigned by Judge Bryan agreed right away we wouldn't make any charge for our services and that we'd ante up necessary expenses. So we sent Herb Scheyer to Puerto Rico and he came up with our one hope to recover some money for the victims. It was narrow and technical as hell but it was our only hope."

The aviation insurance company that had covered Resort Airlines had made its check payable to Golenbock directly because it had been taking a long time to get the necessary court documents covering each widow and her children from the Puerto Rican courts. Meanwhile, as long as the money remained unpaid, interest at 6 percent was accumulating on the payment. In order to avoid further interest payment, the insurance company took a common shortcut and simply made out the check to Golenbock, who was, after all, a leading and reputable attorney.

"In New York this is a common practice when there is a long

list of plaintiffs who are going to share in the award—after the attorney has deducted his fee," Gottlieb went on. "If the children had been living here in New York we wouldn't have had a leg to stand on. But they were living in Puerto Rico and the law was different. We got together with the lawyers for the insurance company and showed them that a technical violation had taken place: the insurance check should have been made out individually to the children and their guardians, their mothers."

The insurance company naturally refused to ante up any more money. They had paid in full in accord with the verdict. When the pressure of the court-appointed special guardians for the children mounted, the company turned on *their* attorneys. If the checks had been made out improperly, it had been done on advice of their attorneys, who should have known better. Let the attorneys pay—or the insurance companies that covered them for malpractice.

"It was a real hassle," Leo Gottlieb recalls. "These were all honest, capable lawyers but a *mistake* had been made. Technical but still a mistake. And there were the widows and orphans."

Eventually a compromise was reached. The widows and orphans would get another $100,000, mostly provided by the aviation insurance company and the rest by the lawyers' malpractice insurance. The only condition: no publicity.

"It was a fair compromise," Leo Gottlieb says. "Of course, if any of us charged them our regular rates they would have gotten a lot less. I figure the lawyers assigned the case by Judge Bryan put in at least $25,000 worth of high-powered time on the case. All donated, of course."

José's uncle, Julio, the Korean veteran who really started the whole case, didn't benefit. He wasn't a widow or orphan. Angelo Cometa went on from the DA's office to another post where he could concentrate on the ethical shortcomings—and occasional defalcations—of personal injury or negligence lawyers. He is now chief counsel of the Coordinating Committee on Discipline of the three bar associations in Manhattan and the Bronx. We will encounter him and his present work in another chapter.

The incident made a deep impression on Eugene A. Sherpick,

who was elected president of the New York County Lawyers Association in May, 1962. After his induction as president he told of what he and several other lawyers had been doing in the matter of the Puerto Rican children. He said if the incident had taken place

in England, in any Province of Canada; in New Zealand or any one of 14 states of this Union . . . these infants would have received some or all of the money they were entitled to. Why? Because in all these places, the members of the bar have established client indemnity funds to take care of those rare instances where one of their brothers commits a defalcation. . . . But when they come to us in the Empire State or in the greatest city in the world, we of the bar say: "Am I my brother's keeper?" It's high time that we catch up, that a fund be set up now. It's an obligation and our duty to go forward.

As a result of his plea the New York County Lawyers did create a Client Security Fund in the fall of 1962. The association contributed $5,000, and with private donations from members it now has $40,000. Actually, the Puerto Rican children did better without the fund, which limits itself to a $5,000 limit in any one case. Of course, the fund would have been wiped out several times over if it had been used to pay the Puerto Ricans.

Recently I visited Joseph Maged, the slender seventy-year-old executive secretary of the New York County Lawyers Association, to find out how the fund had been doing in the past five years. Maged, a veteran attorney, pulled out the Client Security Fund file and told me that only one claim had been paid so far, for $300. The lawyer involved hadn't paid the judgment proceeds of a $694 award to a client. Ironically, the check here, too, had been made out to the lawyer alone, and he had cashed it and kept the money. Before he could be prosecuted, he died. In another case the fund was probably going to pay out $3,200. Here the client was supposed to get the money in a real estate transaction. The lawyer misused the money.

I told Maged I was puzzled that those were the only two claims in the past five years. He laughed: "You can't walk around the world and think everyone is a crook."

"Some years ago Ed Bernays, the public relations fellow, did a survey for us on the public image of the lawyer. He wrote 300 ministers, doctors, officials, architects and engineers: what did they think of lawyers? Well, they didn't think too much. Didn't surprise me. I told Ed he'd made a big mistake. He should have asked them what do you think of your *own* lawyer, and I bet he would have gotten very different answers."

I said there were at least five New Yorkers at the moment who thought very little of their *own* lawyers. I showed him three recent *New York Times* clippings of lawyers indicted for thefts from clients in Manhattan. One was indicted in 1965 for stealing $86,000 of a schoolteacher's inheritance; another had taken $20,000 from a bankrupt estate for which he had been acting as trustee; and a third was indicted in 1966 for stealing $169,000 from three aged clients.*

Maged read the clips carefully and said he too was surprised that no claims on the fund had been made by any of these victims. Admittedly, $5,000 would not have repaid them much of their great losses, but still . . . He phoned a lawyer who was on the County Bar's disciplinary committee:

"You people know about our Client Security Fund, don't you?" Clearly enough for me to hear through the receiver came the lawyer's reply: "Never heard of it."

Mr. Maged was embarrassed. "Maybe it's our fault. We don't publicize the fund. I guess we don't want to get swamped with letters and claims, so we don't shout it from the housetops, but I guess the whisper didn't reach all the people who should know. I was *sure* all the disciplinary committees and the DAs knew about it. . . . Maybe our trouble is that the bar isn't sure yet how much publicity these cases will get us, even if we pay the victim."

As of June 15, 1967, according to the Special Committee on Client Security Funds of the American Bar Association, there were twenty-seven state funds and six county bar funds in opera-

*What happened to these lawyers? The one who took $169,000 pleaded guilty and was given a year sentence in Sing Sing. The one who stole from the bankrupt estate was found guilty and given a suspended sentence with three years on probation. The third had not been tried at this writing. In none of these cases was there any restitution to the victims.

tion with assets of about a million dollars. About $125,000 had been paid out in claims since the funds were begun.

So little has been paid out because even with client security funds, the remedy is hardly certain or even adequate. Many of the funds have inbuilt limitations—usually up to $5,000 per instance of lawyer theft or $10,000 for all the offenses of any single attorney, as in West Virginia. In many states there can be no restitution unless the offending attorney has died, been adjudged mentally incompetent, been disbarred or suspended from practice, or has resigned from the bar. In Arizona and North Dakota the client has to exhaust all his legal remedies—such as suing the involved lawyer in a civil action—before applying to the fund for restitution. Louisiana, where a fund was established in 1961, requires the victimized client to "exhaust all possible remedies against any source legally or *morally* responsible." (Sue the lawyer's minister for not inculcating proper ethical and religious principles?) Understandably the Louisiana Client Security Fund hadn't paid out a dollar as of June, 1967.

Thus, even if there were the most liberal administration of these funds there are still enough exclusions and tightfisted footnotes to eliminate many victims from restitution.

The comparatively small payout to victimized clients was noted in a recent annual report of the ABA's Client Security Fund Committee:

This . . . relatively small amount of claims paid, as to both number and size of claims . . . appears to be attributable to the fact that many of the funds have received little or no publicity in their respective states. . . .

The reluctance of most fund administrators to publicize their fund's operation is based upon a concern for building up the fund to a meaningful amount and a fear that a flood of claims or applications for reimbursement would follow from widespread publicity. . . . Unless some measure of publicizing of a fund is undertaken, at least within the bar itself and to individuals who might be considered to be proper applicants, through the work of the grievance committees, one aspect of the value and significance of a Client Security Fund—the public relations aspect—may well be lost.

The great secrecy of some of the client security funds was illustrated for me when I inquired about a case reported in the April 19, 1966, issue of the Denver *Post*. According to the item, Phillip Gerald Collins, a former Denver attorney now located in Minnesota, had been "publicly reprimanded by the Colorado Supreme Court for unethical legal practice." The court, acting on the advice of its Grievance Committee, found him guilty of "grave abuses." Collins, according to the news item, had accepted a $240 fee to file a bankruptcy proceeding, but never filed the case. He also allegedly received $872 from a client to pay a list of bad checks issued by a relative of the client, but failed to account for the money.

I wanted to know if there had been any compensation for Collins' clients, and I wrote to William B. Miller, executive secretary of the Colorado Bar Association, which has about $27,000 in its Client Security Fund. Mr. Miller wasn't of much help, beyond admitting that the Colorado Bar does have such a fund: "The proceedings of this committee are completely confidential and we have no knowledge as to whether or not its assistance was invoked in the case you cited."

An Arizona friend sent me a clip from the *Yuma Daily Sun* for October 22, 1964:

ATTORNEYS REIMBURSE
DEFRAUDED WIDOW

A Phoenix widow received $4,000 from the Client Security Fund of the State Bar of Arizona to reimburse her for funds misappropriated by an attorney.

It left so much unsaid that at the Honolulu meeting of the American Bar Association in August, 1967, I sought out Robert A. May, who is chairman of the Arizona Bar's Client Security Fund.

I mentioned the size of the item. "Why doesn't the press give us better coverage on this?" he asked. I said without the name of the lawyer and what punishment was meted out to him, the papers didn't have much to go on.

Mr. May was skeptical. "I think the real problem is a lot of newspaper editors in our state don't like lawyers and just won't give us a break when we shell out $4,000 voluntarily as we did in this case."

I said something about it being, after all, simple justice and fair play for the organized bar to recompense victims of thieving lawyers, regardless of the favorable publicity it might garner. Mr. May shook his head: "There's nothing simple about it. There's a real battle in the bar every time one of these funds is established. An awful lot of lawyers are dead set against them."

He wasn't exaggerating. The organized opposition to these client security funds by lawyers is still so strong that twenty-three states have yet to adopt them. How deep-seated lawyer opposition to them still is can be seen by a close look at the battle that took place in the Oregon Legislature in 1967.

Since 1959 some Oregon lawyers have tried to get the State Legislature to institute a fund by permitting the State Bar to tax each member fifteen dollars a year.

One of the earliest points of opposition was that the fund wasn't needed; there just weren't any serious cases in the state of theft of client money by lawyers. The bar's client security fund proponents decided to do a little investigating. Their 1960 report went: "There seems to be an impression that losses from embezzlement, defalcation, misappropriation and the like, by Oregon lawyers, have been minor in amount. Unfortunately this has not been true." And the report gave recent cases in which lawyers had embezzled amounts ranging from $2,000 to $125,000.

But the report was dismissed by lawyers in the legislature after having heard testimony from several prominent attorneys as to why the fund was not needed. One of them, Robert Bennett of Portland, said Oregon attorneys were "overwhelmingly honest." All the bar had to do, he added, was give closer scrutiny of incoming members, and attorneys who were convicted of client fund theft should be "forever disbarred," a backhanded acknowledgment that disbarment of a dishonest lawyer seldom was forever in most states. Another opponent called the bill "a reflection on the profession" and noted that the bar had "repudiated" similar proposals in the past.

That these two lawyers accurately reflected the sentiment of the Oregon Bar was shown in a mail ballot conducted in 1963. Not all the state's 2,500 lawyers replied, but of those that did, 1,079 voted against the establishment of a fund and only 658 for.

For years the bill was introduced and seldom got out of the Judiciary Committee, 90 percent of whom were lawyers. Then came a shocking embezzlement in 1965. A Klamath Falls lawyer, William R. Bradshaw, stole $100,000 from two estates. He was found guilty and sentenced to three years, but there was no restitution to his victims.

Howard Willits, a legislator from Portland who had been introducing client security fund bills since 1965, thinks that this case may have helped turn the tide in the 1967 legislature, which finally voted for the fund's establishment on a modest scale.

"We aren't too proud of it," Howard Willits told me recently. "It's pretty battle-scarred. After the bar puts in $7,500, every lawyer in the state—about 2,600 now—has to put in another $5 a year. This won't take care of many victims but it is a start."

In one form or another the plan has been considered by U.S. bar associations ever since 1946 when a Sacramento lawyer, Kenneth G. McGilvray, did an article for his state bar journal on the operation of the Client Security Fund in New Zealand. McGilvray had been stationed there during World War II.

New Zealand's solicitors were the world's pioneers. There every practicing solicitor has to make a compulsory annual contribution to the fund before he can get his practicing certificate for the year. Queensland, Australia, followed in 1930, and then came Alberta in Canada in 1939. Two years later the solicitors of England and those of South Africa adopted similar funds to protect clients against thieving attorneys. Today nineteen foreign countries have variations on the plan, with Sweden the latest to join in 1960.

The first state to give it even passing consideration was Oklahoma, because the president of the State Bar Association was Hicks Epton, a wise, courtly attorney from Wewoka. When he proposed a client security fund in December 1953 at the State Bar Convention, Epton recalls:

I got the support of seven of the 150 delegates and five of them came to me afterwards and said they wanted it unmistakably clear that they were not for the proposal but had stultified themselves out of long-standing personal friendship. Not since Custer's defeat at the Battle of Little Big Horn has a battle been so decisively lost.

Soon afterward Epton was appointed chairman of the first Client Security Funds Committee in the American Bar Association. "Our success was a little better," he told me. "We escaped with our lives."

Hicks Epton had long felt that the profession "simply could not escape the responsibility of protecting in some way the public from its rare deviates." During the terrible depression days in Oklahoma—so bad that those miserable wanderers, the Okies, had to leave—Epton remembers

passing the hat several times among the more fortunate of our brethren to see that a widow could pay her grocery bill after an almost equally hard pressed and incompetent lawyer had "borrowed" trust funds and had been unable to repay before he died and his defalcation was discovered.

In the United States, Vermont was the first state to institute such a fund, in 1959. For a bright time Graham L. Sterling, then president of the California State Bar, had felt certain that his regime would see the first establishment of a client security fund in a major state. Sterling, the senior partner of one of the largest law firms in the state, O'Melveny & Myers of Los Angeles, campaigned actively, spoke often and persuaded other State Bar leaders.

"I thought it would go through," he said not long ago during a talk in his office, "but I underestimated the resistance to increasing State Bar dues to pay for the fund. The pocketbook nerve was a live one, all right."

He gave me a copy of the talk he delivered many times in 1958–1959 during his presidency. It is in many ways the most cogent and persuasive argument for the fund, and parts of it are worth quoting:

It is because we hold ourselves out to the public as a learned and honorable profession, in whose members the public is entitled to have trust and confidence. We say, "You can trust us, not only with your innermost secrets, but with your money and other property." When one of us betrays that trust flagrantly by stealing the entrustor's money, we are all to a degree responsible for that breach of trust and therefore we should do everything in our power to make restitution to the client. . . . This obligation has been called a debt of honor of the profession and I firmly believe it is just that. . . .

Sterling's opponents had their own cogent arguments as to why the client security fund was not only unnecessary but even dangerous. First they considered the public relations aspects, in one of the frankest expressions of cynical self-interest ever issued by any group of United States lawyers:

If the plan is to be adopted at all it should be because we as lawyers believe that it will benefit our profession through better public relations, and if it does not result in better public relations it should not be adopted.

Having stepped out boldly onto the dangerous plane of very blunt speaking, the plan's opponents went further:

We believe that such a plan would not only fail in its goal of bettering public relations but it might well result in worsening public relations and increase the problems that now confront the bar and its members in their relations with the public.

How could the bar's relations become *worse* by voluntarily paying the victim of a thieving member of the bar? Very easily:

To adopt an indemnity plan . . . would in the eyes of the public be an official recognition of the fact that the legal profession is the one profession in the country whose members are so corrupt that it must assess itself to indemnify the public against the dishonesty of its members. . . . We believe the public would feel that we are doing so, not because of an exalted sense of duty, but because of our own sense of guilt.

Besides, most people, victimized or not, are ungrateful. And after all, not *every* victim of a lawyer's dubious ethics could be helped:

> To adopt such a plan would publicize the dishonesty of lawyers. . . . We do not think the answer lies in providing the free press with a continued source for such publicity from within the profession itself. The majority of the Committee feels that this will be partly offset because the reimbursed client may become a "walking advertisement" for the integrity of the bar. We doubt this. He is more apt to say, "My lawyer was dishonest. Even the Bar Association found him so and had to pay me back. But look how long it took them to do it and what a small part of my loss they repaid. I don't think they would have repaid anything if they hadn't had to. If they owed me anything they owed me all I lost. As far as I am concerned they are all alike."

Further, why make it easier for people to complain about thieving lawyers. Giving a chance to "make money" out of a complaint is very dangerous:

> Such a plan would unjustifiably encourage and increase charges of dishonesty against members of the bar. Normally a client will not make a charge of dishonesty against his lawyer without clear grounds for doing so. To file such a charge results in no personal gain to the client and he hesitates to involve himself in a disciplinary proceeding unless he has a strong sense of public duty or is unusually bitter toward the lawyer. *This is as it should be.* [Emphasis added.] . . . we do not believe that it is in the best interests of the public or the bar . . . to inject into these proceedings the impetus of personal gain.

Besides, once you start this kind of business it can lead to even more dangerous kinds of action by the public against lawyers.

> The adoption of such a plan could well promote not only charges of dishonesty against members of the bar but also actions for malpractice based upon claims of simple negligence. . . . After a client has been encouraged to file charges against his lawyer in the hope of obtaining indemnity under this plan, and is refused such indemnity because the

attorney's conduct cannot be classified as actually dishonest or fraudulent, it is a short step to the courthouse and a civil action based upon a claim of negligence. . . .

And finally the whole plan is a delusion because it could easily become so expensive that *no bar association could afford it:*

> If . . . indemnity is a moral obligation and a debt of honor on the part of the bar, then the plan proposed does not live up to that obligation or answer the problem. . . . We must either inaugurate a system of indemnity that will actually indemnify in full for the total amount of every defalcation, *which will place an almost impossible financial burden on the Bar* [emphasis added], or we must accept a plan that by its very inadequacy will defeat its own purpose.

The extraordinarily frank arguments of the opponents to a client security fund prevailed in California, and the state's 29,000 lawyers still don't have such a fund. (However, Los Angeles' 8,400 lawyers have their own fund of $26,000. To date there have been no payouts.)

In the summer of 1967 the Board of Governors of the State Bar of Wisconsin rejected another proposal to establish a client security fund. A majority committee report said the organization was "not ready to answer for and make good fraud and dishonesty by its fellow lawyers." It said that only nine lawyers had been accused of misappropriating funds in the past five years with losses totaling $70,000: "Embezzlement by lawyers is a rare occurrence, and when it does occur it is due to the weakness and frailty of human nature found in all walks of life, and not peculiar to the legal profession." In a somewhat indelicate combination of news items, the bar also announced that its prosperous state was enabling it to build a $100,000 addition to its State Bar Center in Madison.

* * *

How often does a lawyer steal from a client? No one has the remotest idea. In theory, if you could add up every case of disbarment of a lawyer who had stolen from a client you *might* get a rough gauge. Let's see. In an average year between 65 and 80 United States lawyers are disbarred. But that doesn't get us very far because the reasons for these punishments are seldom given. Say 75 disbarments a year of which, let us assume, two thirds are for stealing from clients. (Former Supreme Court Justice Tom Clark, chairman of the ABA's Special Committee on Evaluation of Disciplinary Enforcement, reported late in 1967 that "the most prevalent disciplinary offense is money defalcation.")

In short, 50 client thefts a year and 212,000 lawyers in private practice would mean, roughly, 1 lawyer in every 4,200 stole money from a client. On the surface, an extraordinarily low rate. For example, a leading authority on bank insurance estimates that embezzlement strikes 1 bank in 20 each year.

But lawyer theft from clients is mounting rapidly, reports Justice Clark—and at a much higher rate than the lawyer population. He said such defaults seemed most often to involve lawyers who have practiced about fifteen years. And, he added, the offender usually is not disbarred permanently.

The Institute of Judicial Administration in New York found that between 1950 and 1958 in New York, Cleveland and Philadelphia $250,000 had been embezzled by lawyers. There is inflation here, too. In 1965 and 1966 alone, more than that was stolen by lawyers from clients just in Manhattan.

Still, there would hardly seem to be a real problem—except for the victim. But as every lawyer who has served on a bar disciplinary committee knows, the known and publicized cases of lawyer theft are far, far exceeded by the instances that are never known. Perhaps, one bar official estimated for me, "as one is to ten. Or worse."

Just after Arizona instituted a Client Security Fund several bar association officers heard of a $50,000 embezzlement by the lawyer-son of one of the state's most prominent attorneys. At first there was some fear that the fledgling fund would be swamped by such an outsize claim—there is a limit of $25,000 for any one claim—but more experienced lawyers assuaged their fears: "The case will never get out; the old man will pay it himself." And he did. Every lawyer I talked to who had ever served on a bar disciplinary committee knew of at least one case of lawyer theft that never was publicized—and often, never punished because *some kind* of restitution was made by the man's partners or relatives.

Ted Voorhees is a brilliant and persuasive Philadelphia lawyer who served as the effective chairman of the American Bar Association's Committee on Client Security Funds for several years and is probably more responsible than any other lawyer for the fact that twenty-seven states now have such a fund in operation. He told me of a case he had come across in Philadelphia while he served on the Committee of Censors of the Philadelphia Bar Association.

"It illustrates why statistics in this area are so hard to come by—and so meaningless. . . . This lawyer was clever, hardworking and trying cases in several states. I'd say he was making at least $50,000 a year, probably more. And he was a helluva liar.

"We had a succession of complaints against him, each charging refusal to pay over funds belonging to clients. After we'd get the complaint and make inquiries the client would get his money. What worried us was not only the dangerous pattern of his conduct but the near certainty that we weren't hearing from *all* of his victimized clients. So we went to court to have him disbarred, offering proof he had been embezzling. But the court showed a hesitance to disbar him as he had enjoyed a good reputation.

"Then while the committee was awaiting the court's decision, still another complaint came in. This time a young woman who was going blind had been given a bad check for $4,000 by the lawyer. She had been divorced by her husband and the lawyer had embezzled the $4,000, all that she was to receive from the husband for the future support of herself and her small child. When the lenient court heard about this, the lawyer was given no way to make restitution and was quickly disbarred. Once disbarred, of course, he was under no pressure to repay her. She never got a dime from him."

This Philadelphia story brings to mind a notorious case read by millions of Americans who encountered it in the 1957 best seller *By Love Possessed*. In it James Gould Cozzens told of forty-nine crucial hours in the life of Arthur Winner, a middle-aged lawyer who lives in and practices in "Brocton," a "rural county seat" somewhere between Philadelphia and New York. Winner has two law partners. In the last 20 pages of the 570-page novel Winner discovers that his oldest partner, Noah Tuttle, has taken some $200,000 from trust funds he has managed, funds whose prime beneficiary is the local Episcopalian Church. Worse, Winner discovers that his other partner, Julius Penrose, *had known about the defalcations for twelve years* and had never even hinted at it. His world shattered, Winner is all for calling in a CPA and getting a long overdue audit of the funds. His partner, Penrose, points out that at the very least it would mean five years for their older partner. No, he has a better, trickier solution. They won't tell their guilty partner that they know.

"We aim to buy time," explains Julius Penrose. "We hope to see Noah live long enough to get the accounts squared. Intelligent recognition of the risks must include giving thought to what happens if time runs out, if our hope is not realized. If luck should fail us, if the law overtakes Noah, I would like him to be able to testify that we knew nothing of these shortages. . . ."

There are seldom sequels to popular novels, and we'll never know how the firm of Tuttle, Winner and Penrose managed the considerable feat of hiding a $200,000 defalcation, or somehow making it good.

Obviously no one knows how many real life cases like this exist. Nor do we know how many thousands of lesser thefts there are of a kind Graham Sterling, the former president of the California State Bar, described a few years ago.

There are, he wrote, many instances in which for various reasons there has been

no criminal proceeding or no conviction and yet the client in a complaint to the State Bar alleges facts, which at least in the client's opinion are tantamount to misappropriation, embezzlement or defalcation, and establishes enough of the alleged facts to constitute grounds for discipline but not enough to warrant disbarment.

He provided a typical instance:

The client gives his attorney money for legal costs; the money is not applied to costs; the attorney asserts that it was not all required for costs, so he pocketed the balance as payment for his services pursuant to an oral agreement which he claims with the client; the client denies any such oral agreement; and the attorney has never rendered a bill for the services or a statement as to the purposes for which the money was used.

Doesn't a client security fund also owe this mistreated client some payment, if "our primary object is the discharge of a debt of honor which the profession owes the public?"

Another instance, says Graham Sterling, is that of a client who gives a lawyer $300 for filing an action in some case. The attorney does nothing

except to stall the client's questions as to the progress of the matter and it turns out later that the complaint was never filed and the statute of limitations has run; the client wants his $300 back and no explanation will convince him that the attorney has not . . . "stolen" his $300; nor is the client satisfied to be told that he has good grounds for a civil action against the attorney which he can probably prosecute successfully by hiring another attorney to sue the first attorney.

In neither case, argues Mr. Sterling, would there be any real chance of disbarment for the attorney; in fact, in the second instance there might well be no discipline imposed on the attorney at all. Yet, asks Graham Sterling of his fellow attorneys, "Would there be any doubt in the mind of any decent lawyer that the client should get his $300 back without having to hire another lawyer to collect it?" Thus, he favored letting a client security fund consider payments to such victims, too. But since California lawyers still have to vote themselves *any* kind of a client security fund, let alone such a proposed comprehensive one, it is all academic.

In New York recently, another kind of commonplace but invisible lawyer theft was described by Angelo Cometa, the former prosecutor who built the case against embezzling lawyer Jerome Golenbock. Cometa is now chief counsel of the Coordinating Committee on Discipline of the three bar associations in Manhattan and the Bronx, New York City.

"It happens here several times a year that we *know* about. I don't want to even think about the unknown times. A lawyer calls me. He needs a little help. An important client asks him to check into a case involving the client's *mother*. She had been injured in a car crash in Brooklyn in 1961—seven years ago. Years pass. The son asks his mother's lawyer: what goes? The lawyer stalls. Court congestion and all that. Now two weeks ago the lawyer called him: well, at last the insurance company is offering $1,000. The son is indignant: his mother had been in the hospital fifteen days and out of work for months. A thousand bucks! Ridiculous! The lawyer says that's the best he can do. A few days later the mother gets a check for $500. The lawyer is entitled to up to 50 percent if the total recovery is $1,000 or less, so the arithmetic is straight on that part. But the son is very suspicious and no fool. "How come the check? My mother never endorsed any check the lawyer got from the insurance company and she never had to sign a release, so how can he be paying us this way?"

As the son's lawyer provided the details over the phone, Angelo Cometa was pretty sure he knew how; just as he knew the lawyer at the other end of the phone knew. Cometa said he would check it out.

Later that day he called the insurance company's counsel. They checked the case. In the summer of 1966—two years prior—the case had been dismissed by the court for failure to prosecute. The negligent lawyer had accidentally—or stupidly—allowed his client's case to lapse. Now in order to prevent her from finding out about it he was offering her a picayune $500.

I said, $500 was better than nothing. Cometa shook his head: "You don't understand: her case was worth $4,000 to $5,000 at least. The insurance company had offered her lawyer $2,200 back in 1962. He held out for more and then just forgot about the case. Now she's out in the cold: the case can't be reinstated. Sure, she can get another lawyer to sue this character for malpractice, but I'll bet he doesn't carry any insurance. So what we have here is a case of 'theft' by a lawyer—'theft' of several thousand dollars, just as if he had taken it out of her savings account."

Some time later I called on Angelo Cometa again to find out what had happened in the case.

"No surprises," he said. "We checked him out carefully and found he has also 'borrowed' from several clients' insurance settlements without telling them. And he doesn't have any malpractice insurance. I recommended disciplinary proceedings against him and he was prosecuted.

"Generally when you find a lawyer has failed to prosecute a case he's been hired to handle you'll find other kinds of professional misconduct. These are the lawyers who shouldn't be practicing at all. You'd need a special giant Client Security Fund all by itself to cover the losses these characters generate for their trusting clients."

I suggested that surely the insurance company involved had some responsibility here: at the very least they should have notified the bar grievance committee two years ago when the case was allowed to lapse.

Cometa shook his head: "I agree, but there isn't any such requirement on the books right now. They don't have to notify me or the courts or anyone. As far as they're concerned, a stupid neighborhood lawyer who doesn't have a system of keeping track of his cases let a case go by default—a case that might have cost them $4,000 to 5,000. They can't be mad at him. He's saved them a small bundle by his stupidity. A man like that in the course of a professional lifetime might forget several times. If you had enough men like that in the negligence field—why, they're great hidden assets for the insurance carriers. Blow the whistle on them? Forget it. The carriers can only wish him a lot of accident clients—and a long life."

Cometa feels that the insurance companies *should* be required to report all motions to dismiss cases for lack of prosecution by the plaintiff's lawyer. I suggested that perhaps the courts should be required to notify his office of such cases. By not passing on word of an attorney's dereliction of duty to a client the court was, in effect, helping conceal abuse of a client.

In at least one case I studied, the court's responsibility in the theft of client funds was much greater.

The year 1966 was a particularly disturbing one for D. Lowell Jensen, a tall, dedicated assistant district attorney of Alameda County (Oakland), California. First, he had to prosecute a fellow lawyer on a charge of stealing $150,000 from the estate of a helpless widow. That the lawyer happened to be Oakland's most recent mayor, John C. Houlihan, didn't help. But what bothered Jensen most was the discovery—and Houlihan's admission—that *the former mayor had been stealing from estates entrusted to his care by the courts for more than twenty-one years.*

"Obviously something's wrong here," Jensen told me recently. "How could court accounting procedures have been so lax as to allow this to happen for so many years?"

Houlihan, an auburn-haired, hard-drinking fifty-six-year-old lawyer, made himself an "active" mayor in Oakland, which is run essentially by a city manager. Oakland's mayor, who is paid $7,500 a year for part-time work, was traditionally a ceremonial figure. Houlihan changed all that when he was elected in 1961. He worked hard to bring new industry to the city and to get public projects built. His efforts brought him articles in national magazines and many invitations to speak. He made official visits to all parts of the United States, and to Europe and Japan, and the San Francisco *Call* termed him "the Golden Boy of Bay Area Politics." He was made a consultant on core cities to the Center for the Study of Democratic Institutions in Santa Barbara. This paid $16,000 a year for part-time work, but it wasn't enough.

He had begun stealing from estates entrusted to his care in 1945. Between that year and 1961 when he was elected mayor, he managed to put the money back. But as an active mayor his law practice diminished, and paying back the money taken from Mrs.

Sarilla Whitlock, the widow of a former Safeway Stores executive, became impossible.

Houlihan handled her husband's estate. In October, 1960, Mrs. Whitlock fell and broke her hip, requiring hospitalization. Soon afterward she went into a convalescent hospital, and Houlihan's thefts from her estate began almost simultaneously. This was risky, he knew, but there was a way to lessen the risk. Besides, he was going to need quite a bit of money soon: he intended to run for mayor.

In April, 1961, he persuaded Mrs. Whitlock's relatives to let him become the conservator of her estate, that is, a guardian.

"Conservatorships are popular here," explains Al Hymer, research clerk of the probate court in Oakland. "For one thing the conservatorship doesn't have the stigma of a guardianship. For a guardianship case the court has to find that the person is *incompetent*. For a conservatorship the court only has to believe that there is a likelihood that the person might be 'deceived or imposed upon by artful or designing persons.' "

Houlihan easily convinced the court that Mrs. Whitlock might be so deceived or imposed upon. Understandably, he didn't add that *he* was going to do it.

As the District Attorney put it later:

> It appears that the entire conservatorship was created not to protect Mrs. Whitlock but rather as a mechanism to enable the defendant to obtain the monies of Mrs. Whitlock, an extraordinary use of a court process designed to protect those who need help.

In California the law requires annual accountings by the conservator of the funds entrusted to him, but there was then no independent checking as to whether or not he actually filed an accounting. Houlihan didn't.

A good deal of the stolen money went to pay for Houlihan's campaign expenses. He was elected in 1961 after a tough primary fight, and he spent some $20,000 of his client's money here.*

*After studying the details of some fifty lawyer thefts from clients around the country in the past few years, I was impressed by the number of times

He took another $33,000 to pay his back income taxes. His thefts were uncovered only after the death of Mrs. Whitlock in 1965. Her heirs asked for an accounting through their attorney. Houlihan stalled, and they filed a suit demanding an accounting. The day he was ordered to attend a hearing in probate court he failed to appear, and the case was sent to the District Attorney. That day Houlihan resigned as mayor with the excuse that the job simply didn't pay enough.

He was indicted—the foreman of the grand jury had been his campaign manager—and he pleaded guilty.

Before he was sentenced a vigorous campaign on his behalf was undertaken by friends. Hundreds of letters urging probation instead of a prison sentence were sent. The judge, obviously impressed, postponed a decision, and the San Francisco *Call* felt that the judge ought not let himself be swamped by the appeals. In an editorial the paper set the record straight:

> While compassion should never be withheld from any man, the fact remains that Houlihan's crime is unforgivable. He violated not one trust, but three.
>
> He stole money placed in his hands as trustee to conserve and protect.
>
> He violated the trust of the people of Oakland, for he was stealing from a widow while standing before the people as their mayor of unblemished character. . . . He tried to deny his crime and confessed it only when the evidence of guilt was overwhelming. His promise of restitution lacks conviction.

On January 4, 1967, he was sentenced to one to ten years in a state prison. No restitution was made. At the time he entered prison he owed the heirs of Mrs. Whitlock $144,000. In theory he could be tried later for a federal crime—forging Mrs. Whitlock's signature on $24,000 worth of U.S. bonds—but the federal prosecutor seems unlikely to press that action.

Since California doesn't have a client security fund, the heirs cannot look there for any payment. Ordinarily they might have

---

in which the lawyer had political ambitions. Often the stolen money was used to help finance his campaign for office.

been able to turn to the bonding company used by the conservator. In this case Houlihan should have had a $150,000 bond to cover the estate, but to save money—he looked upon it as *his* by then—he got the bond reduced to $50,000 by claiming he had deposited U.S. bonds in a safe-deposit box controlled by the court. But no one at the court checked this; the bonds were actually in Houlihan's own safe-deposit box. He took them out as he needed them and forged Mrs. Whitlock's signature to cash them.

The much publicized case did result in one reform in the probate court which supervises conservatorships. Now all annual accountings in these cases are actually checked by the court. This is a help, of course, but as one Oakland lawyer told me, "The only trouble is that a crooked lawyer could just as easily swindle an estate between two annual accountings."

There are better ways to protect a client's funds.

New Zealand's lawyers, who were the first to set up a client security fund, also devised this plan: There all solicitors must provide a *monthly* accounting of funds held in trust for their clients. And audits of the funds and the accountings must be conducted at least three times a year. In case there is even a hint of suspected irregularity, the Law Society of New Zealand can demand production of a solicitor's private records and conduct its own audit. It does not have to get a court order to do so, either.

In England, solicitors have had a quite gamy reputation for taking clients' funds—before and after Dickens. In 1888 and 1889 Benjamin Greene Lake, who was president of the Law Society— equivalent to the presidency of the American Bar Association— was also chairman of the society's disciplinary committee. For twenty-five years he lived in great luxury by the steady systematic looting of estates his office handled. When he went bankrupt during a stock market crisis, his clients were out several hundred thousand pounds (the equivalent of some five million dollars today). There was no restitution but he did get a twelve-year sentence.

In spite of this horrible example, English lawyers bitterly resisted any attempts to protect clients from thieving solicitors. Not until 1942 did the English Law Society create a client security fund to which every practicing solicitor had to contribute $25 a year (now $28 a year). In addition, every solicitor has to produce an auditor's certificate of his accounts when applying for his annual license to practice.

England's 20,000 solicitors add about $500,000 a year to their compensation fund. Payments from the fund have been averaging about $456,000 a year, according to a survey made recently by Quintin Johnson of Yale Law School, and Dan Hopson, Jr., of the University of Kansas School of Law. (In the United States a comparable rate of restitution for our 212,000 lawyers in private practice would mean an annual payout of about $5,400,000 to victimized clients. So far all the client security funds in operation in the United States have paid out about $125,000 since they have been in operation.)

The worst blow to the English fund came with the death in 1957 of an esteemed, prosperous London solicitor, Robert Eicholz. A client was suing Eicholz for the return of some money just before the solicitor died. Inquiry into his books and client relationships disclosed that the solicitor had been stealing steadily and grandly from hundreds of Jewish refugees from Nazi Germany. The Law Society spent $140,000 on the investigation of the case before it found out that Eicholz had stolen $1,680,000 from clients. The money was paid them or their heirs—but it was *all* paid. There was a lot of grumbling and many solicitors advocated abolishing the fund entirely. In spite of the payments made, they felt that the fund did not increase public prestige of the profession but "instead raised suspicions as to why it was needed and gave added notoriety to dishonesties that occurred." But the fund is still operating.

Canada has also gone much further than we have in protecting clients from lawyers. In 1954 the province of Ontario instituted a client security fund. (Alberta had been the first in 1939.) But in 1960 the 5,200 lawyers of Ontario and the Law Society of Upper Canada had to do some painful self-examination. Between 1954 and 1960 the fund had paid out $286,548 to victims of thieving

Ontario lawyers, eighteen of whom had been disbarred for their thefts.

To appreciate the enormity of the sums stolen—and repaid— and the number of lawyers disbarred in the one province, which has only 5,200 lawyers, let me project it into U.S. terms. Between 1954 and 1960 there were 34 times more lawyers in private practice in the United States. If the Canadian lawyer theft rate had taken place here, there would have been about $9,700,000 stolen from U.S. clients in that period. If their disbarment rate had been attained here, it would have meant that some 580 U.S. lawyers would have been disbarred. In fact, during that period there were only 277, or less than half the Ontario rate.

We haven't the faintest idea of how much U.S. lawyers stole from clients in this period before any U.S. bar association had a client security fund; nor do we know how many lawyers who should have been disbarred weren't. It could be, of course, that U.S. attorneys are more honest than their Ontario counterparts; or possibly, that the lawyers of Ontario, hit by heavy claims against their client security fund, had good reason to be far more diligent in weeding out dishonest lawyers than U.S. bars, which then didn't have to pay out any money to victims of lawyer thefts. I once discussed the great gulf between the Ontario figures and the U.S. equivalents with a wise Toronto lawyer. "It is odd," he admitted. "All the more so because Ontario and Toronto, in particular, are considered the most Americanized portions of Canada."

The "run on the bank," as the Ontario Law Society officials termed their plight in 1961, stemmed mostly from lawyer involvement in speculative land deals. In investigating the cases that led up to the many disbarments in the 1954–60 period, auditors found that the temptation of quick-and-easy land deals was too great. Especially when there were client trust accounts to be used. One solicitor came within a day of closing a land deal on which he would have made $200,000. He was disbarred and jailed instead. Another was using client money, without permission, to lend money to land speculators at 2 percent a month. When the new home market died, his borrowers couldn't repay; neither could he.

The Ontario Law Society at this point began examining a plan used by the provinces of Saskatchewan and British Columbia— the spot, or blitz, audit. The names of all attorneys in these provinces are placed in a hat, and a draw is made every month. The lawyers whose names are drawn have their books scrutinized immediately. Presumably, since no lawyer knows when his turn will come, all have to keep their accounts current—and honest.

In 1964 a majority of the members of the Ontario Law Society agreed to adopt the blitz audit. That year, outside auditors working under the direction of the society's own auditor, Robert L. Anderson, visited 243 firms in East Toronto, Windsor and Ottawa. Out of these sharp-eyed skimmings the auditors were able to spot 12 lawyers' offices that indicated some unsatisfactory accounts. Full-scale audits were given these accounts, and 5 were found to be worthy of a sharp look by the society's disciplinary committee. Another 169 firms had been guilty of technical breaches in the way they kept their client funds.

In 1965 the plan was expanded, mostly in Toronto itself. More than 1,000 firms with 2,346 lawyers in them were visited. This time 8 full-scale audits were ordered because of suspicious items uncovered in the blitz. And after these audits 3 law firms were called before the disciplinary committee. By the middle of 1967 more than 65 percent of all lawyers practicing in Ontario had been visited and given a blitz audit.

In August, 1967, Ralph Hyman, in the Toronto *Globe and Mail*, described the blitz operations this way:

Zero hour is 10 A.M. Monday. Sharp on the dot, a stranger appears at the office of a Toronto law firm and produces a letter which says he is empowered by the Law Society of Upper Canada to examine the firm's trust fund account. The books are produced at once.

This is the technique of the blitz. At the same hour, every law firm in a designated area of the city is visited by a society investigator in a swift, unheralded descent. . . .

The results have been good, points out Kenneth Jarvis, secretary of the Law Society. In 1966 only three lawyers were disbarred, the lowest number since 1958. In 1962 and 1963—before the blitz began—twenty lawyers were thrown out. A year later the blitz was started and the improvement was immediately visible: disbarments fell to six.

If you go looking for trouble you're bound to find it. Before the blitz was instituted, Ontario's lawyers were paying $45 a year into their compensation, or client security, fund. But in 1965, because of the large sums paid out, the levy had to rise to $100. In 1966–67 it dropped to $65. On June 30, 1967, the Ontario Client Security Fund held $702,682. Against this there were outstanding applications by aggrieved clients of $1,027,629. But Kenneth Jarvis believes that only a third of this, about $325,000, "will stand up to scrutiny as being worthy of consideration for compensation."

As I pointed out earlier, all the existing 27 statewide client security funds and the six separate county funds have paid out only $125,000 since they began. Either our lawyers are much more honest than their Ontario counterparts, or the Canadians are much more thorough in their publicizing the existence of their funds and in allowing claims against it.

Another big difference, of course, is the presence of the blitz audit in Ontario. Several bar officials I talked to simply didn't think that the American bar was ready for it. When one of them countered, half-seriously, that the idea of the blitz sounded "un-American," I pointed out that the New York Stock Exchange had been doing it with member firms for more than thirty years, and those apostles of free enterprise, the Wall Street stockbrokers, accepted the idea as both necessary and useful.

Banks are probably an even better example, commented the *Washington Post* editorially on November 15, 1967. Like lawyers, they are licensed to accept deposits but are not

left free of regulation. Why should lawyers holding clients' funds in escrow, be exempt from occasional examination of their books? If the judges feel that they do not have sufficient authority to order spot checks of lawyers' books, they could render a great service by seeking such authority and machinery to make the policy effective.

But no judges, in Washington or elsewhere, have as yet tried to initiate even an attenuated model of the Toronto "blitz" audit technique.

There *is* another way for each lawyer to pay the penalty for his own wrong against a client. Why not require each practicing lawyer to obtain and pay for a large annual bond, commencing, say, at the $50,000 level for the beginning single practitioner and rising to the multimillion-dollar level for larger firms which, on the basis of experience, probably need it least? Bonding of people who handle money is a normal, everyday experience in the United States. Surely there is no real reason why it should not be required of lawyers, who increasingly handle more and more of their clients' money—accident awards, estate settlements or business deals.

After all, "Law is the only profession," points out James C. Sheppard of Los Angeles, a former president of the California State Bar, "that handles a client's money."

It seemed so obvious an approach that I wondered why insurance firms that do a lot of bonding work hadn't thought of it. I asked the vice president of a leading firm—one that has already had experience in the field of underwriting lawyers' malpractice insurance. He smiled wryly:

"Everybody in the business has thought of it, but there isn't a one of us who'd dare suggest it to lawyers or bar associations. We have to live with them, sell them and their clients bonding insurance. They send us a lot of business. Can you see me turning around and suggesting a permanent bond for lawyers that not only would cost them but carries with it the clear implication that they *need* such bonding? Come on. Sure, you talk to lawyers over a few drinks and they'll tell you about four, five lawyers in town who, by God, should be bonded. Naturally, they always exclude themselves. It's always: that other bastard needs it; me, I'm honorable and I'll sue the first man who even suggests I need it."

A bar association official nodded when I mentioned the bonding proposal.

"Oh, we've thought of it. The only trouble, besides the expense, is that the bonding companies would automatically replace our bar admissions committees. If you have to get a bond before you can practice law it means the bonding companies become the ultimate arbiters of who can hang up a shingle and who can't. You honestly don't think we're going to give them that kind of power, do you? No, we're just going to have to make the client security funds more comprehensive, better endowed—and better publicized. Don't hold your breath. It will take quite a while."

But the most direct, the simplest way of ending lawyer theft of client funds has been suggested by Robert C. Abel, Jr., a Fort Lauderdale, Florida, attorney who is active in his bar association's grievance work.

We punish the wrongdoer for what *has been done*. In nine cases out of ten brought before the grievance committees, the wrongdoer was motivated by economic shortcomings of his practice and our profession. I say let us cure the disease, not the symptoms. Let us improve our economics and we will. Improved economics can be to our profession and its ethical maladies what Salk vaccine has been to polio.

In short, if your lawyer asks for a bigger fee, for God's sake give it to him. He might steal.

2 *DIVORCE IS GOOD BUSINESS*

Draw up the papers, lawyer, and make 'em good and stout,
For things are running crossways, and Betsey and I are out.
              —WILL CARLETON, *Farm Ballads,* 1873

I am writing this book in a New England village. Twice a week I leave my cottage for a shopping visit to town a mile away. Just before turning back I often drop in for one or two items and small talk with Mike, our local pharmacist. Mike, a handsome, plump, white-haired merchant who takes his calling seriously, recently becoming the first druggist in his state to stop selling cigarettes. "Why should I *help* my customers get lung cancer?"

This afternoon his normally friendly, outgoing manner was missing. I asked what was wrong. "Every time I see that son of a bitch I get mad all over again," he said with surprising vehemence. "I don't know what you're writing this time, but you ought to do a book about lawyers and their so-called ethics." When I told him I *was* writing about that, he was momentarily put out that I hadn't confided in him. That passed quickly as he sat down to fill me in.

In 1963, after eighteen years of marriage and two children, he asked his wife for a divorce. The marriage had been rocky for more than ten years, but he had recently met another woman he wanted to marry. At first his wife was reluctant, but before long she agreed that maybe it would be best for both of them. She got a lawyer in another town and so did he: the lawyer he normally used was a friend of his wife's and didn't want to handle the divorce.

The two lawyers got together and the division of the couple's property, which had been held jointly by them, was agreed upon without much trouble. She got half of their property—which was worth about $150,000, including the building in which the pharmacy is located—and $125 a week for herself and $50 a week for the children until they were twenty-one. Mike would pay for their college education.

"The first thing that bothered me," Mike recalled, "was the little con job. He was always telling me how difficult it would be to get the divorce. He had advised me to let her get it—on grounds of mental cruelty which is about the commonest reason up here. I'd asked how could it be so difficult if we both wanted it?"

Just before the divorce was to be granted the lawyer threw a little party to which he invited Mike and his date and several others.

"When I showed up he was very jovial. It was a nice party, I told him. 'Enjoy it, you're paying for it,' he said. You know, one of those kidding things you say when everybody has had a few drinks. After that I suddenly started wondering: how *much* was I paying for it? Like a fool, I had never asked him how much the divorce was going to cost. And he never mentioned the subject."

The next day Mike asked. He was told the fee would be $2,000. "I asked him how he happened to pull *that* figure out of the air. He said it was a percentage arrangement: $150,000 in property held by the couple called for a $2,000 fee. I said I'd also have to pay my wife's lawyer. He said, yes, that will probably cost you another $2,000. Which meant that two people who *wanted* a divorce had to pay nearly three percent of what they had accumulated during their marriage to have lawyers take it through the court routine.

"I got pretty mad: 'Listen, I didn't take you and your *dear Brother* in to be my *partners.*' Then I asked him how much time he had actually spent on the divorce. I knew he generally charged $18 an hour for legal work in connection with a business, and on that basis he would have had to put in 110 hours on my divorce which was crazy. He couldn't have put in 20 hours.

"I said I'd love a chance to fill his prescriptions on the basis of what *he* owned. I figured he was making $35,000 a year or so, so that he should be paying at least seven times more for drugs than somebody in town who was only making $5,000. I kept coming back to: who made you my *partner?* And he'd say, that's the way lawyers figure their fees here.

"He wouldn't give me a time sheet or anything. I refused to pay him. He got a court order attaching my bank account. Then I cooled off a little and started thinking: I couldn't win this kind of battle. He was on his home grounds in the court, the judge was an old buddy he grew up with. I've been here about twenty years but to a lot of them I was still the fella from Boston, not one of the locals, really. So, in the end I paid. And my wife's lawyer, too. Another $2,000.

"Afterward I asked some lawyers in town—we have seven full-time ones here—and all of them said the first mistake I made was not *asking* the fee in advance. None of them would knock my lawyer, of course, but a few of them said that they thought $500 would have covered it in their office. That might not be too much dough in New York or Boston but that's still money around here. Oh, I see the lawyer from time to time but I don't talk to him. I just saw him in town today and I'm still mad. You know, I can't figure out if what makes me boil is that I let him take me or that I was such a damned fool in not shopping around."

Like many other Americans who have been through the divorce experience, Mike really doesn't think of himself as part of a vast, alarming army of men and women who have been broken from their former ranks. Nor does he worry overly that the United States has the highest divorce rate in the world; that every day more than 1,300 marriages are dissolved in divorce; that in California there is one divorce for every two marriages and in one wildly unstable county, Napa, more than seven of every ten marriages teeter-totter into divorce.

These are the mournful bits Mike expects to find in his store's magazine rack when he sees cover titles such as: DIVORCE—THE SHAME OF AMERICA; or LET'S END THE (DIVORCE) (ANNULMENT) (ALIMONY) RACKET. You might get Mike a little worried if you told him that the divorce rate is three to four times higher among teen-age marriages than among those married later. But that's a gut item: his two children by his first marriage *are* teen-agers. And in small towns they do marry younger.

No, for Mike his divorce was simply like some of the viscous brown medicines he has in the back room: bitter but necessary. What galls him, *infuriates* him is that two of his neighbors were legally able to take him for $4,000 for a service that should have cost a few hundred at most. He always translates it: "That's a year-and-a-half of college for my oldest."

When weighed against the frightening social costs of divorce— 600,000 children are affected by our 500,000 divorces each year; most juvenile delinquents come from broken homes; children of broken homes are likelier to get divorces of their own later in life—Mike's concern with $4,000 surely seems pretty narrow. Yet he is not alone. The high direct, legal cost of divorce is a mounting concern for hundreds of thousands of middle-class Americans as well as many more poor, who want and need divorce but can't buy one.

There are still some who say, good: divorce *should* be hard to get, *should* be expensive, or what will happen to marriage? But these were invalid arguments long ago. Divorce is an artifact of our times like smog, neon lights and colitis.

The increasing personal-dollar cost of divorce helps make it clear that the real jumbo obstacle to *basic* reform of the divorce process is the fact that for thousands of U.S. lawyers the occasional divorce proceeding can be the difference between making a fair living or making a really lucrative one. In a way, then, the legal profession has acquired a substantial stake in preventing any of the *far-reaching* reforms from being tried. I know lawyers have been in the forefront of divorce reform in New York, and the fact that adultery is no longer the sole ground for divorce in that state is a tribute to much bar association effort and lobbying. But merely adding newer and easier grounds for obtaining divorce doesn't do anything to the process itself. Yes, the game has been changed slightly: two can traverse the gameboard hazards more easily now, but the old iron rule is unchanged. Each of the divorce-game players still needs one lawyer, *paid,* to guide him or her across the board. Otherwise, no game.

"There has been much criticism raised and a substantial portion of it is valid," says the New York Committee for Fair Divorce and Alimony Laws, "that under any new divorce law, [in New York State] the legal fees that would be borne by the parties to a separation and/or divorce would be too costly."

•   •   •

A few years ago I was sitting in a lawyer's office in Beaumont, Texas. Waiting for him to finish a phone call, I was leafing through his copy of the current *Texas Bar Journal*—writers read anything—when I was stopped by a full-page ad of one of the leading law publishing companies, Bancroft-Whitney. Half the ad was a drawing of a large slice of buttered bread. The text went: "Divorce, alimony, real property, wills and contracts are the bread and butter of practice. But spending too many hours researching such cases can make them disastrously expensive." The thing to do, of course, was to buy their set of Texas law reports.

It was quite a surprise. I had no idea most lawyers looked upon divorce cases as *good* everyday bread-and-butter cases. Everyone knew what "divorce" lawyers looked like: on the late, late TV movie he was Warren William gone to seed a bit but still jaunty with a gardenia in his buttonhole as he enters the courtroom Homburg in hand.

Like a lot of people I had the idea that decent lawyers just don't handle divorce cases because they're too messy and unprofitable, and if they did it at all it was only to accommodate clients of long standing.

In a way it was fitting that this old notion should be discarded in Beaumont. I was in the city on a magazine story whose real premise was that you shouldn't trust old notions.

On the surface Beaumont was a prosperous city of 120,000 in southeast Texas. It made its money through cattle, oil, lumber and ships—and by being the widest-open city in the country. A lot of cities are extraordinarily tolerant of prostitution, gambling, narcotics and general corruption for varying periods. But in all of them civic disgust mounts in time and another reform movement succeeds in closing the city down—for a few years. Beaumont was unique. For more than forty years it had gone without reform. That interested me.

One of the men I talked to there was William G. Walley, a local lawyer who had worked with the successful reform group. He was the new acting District Attorney. "It wasn't a secret here," he explained. "Everybody knew what was going on. No one seemed to care. Maybe one of the reasons was that a lot of people were profiting from the mess, besides the corrupt officials and the gang. But what got me was the complaints I heard from fellow lawyers.

"It seems that they missed the heavy flow of young prostitutes in and out of the twenty houses running openly in the county. During the year several hundred girls would be shuttled in and out. Most of the prostitutes were unhappily married and wanted divorces. The lawyers here would charge them twice the going rate—and the girls would be happy to pay. Then some of my shrewder colleagues built up a profitable sideline acting as 'investment counsel' for some of the madames and prostitutes. They'd invest their money in mortgages and securities and get a healthy percentage for handling the money. Oh, a surprising part of the local bar missed the girls and the madames. Put a real crimp in their incomes."

You could if you wanted also prove that divorce law was a poor way to make a living. For example, a recent survey by Daniel J. Cantor & Company of Philadelphia—a unique specialist in the economics of law practice—found that lawyers who specialized in "domestic relations," mainly divorce and alimony cases, had the lowest median incomes. In Florida, in 1965, such divorce specialists only averaged $9,000 a year when other lawyers who specialized in banking law were averaging $20,000 and lawyers who stuck largely to probate and wills were making $18,700. In Pennsylvania, divorce specialists made only $10,000 a year in 1964 when their colleagues in corporation law were pulling down twice as much.

I showed these figures to a prosperous New York divorce lawyer. (They don't like to be called that: the preferred expression is, "I specialize in matrimonials.") He made a face. "A lawyer who *nets* less than $20,000 a year is not specializing in *anything*. He's just getting by. A man concentrates on one kind of practice because that's the kind he's getting and *there's money in it*. We have 500 men around the country in our American Academy of Matrimonial Lawyers. We don't want characters who have to buy their suits at Robert Hall."

When Hubert J. O'Gorman, who teaches sociology at Hunter College in New York, surveyed matrimonial law specialists in New York he found that "all but one of these attorneys expressed a marked preference for such cases."

But even neighborhood lawyers also like "matrimonials," explains lawyer-sociologist Jerome Carlin, because "divorce cases bring relatively large fees for what is often only a perfunctory service."

Leroy Blackstock, past president of the Oklahoma Bar Association, told some lawyers gathered for an Economics of Law Practice meeting in 1967 just how some lawyers made a lot of money out of divorce. He was against their method, however:

It is, in my opinion, wholly unprofessional to simply handle these cases in bundles with printed forms of petitions, answers, motions and decrees . . . some practitioners gloat in the fact that they can interview the client in a matter of minutes and get the divorce summarily. . . .

In California which has our highest divorce rate, a State Assembly Committee on Domestic Relations surveyed the divorce business and found, among other things:

There is some evidence to indicate that 8 percent of the lawyers handle about 80 percent of the divorce business in some cities. For them divorce is their rent, their stenographer's salary, their baby's shoes, sometimes their solid-gold Cadillac. The simplest uncontested case is generally worth a couple of hundred dollars; a case involving even a moderately well-to-do husband accused (not necessarily guilty) of infidelity is ordinarily worth a few thousand to the lawyers. How unrealistic to expect them to forego anything like that for mere considerations of ethics or morals.

Just how much does "anything like that" amount to nationally? National divorce statistics are merely cumulative state-by-state approximations. The most recent national figures indicate that about 494,000 divorces were granted domestically in 1966— plus at least another 25,000 granted to U.S. couples who went to Juarez, Mexico and other foreign easy-divorce meccas. Since a U.S. lawyer was required for some aspects of these foreign divorces, it seems likely that in 1966 our lawyers were paid not for 520,000 divorces but for representing the more than 1,000,000 Americans who were involved in divorce actions.* Admittedly most of these payments were made by the husband, who paid his lawyer as well as his wife's, but they were two separate and fairly equal payments.

What should lawyers charge? The only and barest guidelines are provided by the ABA's 1966 survey of recommended minimum fees in all fifty states and many counties. More than 700 state and local bar associations' scales were covered. The legal services considered were "typical nonlitigious matters for which the amount and work requirements would be reasonably foreseeable." Under the heading "Domestic Relations—Uncontested Divorce" there were minimum fees ranging from a low of $75 in two Texas counties to a high of $500 minimum in New York and New Jersey. In between was $100 for Montgomery County, Alabama, and the same fee for seven of nine counties in Arkansas. Naturally, the more urban areas were higher. The median figure for the United States according to the survey was $200. And if every U.S. divorce were obtained on this median fee, our lawyers would

*The Committee for Fair Divorce and Alimony Laws estimates that another 167,000 couples secured annulments in 1966. These, too, required the services of lawyers.

be earning about $200,000,000 a year from divorce. But, of course, few divorces are provided just for minimums. One estimate is that we actually spend about $800,000,000 in legal services for divorce, annulments and separations.

To get an idea of how much higher the fees might be, we can look at the suggested minimum fees published in December, 1966, by the Lawyers Club of San Francisco. For obtaining an uncontested divorce it recommended minimum fees between $300 to $1,000. Added to this would be:

$75–$100   for appearing at order to show cause hearing
$75–$100   for publication of a summons, and
$75–$350   an hour for working out a property settlement with the other side.

The last figure is interesting. Ordinarily the range of time charges by a lawyer can go all the way from $10 an hour up to $100 for the highest priced man. Obviously if a lawyer is asking up to $350 an hour for his time during a property settlement he is, in effect, making himself a partner in the settlement.

Other useful clues are provided by Morris R. Ploscowe, a former New York City judge who now teaches law at New York University. In April, 1967, he estimated that in the United States the real range of divorce costs where the husband's income is between $10,000 and $20,000 a year—some 20 million U.S. families are in this range—the costs would go from $500 to $2,500 for *each* lawyer involved. In effect then, $1,000 to $5,000 for *a* divorce. In the higher brackets, Professor Ploscowe admitted, "lawyers often charge whatever the traffic will bear."

Sidney Siller, a New York divorce lawyer—separated from his wife—is counsel of the Committee for Fair Divorce and Alimony Laws. He proposes that every New York bar association "adopt schedule of *maximum* fees in separation and divorce cases so as to protect the public from what may be in some cases an excessive fee." First, he wants all families with $3,500 and more in income to require the services of a private lawyer for divorce. (In short, he doesn't want Legal Aid providing free services for families with $4,500 income, as is true at present in New York City.) For a family with $5,000–$7,000 income the maximum fee would be $650 for each party in a separation or divorce trial. At the $7,500–$20,000 income level the corresponding fees would be $1,000 *each;* and $1,500 *each* for couples in the $15,000–$20,000 range. Above $20,000 there would be no maximum fees: whatever the lawyers thought they could get.

Possibly a record was the $500,000 received by attorney Robert A. Neeb of Los Angeles in 1966 for obtaining a divorce for a seventy-four-year-old woman, Ednah Race Capron, from her eighty-year-old husband who had made a $32,000,000 fortune in Orange County land. That same year New York attorney Louis Nizer received a fee of $360,000 for brilliantly handling a long drawn-out divorce for the wife of liquor millionaire Lewis Rosenstiel. Nizer had asked for a fee of $683,000.

Obviously, there are temptations when a great deal is at stake, and some weaker lawyers, says Professor Ploscowe, have succumbed by "encouraging litigations in order to earn high fees, without considering the potential damage to the families involved in the suit."

Offsetting these occasional golcondas are the cut-rate and free divorces secured through some of the newer organizations set up by the OEO to help the poor get legal services.

When Judicare was established in the hard-hit twenty-six northern counties of Wisconsin in June, 1966, it set out to provide legal care for the 37,000 families there who had incomes of less than $3,000 a year. Judicare officials were surprised, and a little embarrassed, when the biggest single request was for divorces. Out of the first 426 completed cases, some 161 (35 percent) were divorce actions. Under Judicare, lawyers are paid at lesser rates, and most of the divorces obtained were for $160 to $250. (A family of four is eligible for Judicare if its net income is below $4,160 a year.)

Some large city Legal Aid offices will handle divorces, but many more will not. ("Divorce for the poor is a privilege, not a right," is their guiding principle.) But in recent years the Detroit Legal Aid Bureau has averaged about 350 cases a year, and the Boston bureau about 160. In Philadelphia, Community Legal Services which provides free legal help only if the applicant's income is below $3,400, warns its attorneys:

The policy with regard to handling divorce is a delicate one in which you must be extremely circumspect. No divorce case is to be taken unless both parties would be eligible under the standards of poverty . . . it means that if the wife is poor but her husband is not, the case must be referred to a private attorney. Also, since the court costs of an undefended personal service divorce in Philadelphia are $215, you must inquire of any applicant where the costs are coming from, and why, if the person can raise the $215 for costs, a fee cannot also be paid to a private attorney.

One of the elements that make up the $215 in court costs in a Philadelphia divorce is a $15 fee that every divorce applicant has to give to the Philadelphia Bar Association. The custom was begun quietly by the city's Board of Judges in 1959 and now provides the bar with some $50,000 a year. What does the money go for? To maintain the bar association's midtown luncheon club on the lobby floor of the Adelphi Hotel. For years the association kept its secret until U. S. Divorce Reform publicized it. As a result Philadelphia divorces not only literally provide the city lawyers with their traditional "bread and butter" but also throw in a lot of French pastry for the bar association's luncheon club.

For many lawyers in Nevada, divorce is the very basis of legal life. In 1965 the state had 20,000 divorces, most of which were provided for out-of-state residents who came there for the required six-week stay. Divorces slumped to 10,000 in 1967 and a lot of lawyers were hurting. In a recent Nevada Bar Association poll, two thirds of the lawyers responding said they favored granting uncontested divorces after one day's residence—as in Mexico— *providing both parties hired individual lawyers.* (At present only the party in residence, usually the wife, needs a *local* lawyer.) Such a move, many lawyers said, "would boom the divorce business in Nevada and add to the income of the legal profession."

"You don't need a lawyer to get married. Should you need even one lawyer for a divorce?" asks Clark W. Blackburn, general director of the Family Service Association of America, which represents 300 local social service agencies working with families.

"Getting married is a reasonably simple procedure," he said. "You get a blood test, you go down to the license bureau, pay maybe five dollars and that's it. I don't see why, when a marriage is on the rocks and every effort to save it has failed, you shouldn't go down to a 'divorce license' window and pay five dollars for a license signifying your marriage is ended."

Blackburn's suggestion came after he had gone through the returns from the FSA member agencies which had been asked to speculate on the changes we could expect in marriage, divorce and family in 1975. Most of them thought that divorce would get simpler and its frequency would probably increase; that there would be much greater acceptance of divorced persons.

Some specific replies were:

- Divorce should be automatic, not a matter of proving one wrong and one right.
- The law assumes one "guilty" party and one "innocent" party, which is unrealistic in the light of our increased knowledge of human behavior. Hopefully by 1975 the law may become more realistic in recognizing that in most divorces it is a mutual decision.
- Divorce laws will be liberalized so that people don't have to engage in fraud or be rich to dissolve marriages . . . the prohibitive cost of divorce penalizes couples living on marginal incomes . . . I hope that by 1975 low income families will be able to obtain divorces cheaply rather than the man deserting his family completely as often happens now.
- If we could get lawyers out of the picture, maybe the divorce process wouldn't be given over to proving each other's weaknesses and thus give the divorce process a destructive rather than constructive connotation.

Lawyers today are an integral part of the divorce picture because of a historical accident. In the United States after the American Revolution, we took over much of the ecclesiastical law of England as developed in their church courts, which handled marriage and divorce. In these tribunals, established by William the Conqueror nearly 1,000 years ago, divorce could be granted if somebody was at fault and had hurt "an innocent and injured spouse." In short, there had to be a good party and a bad party to the marriage, a guilty one and an innocent one. Obviously, the courts had to decide which was which, and that meant, in turn, each party had to have lawyers, just as they would if they were involved in criminal trials. This "adversary procedure" continues today even though we know that 90 to 95 percent of all divorce cases are uncontested. ("Divorce by mutual consent" is the commonest description.) The "innocent and injured" spouse's allegations of grounds—adultery, cruelty, etc.—are "undenied, unexamined and rubberstamped," says one authority. And even in the 5 to 10 percent of litigated cases, points out the California Assembly's report on divorces, "the contesting spouse is actuated by hatred, spite or greed rather than a sincere effort to save the marriage."

The adversary procedure in divorce, continues the California report,

is inappropriate and destructive to those involved, often requires dishonesty, and always creates disrespect for the law . . . the law actually suggests that they "fight" one another to the finish, and until one is judged officially as the good one, the right one, and the other is declared publicly by authority to be the bad one, or the wrong one. . . . This is not a healthy system.

The involved lawyers, the report continues, are forced

to function in ways which serve to intensify the anger of their client toward their mate, the attorney, the law, the court, and even the state. The position they hold, also grants the attorneys power which is used in inappropriate and destructive ways on occasion, to the detriment of all concerned.

There have been many recent reformers who would eliminate the "adversary procedure" in divorce completely. Let's take divorce out of the courts, they say. Let's stop this piecemeal reform of divorce by simply providing *more* grounds on which a guilty party may be guilty, as New York has done recently. And above all, let's take the lawyers out of the picture, they plead.

•   •   •

One of the very first items to be decided in a divorce case is how is the wife's lawyer to be paid. Shirley R. Levittan, a New York lawyer, explains the process. The first step is usually

the wife's motion for temporary alimony and lawyer's fees. American courts are generally overcrowded, with matrimonial cases taking up 50–60 percent of the court's work in many places. The temporary alimony proceeding is often brief . . . a matter of 15 minutes. The judge often has to fall back on a conventional formula, which is one third of the husband's income . . . the law also requires the husband to pay his wife's legal fees, about ten times the weekly alimony, because husbands traditionally are supposed to pay the family bills.

Judge Morris R. Ploscowe of New York spells it out more incisively in discussing "suit money," as the husband's payment to the wife's attorney is called in some states:

In the eyes of a husband, the fact that he must pay for the divorce action or defenses of his wife may appear to be unmitigated gall . . . a husband may not only be compelled to support his wife but her lawyers as well.

Inevitably abuses emerge in such an anomalous situation. In California, for example, the wife who goes to a lawyer for a divorce usually has to sign an agreement with him to pay his fees. Then he seeks a court order asking an award of fees from the husband without telling the court that the wife has already signed such an agreement with him. Under California law, once a wife has signed such an agreement to pay her attorney, the husband cannot be ordered to do so. Naturally, the attorney doesn't disclose the agreement to the court. The investigators of the 1965 California Assembly Committee on Domestic Relations found the State Bar has had numerous complaints about certain unethical practices, many of which are unfortunately well founded, whereby an attorney will prepare an affidavit for the plaintiff in a divorce case to file, alleging she has no arrangement with her attorney for the payment of court costs or fees, and then immediately thereafter have that client sign a retainer agreement providing for fees. There appears to be no question that such practices are a fraud on the court and are most certainly unethical.

Still, it can be argued, the lawyer is simply taking a sensible extra precaution to make sure *someone* is going to pay him. If by some chance the divorce doesn't go through, why, then, the wife is committed to pay. But the possibilities for a little chicanery are too tempting here, points out the California report:

> Of course, there are attorneys who take advantage of wives by obtaining their agreement to pay fees and then charging unconscionable amounts, *often in addition to those awarded by the court and paid by the husband.* [Emphasis added.]

"It happens pretty often," says George Partis, a lightly built sixty-year-old retired U. S. Naval Commander who is a founder and now national chairman of U. S. Divorce Reform, Inc. (Slogan: "Take the Fight Out of Divorce"). Partis is divorced—after twenty-seven years of marriage. He pays $150 a month alimony and got a divorce for about $6,000 in legal costs, because his wife converted to Seventh Day Adventism and wouldn't have anything to do with her unconverted husband. U. S. Divorce Reform, he adds, has prevented

"double fee" collecting lawyers from extracting a fee from the wife, when the husband has already paid in compliance with a court order. The lawyers rely on the fact that a divorced couple will not communicate and discover this trickery. When a protest is made the lawyers blame it on a mistake or misunderstanding.

Partis has another complaint about legal fees in divorce:

Our judges, whose salaries are paid with our tax dollars, act as collection agencies for attorneys. How? Just let anyone go to the County Clerk to pick up their final divorce decree. They will often find that because of a stipulation by the judge, attorneys' fees must be paid before the final decree is issued, even though the required time has elapsed.

U. S. Divorce Reform, which started in 1961 with 20 members, now has 6,000, including one unnamed multimillionaire whose own divorce cost him $2 million. Each USDR chapter gets out newsletters and writes editors demanding "change, revision, mercy and justice." And occasionally they picket courts which they feel shouldn't be in the divorce picture at all. Their basic goal is a Family Arbitration Center to replace the present divorce system. The centers would be staffed by social workers, psychiatrists, accountants and lawyers—to handle the property divisions. They would work to save a marriage by counseling and guidance, and if a marriage couldn't be saved at all, it would be dissolved "with a minimum of bitterness and a maximum of dignity."

Alimony, that traditional fury, would be eliminated. However, "if either party is unable to support herself or himself, because of physical inability, support payments shall be in keeping with the ability of the party to pay." Parents would be held mutually responsible for the support of their children, and arrangements for their care would be under continual review by the centers.

And there would be *no* lawyers on either side when the husband and wife come to the center. The only fees they would have to pay would be a filing fee of $25 and certain other small costs. The centers, which would be fairly expensive to run, would also be financed by increasing marriage license fees.

At first the USDR was looked upon as a bunch of angry cranks and disgruntled fathers who wanted to avoid support payments. One writer called them "a crippled army of weaponless giant killers."

Then in 1965 the "crippled army" started finding weapons. Several of their members ran for office. None were elected but they got respectable vote totals. And in 1966 USDR came up with a potential blockbuster—an initiative measure. In California, as in several other states, a state constitutional amendment can be placed on the ballot if a large number of voters sign a petition for it. About 500,000 signatures are called for. The proposed initiative would strip the California courts of their powers to adjudicate domestic relations matters and replace them with the USDR's pet Family Arbitration Centers.

Now for the first time the organized Bar of California and the ABA itself began to take the USDR and its initiative proposal seriously. On March 1, 1966, the ABA accepted the challenge that might end all legal fees in divorce actions. One press release went: "Any attempt to create nonlawyer state agencies to handle domestic relations will be vigorously opposed by the American Bar Association." The release went on to mention that the ABA's all-powerful House of Delegates had unanimously adopted a resolution introduced on February 22, 1966, by Los Angeles Superior Court Judge Alton Pfaff, chairman of the ABA's Family Law Section. The resolution warned against adoption of currently proposed constitutional amendments and other legislation which would remove all domestic relations matters from courts and legal profession and "have such matters heard and determined by a state agency other than in the courts."

The resolution pointed straight to the culprits behind this. They were "nonlawyer groups in several areas of the United States, antagonistic to the legal profession and the judiciary." The whereas-besprinkled resolution closed with a recommendation that "a program of education be instituted to alert the general public to the dangers inherent in any such unwarranted departure from present procedure in family law."

Always ready to turn the enemy's weapons against them, the USDR sent thousands of copies of the resolution to its members:

Please write your newspaper editors, legislators, etc., telling them about the above Resolution of the American Bar Assn. Tell them that by their actions the Am. Bar Assn. seems more interested in preserving their existing profitable system of divorce whereby the lawyer is "paid to kill" the marriage rather than supporting our proposed system whereby people trained and experienced in human relations would be "paid to save" the marriage.

Apparently the divorce reformers didn't reach enough editors, legislators, etc., or even plain petition signers. The first initiative attempt didn't get nearly enough signatures and it died. Experts consider that it takes about $275,000 to get enough signatures for an initiative in California. "Obviously this kind of operation cannot be financed by our $10 yearly dues," mourned George Partis in a recent issue of his newsletter, *Divorce Chats*. He expects that family arbitration bills will be introduced in the California and Michigan legislatures in 1968.

But the divorce reformers' activities did bring forth a lot of editorial comment all over the state that *something* had to be done about the situation. Governor Brown appointed a Governor's Commission on the Family on May 11, 1966. On it were judges, law professors, ministers, lawyers and social workers. The commission was asked to report by December 31. The Governor told the appointees that "the time has come to acknowledge that our present social and legal procedures for dealing with divorce are no longer adequate." On January 1, 1967, Governor Brown was replaced by a *divorced* former actor, and the commission report got wide circulation.

It proposed establishing a family court within the framework of the existing Superior Court. A husband or wife would file a petition for dissolution of the marriage. A staff of trained counselors would provide help to the court in "a therapeutic, nonadversary proceeding seeking to hear vexing problems with understanding and helpfulness." The existing fault "grounds" for divorce or annulment would be eliminated. Provisions for support of the parties and the division of their property would not be determined on the basis of fault but rather on the needs and financial circumstances of both parties. Custody of children should be awarded only in the best interests of the child.

At first the court staff would try conciliation. If that didn't take or wasn't feasible, the assigned counselor would, no later than four months after the first interview, file with the court a written report—*"to be prepared only after consultation with the attorneys for each party."* Then would follow a private hearing, and if the court concluded that the marriage was irreparable, it would enter an order dissolving it. If the court was in doubt it could order a ninety-day waiting period during which the professional staff might work anew with the troubled couple. But if it still didn't take, the marriage would be terminated. All "orders of dissolution"—which already sounds much worse than divorce does—would be effective immediately without any of the traditional waiting or "hangfire" periods. If necessary, the professional staff would help the couple adjust to their post-dissolution state.

In many ways this is a broad, even novel approach to an enormously vexing social problem. But the occasional references in the report about the "attorney for each party" soured U. S. Divorce Reform. *No* lawyers, they cried. "If you have lawyers you still have adversary procedures. . . . Trickery is being resorted to."

For a long time to come, divorce will still be, for our lawyers, "their rent, their stenographer's salary, their baby's shoes, sometimes their solid-gold Cadillac." Why on earth should most of them *want* anything basic changed?

3 STUPID, LAZY OR INEPT

Lawyer: the only man in whom ignorance of the law is not punished.

—ELBERT HUBBARD

There are not competent people enough in the world to go round; somebody must get the incompetent lawyers and doctors.

—GEORGE BERNARD SHAW

. . . widespread knowledge that lawyers are insured would probably promote promiscuous claims and herald the birth of a new negligence industry—setting lawyer against lawyer for a percentage of the insurance proceeds—an ugly prospect indeed.

—PROFESSOR JOHN J. MEEHAN
Brooklyn Law School

The law—which is made by lawyers, administered by lawyers and adjudged by lawyers—is inevitably protective of the stupid, lazy or inept practitioner.

•   •   •

Item. Your mother pays a lawyer to make her will, in which she leaves everything to you and your brother. You go with your mother to the lawyer's office, and while you're there he says, "Joe, here, you sign as one of the witnesses." You do—and that costs you $85,000. The lawyer was appallingly stupid about a basic rule. Can you sue him and get your money back? No.

Item. Your lawyer is handling a personal injury case for you. Time goes by, he is disorganized, and it becomes too late to get the case on the court docket. He doesn't tell you about his forgetfulness. Instead he lies to you and stalls and years go by. You're out a likely $10,000 the case was probably worth. Can you sue him and get your money? No.

• • •

Because the law largely favors the lawyers in such matters there is enough law work in the country for only a few men like Nathaniel Rothstein of New York City.

A slender, gray-haired, gray-moustached suburbanite, Rothstein is New York's great repository of the costly sins of omission and commission of the city's lawyers. He is a busy trial lawyer with a specialty lawyers don't like to talk about: he defends lawyers who are sued for malpractice by their clients.

"No lawyer likes these cases," Rothstein told me. "But there are going to be more and more of them. Until recently, when lawyers spoke of malpractice actions they invariably meant *medical* malpractice. No more."

Most of Rothstein's cases come to him from the Continental National American Group Insurance of Chicago, which is the nation's second largest underwriter of lawyers' malpractice insurance. In 1966 the company took in about $700,000 in premiums from lawyers. One of them is *not* Nathaniel Rothstein, who has a $300,000 malpractice policy coverage that costs him about $150–$200 a year. His policy is underwritten by the St. Paul Fire & Marine Insurance Company of St. Paul, Minnesota. Nothing disloyal: he had the policy even before he began handling Continental's cases in this area.

St. Paul Fire & Marine writes about $2,500,000 worth of premiums in the lawyers' malpractice field and has become the largest in the field. Neither St. Paul nor Continental likes to give out figures, so outsiders can only guess. Assuming that the average attorney-policyholder is covered for about $25,000–$50,000, and his annual premium is around $50, there are probably fewer than 100,000 attorneys—out of the 212,000 in private practice—covered by malpractice insurance. A couple of other insurance companies write these policies—until 1956 *only* Lloyd's of London did—but there's no great push. For one thing, it's doubtful if either St. Paul or Continental has made any money out of this form of insurance. "The rates are too low and the claims too frequent," complains an executive at Continental. And the statistics are too uncertain, he might add.

No one has the remotest idea of the incidence of these cases, which the insurance companies *must* know in order to build their rate structure. Sterling Hutcheson, a San Diego lawyer who defends many lawyers' malpractice cases on the West Coast, listed the difficulties in the way of obtaining accurate statistics in the field.

Any such statistics . . . probably would not even be one ninth of the "mass" of cases of bad results or potential losses caused by lawyers' "errors" of which clients are ignorant or else for which they do not wish to sue.

Remarkably few cases go to trial. "At first the accused lawyer is adamant: 'I didn't make a mistake and I'm not at fault,' he tells us, but often when the trial date approaches he crumbles and urges a settlement," says a Continental executive.

Continental's biggest payout to-date was a $40,000 settlement in a case where a lawyer failed to file a client's negligence action in time. Nathaniel Rothstein, who has handled about seventy-five malpractice cases, recalls his worst payout as a $20,000 settlement. This was a case in which the plaintiff said that he had lost $200,-000 because of an error his lawyer had committed in a real estate closing. Rothstein thinks the lawyer involved "was probably in error." When I talked to Rothstein, the biggest case pending was one stemming out of a killing in the New York subway. A man had pulled a knife on a Transit Authority patrolman who shot the attacker. A grand jury wouldn't indict the patrolman, so the dead man's wife hired a lawyer to sue the Transit Authority for $1,000,000. But the lawyer didn't know—or forgot—that claims against the Transit Authority have to be filed within a year. His belated action was thrown out. Now the dead man's widow had hired another lawyer to sue the first one for malpractice.

Under its policy Continental won't *settle* a case without the consent of the lawyer involved because, as one of its selling brochures puts it, "unwarranted settlement of a claim against any attorney would do irreparable damage to his professional reputation." The brochure also explains why *every* lawyer needs malpractice insurance: "This policy protects against claims which the most competent attorney may not always avoid nor the wealthiest attorney always afford."

The policies are often sold with the help of bar associations. In turn, the insurance companies agree not to publicize malpractice insurance just so the public won't get ideas.

Occasionally, though, the victimized client may get the idea from the lawyer himself. Nathaniel Rothstein explained how: "He just tells a complaining client: 'I have insurance. Go after me.' The client often does."

But the client's chances are not very good in court. To understand why, let's take a look at one of the landmark cases which took place in California.

A lawyer named Gray was hired to draw up a will for an aging widow, a Mrs. Buckley. In it she left her sizable estate to her two sons. The lawyer drew up the will and then asked one of the sons to witness it. As any lawyer should know, that was a terrible mistake. The law is that an attesting witness to a will *cannot* be a beneficiary. When the will was offered for probate on the widow's death, the probate judge ruled the signing son was thereby excluded as a beneficiary. The victimized son sued lawyer Gray for $85,000, the inheritance he lost. The court held that he didn't have a case because *he* had not hired attorney Gray. In the law's inelegant language he wasn't "privy." The privy, or privity, rule is that the lawyer is liable to his client for negligence in his duties but *not* to any third parties. In effect, the only one who could have sued attorney Gray was the widow, Mrs. Buckley, who had hired him. But she was dead, so no case.

This 1895 case of Buckley vs. Gray became part of every legal text on contracts and came to the fore again in 1961 when California had another will case where it seemed the lawyer should have known better. It started when Eugene H. Emmick, who had made his money in movie theaters, left $2,300,000 in a will to several beneficiaries. The will had been drawn by his attorney for many years, Lisle S. Hamm, of San Francisco. He had been in practice more than forty years, and in that time had drawn hundreds of wills and trust agreements for clients.

Emmick wanted to do something nice for a friendly cigar-store owner named Lucas. Emmick had been coming into the store daily for many years, and in time learned all about Lucas' five children. In his will Emmick left the Lucas children a $200,000 trust fund to provide for their college education. When Emmick died, some of his blood relatives contested this trust fund to the outsiders. Their lawyer had found a serious technical error in the way Hamm had drawn the trust agreement. Since he was beginning to have doubts himself about the trust agreement's legality lawyer Hamm suggested a $75,000 settlement. The Lucases took the $75,000 and now hired lawyer Reginald Hearn to sue Hamm for negligence on the ground that his drawing of a faulty trust provision had done them out of some $90,000. (There were technical reasons for not asking for $125,000.) The first court that got the case threw it out without even listening to arguments. Hearn took it to the District Court of Appeals, which overruled the Superior Court and said the case should be tried on its merits.

The judges here added that Hamm could have consulted an expert in the drawing of trust agreements so that it would have been valid:

The law today has its specialties and even as the general practitioner in medicine must seek the aid of the specialist in his profession, so the general practitioner in law, when faced with a problem beyond his capabilities, must turn to an expert in his profession to the end that his client is properly served.

Lawyer Hamm carried the case to the state's highest court, the Supreme Court of California. In a unanimous decision that court decided Hamm wasn't liable for damages to the Lucas children.

The reasoning was a little peculiar. The court said, in effect, that the law governing certain aspects of trust agreements was murky and difficult, and an ordinary general practitioner of law couldn't be expected to be an expert in it.

("Ignorance of the law excuses no man," wrote John Selden, the great English jurist and scholar of the seventeenth century. "Not that all men know the law, but because it is an excuse every man will plead and no man can tell how to refute it.")

Hearn, the attorney for the Lucas children, was outraged, of course. But several other lawyers, unconnected with the case, also thought the court's ruling was dangerous and even silly. Writing in the *University of Richmond Law Notes*, D. Orville Lahy of Virginia saw it analogous to a case where

a physician-surgeon is not liable for malpractice where he negligently performs a very difficult operation, such as brain surgery on his patient, for the reason that such an operation is considered very complex in the medical profession. . . .

There is no doubt that the Supreme Court of California went to extremes to rescue the legal profession from a precarious area of professional liability. . . . Such judicial protection for a fellow member of the legal profession seems to be entirely without justification. It introduces a foul odor in the output of the fountain of justice and will inevitably evaporate in the arena of public opinion.

Recently, New York had a replay of the classic Buckley vs. Gray will case. In January, 1953, Benjamin Bosworth, a Brooklyn lawyer, drew a will for a widow, a Mrs. Goldberg. Bosworth had Harvey, her son and one of the main beneficiaries, sign it as a witness. The lawyer was paid by mother and son. When Mrs. Goldberg died in December, 1959, Harvey Goldberg found that he could not inherit a valuable piece of real estate because he had, at the lawyer's suggestion, signed the will as a witness. When Harvey sued lawyer Bosworth in 1961 the court said, too bad, but there was nothing to be done about it. More than eight years had elapsed and the statute of limitations had come into play. Goldberg's attorney argued reasonably that the negligence took place only when the will was offered for probate in 1959, and thus there was plenty of time to sue for negligence. Not so, said the court. The statute started running the moment the will was drawn in 1953.

Even Nathaniel Rothstein, whose sympathies are ordinarily with the defendant attorney in these actions, felt the court had really stretched to reach its conclusions:

. . . it is not so easy to accept the concept that the plaintiff [Goldberg] sustained damages as soon as the will was drawn. It would seem that actual damage . . . did not occur until the death of the testatrix [Mrs. Goldberg].

Rothstein suddenly got a large batch of lawyer negligence cases to defend in 1964 when the Appellate Division ruled the lower courts should dismiss cases in which lawyers hadn't diligently prosecuted their cases. Most of these were personal injury cases. When the clients' cases were dropped by the courts because their lawyers had been too tardy, some of the more sophisticated accident victims turned around and sued their lawyers for negligence.

"Many members of the legal profession," sighs Rothstein, "got caught." It was, he recalls, a nightmare period.

Every client has a "dream" figure which he expects to realize out of his accident case, and this does not facilitate the task of settling with the former client his claim in malpractice. Such a client is very much like a woman scorned, and not infrequently he seeks to cause disciplinary action to be taken against his erstwhile attorney in addition to suing him for damages.

It might be the long way 'round—but still, if clients were able to get compensated, one way or another, for their accidents, surely things weren't too bad. Rothstein shook his head.

"No, at best clients who were wronged by lawyers can't get a *complete* remedy. Don't forget they have to hire a lawyer to go after their first lawyer. That's going to be on a contingent fee basis, which means here at least a third or even 40 percent of what the client eventually gets is going to the second lawyer—*after* the case has been tried and won. The lawyer's fee can't be included in a malpractice suit."

So the poor client is still victimized financially in addition to undergoing a fair amount of aggravation and delay. U. S. Supreme Court Justice Hugo Black in November, 1966, denounced this resulting injustice to litigants who lose their day in court because of procedural difficulties:

> I find it inconsistent with a fair system of justice to throw out a litigant's case because his lawyer, due to negligence, or misunderstanding, or some other reason, fails to satisfy one of the procedural time limits. If a pound of flesh is required because of negligence of a lawyer, why not impose the penalty on him and not his innocent client?

Nathaniel Rothstein suggests another solution.

> Why should any litigant be given a pound of flesh? Wouldn't it be fairer to keep a litigant's case in court and perhaps penalize his attorney to the extent of charging him personally with costs up to, say, $250.

What happens when a lawyer knows his case has been thrown out of court for not acting in time and doesn't *tell* his client? Instead he stalls and fraudulently conceals his costly inaction by talking about the court calendar congestion and telling him not to worry. In New York there is a three-year statute of limitations on malpractice actions, so that if the lawyer can stall long enough . . .

Can the client then do anything about the lawyer who not only failed to act on his case but also lied to him regularly? All the reported cases so far favor the lawyer, fraud or no. Rothstein thinks this is unfair. "There should be a course of action against a lawyer who has practiced fraud against a client in concealing from him the facts in the case."

How could New York courts *not* see the injustice of the decisions against the aggrieved clients? I asked. "Well, judges can look kindly on lawyers, particularly those they know," Rothstein said.

The "kindly" look certainly didn't hurt a St. Louis lawyer, John J. Relles. He was sued for $75,000 by a former client, Charles Dorf, who runs a filling station in East St. Louis, Illinois, just across the river. Dorf had hired Relles to represent him after he had been badly hurt when his car was hit by a tractor-trailer. (An Illinois lawyer was associated with Relles, who wasn't qualified to practice in Illinois.)

During the trial Relles got an offer of $75,000 to settle the case. He didn't tell Dorf about it. The case went to the jury and it found against Dorf. Not a dime, let alone the $75,000 he might have had if attorney Relles had told him about the offer.

Dorf now hired another lawyer and sued Relles for negligence in having failed to discuss the $75,000 settlement offer. Relles denied there had been such an offer, but a jury in a U. S. District Court believed Dorf and awarded him a $75,000 verdict. Now lawyer Relles appealed to the U. S. Circuit Court of Appeals in Chicago, and the three-judge court unanimously decided in favor of the St. Louis lawyer on January 31, 1966. They held Relles' failure to inform his client about the offer didn't give rise to damages. They added that no attorney could be liable for an error in judgment. All that he owed his client is good faith and reasonable skill and diligence in prosecuting the action.

If a judgment against an attorney, on a record such as is before us, can be justified, the legal profession would be more hazardous than the law contemplates. An attorney could hardly afford to take the chance of communicating with his client by any means other than in writing or by having a record made of every conversation between them. . . .

In another recent case against a lawyer, Paul Sitton, a thirty-seven-year-old Knoxville, Tennessee, sheet metal worker, was "luckier." On December 4, 1959, Sitton was shot by John E. Fuller, the business agent of his union, Local 51 of the Sheet Metal Workers. The bullet entered Sitton's spinal column and caused permanent paralysis from the waist down.

Fuller was prosecuted and found guilty. He got a $500 fine for assault and a few months in jail for carrying a pistol. Sitton's lawyer, Hal H. Clements, Jr., had a contingent fee contract in which it was agreed he would represent Sitton in a civil action against Fuller and be entitled to 50 percent of any award. Clements didn't file any civil action within the one-year period allowed under Tennessee law. Sitton now hired two Nashville lawyers to sue attorney Clements for his inaction.

During the jury trial, Clements said he decided not to sue Fuller because (1) there was no chance for recovery against the union, and (2) any judgment against Fuller wouldn't have been collectible. The jury was told by the judge that the burden of proof was on Sitton to prove (a) that he was entitled to damages from Fuller and (b) that Fuller was solvent. (After his jail sentence was served, Fuller returned to his union post, which pays him $12,000 a year and expenses.) The jury believed Sitton and awarded him $162,500. At the time of the trial Sitton's medical and hospital expenses were $17,000.

Lawyer Clements asked the U. S. District Court in Tennessee to set aside the verdict. On May 11, 1966, the court ordered the Sitton award cut back to $81,250 because it was excessive and substantially more than Sitton could have recovered and collected from Fuller. Still, it was a victory—an all-too-rare one—for a client who had some reason to think he had been victimized by his lawyer. Admittedly, Sitton had to hire two other lawyers to prove his point, but the case does show that the courts are beginning to take a more stringent view of a lawyer's carelessness.

•   •   •

In going through U.S. legal records, attorney Sterling Hutcheson of San Diego could find only one judge who had publicly advocated *more* malpractice claims as being good for the practice of law. This was an Indiana justice who made the atypical comment back in 1868. "Fortunately for lawyers," wrote Hutcheson in the July, 1963, issue of *Insurance Counsel Journal,* "this theory has not taken widespread hold in the intervening century."

Quite the contrary. He adds, "In considering lawyers' malpractice cases as a group, the judge's protective attitude has been made apparent in almost all elements."

Then he goes on to list five major "doctrinal" barriers courts have erected that a plaintiff has to hurdle successfully before he can get a verdict in a lawyer malpractice case. And, he adds:

> There are numerous other minor ways in which judges have protected lawyers in legal malpractice suits—ways which are not reflected in the appellate decisions. For instance, in a recent West Coast case a judge in exercise of his discretion repeatedly sustained objections to the form of proposed hypothetical questions directed to an attorney witness who had been called by the plaintiff. . . . At the end of the case the judge reportedly told the attorney, "We don't testify against lawyers in this County."
>
> Any experienced or imaginative attorney will be able to think of a myriad of other breaks which "sympathetic understanding" from a judge could give him. And why not . . .

A cool, authoritative survey of "attorney malpractice" in the November, 1963, *Columbia Law Review* came to a similar conclusion—that a client wronged by his lawyer didn't have too good a chance to collect in court:

"The majority of decisions reflect a superficial analysis that is almost certainly colored by the fraternal concern of the judiciary for members of the practicing bar."

The anonymous author of the *Law Review* article was particularly unhappy that so many sued lawyers were able to win verdicts with their defense that they had simply made an "error of judgment." He felt that judges were accepting this much too readily, and went on to point out that none of us is allowed to get away with this excuse in one everyday situation: "In a case involving negligent operation of an automobile, it would be absurd to relieve a defendant of liability merely upon his assertion that he made an error of judgment. Virtually all actions for negligence are predicated upon errors of judgment."

Sterling Hutcheson, who defends lawyers in lawyer malpractice actions because he is usually hired by their insurance carriers to do so, has some mixed feelings about malpractice insurance. For example, he writes, ". . . a strong case could be made that malpractice insurance has in fact *aggravated* the [malpractice] problem."

Hutcheson has other unorthodox opinions about the rising number of malpractice cases. He thinks the bar itself might be partly to blame for the rise in malpractice cases against lawyers. He points to various programs to educate the layman about the law. As a result of such well-meaning programs, we now have

many laymen who are as informed or perhaps even more informed as to the law in a particular area than a sizeable number of lawyers. Here again we have a well-intended generally beneficial public program which nevertheless has a potentially disadvantageous by-product the tendency of a party to be more critical of an attorney and to be more apt to file a malpractice claim against him when he has demonstrated ignorance of a law.

Lawyer Hutcheson thinks the public relations campaigns bar associations have conducted in the recent past to improve the lawyer's image are also responsible for the rise in malpractice suits:

As efforts to improve the image of the lawyer in the public eye have been made by public relations experts, the populace has grown to expect more of the lawyers, and, therefore, when unsuccessful results occur or an error is committed, the claimant is more aware of the situation than in a climate where less would be expected of the lawyer.

Obviously, the public relations men employed by the bar have been following the wrong line. What lawyers need is a campaign that shows them as lazy, stupid, larcenous and altogether the very model of imperfect man. Says Hutcheson:

If you have a climate of opinion where people expect imperfections on the part of lawyers and do not expect to be able to get compensation in courts controlled by lawyers or former lawyers, the natural results would be fewer lawyers' malpractice claims. The disappointed client is obviously more apt to tell himself, "What else could I expect?"

Perry Mason has to start *losing* cases. When a script shows a lawyer stealing from a client's estate or otherwise diddling him, there shouldn't be any cries of outrage and great pressure on the TV producer in Hollywood, as now happens when the ABA's Legal Advisory Committee on Motion Pictures and Television gets to work there. The committee was miserably unhappy when it learned about a new TV show, *Trials of O'Brien,* that opened in the fall of 1965. O'Brien not only was divorced but refused to pay his wife alimony; he was generally rambunctious and fairly disrespectful of institutions lawyers are supposed to respect. If Sterling Hutcheson's hunch about a needed image of "the imperfect lawyer" is correct, surely the ABA should have secretly subsidized *Trials of O'Brien* when it was dropped for lack of popular appeal. In time, O'Brien properly guided by the new PR philosophy would have lost most of his cases, flaunted some simultaneous love affairs, avoided paying income taxes, cheated clients whenever possible, and bribed a few judges—who wouldn't stay bought. Then, surely the thousands of Americans who might feel they have a gripe against their lawyers would be constrained, in all fairness, to say to themselves: "Sure, I know, he's a stupid bastard (or a lying thief, or a lazy no-good), but still when I think that I might have gotten a lawyer like O'Brien—boy, *am I lucky.*" With the psychological groundwork handled so cleverly, lawyers' malpractice cases might fall away to nothing.

There was another possibility mentioned by lawyer Hutcheson. If only people did not *expect* "to be able to get compensation in courts controlled by lawyers or former lawyers, the natural results would be fewer malpractice claims."

I am surprised he missed still another way for people not to expect so much from lawyers, or justice in general. Hutcheson, who was born in Nanking, China, of medical missionary parents, surely knows that in the ancient days in China anyone with a complaint was entitled to beat the large cymbal that hung in the inner courtyard of the tribunal. Day or night, the mandarin had to come out to hear the complainant. But when the fierce Manchus took over the country they set out to break the authority of the mandarins. How? They ordered that *all* plaintiffs be whipped without mercy.

4 LOSER OF THE YEAR

May you have a lawsuit in which you know you are in the
right.
                    —Gypsy curse

On December 30, 1967, Clarence O. Jackson of Phoenix, Arizona,
was easily the Loser of the Year, America's own Job. His wander-
ings through a monstrous wasteland of evil, inept or listless lawyers, uncomprehending courts and an impersonal corporation's
set ways led to his staggering losses—of a $250,000 competence,
a wife, a home, a business and, nearly, his sanity. A local reporter
summarized the events: "Clarence Jackson fell into a legal meat
grinder and came out in shreds." Jackson's own coda is equally
incisive: "Somebody up there must sure hate my guts."

As the year was ending, Clarence Jackson was hopefully awaiting
a sign that his long, terrible time was over, that the overdue
good years were about to begin. The mailman gave him a thin
letter from Sears, Roebuck in Chicago. It had the uncrinkly stiff-
ness of money in an age when currency is transmitted in the form
of carefully punctured cardboard. At last a check from the company that had quite unconsciously and unintentionally helped
encompass his ruin. He opened the envelope and stared at the
check made out to Clarence Jackson. It was for—$1.35. There was
no letter of explanation.

He took the check to an acquaintance, Paul Dean, a skillful
newsman on the *Arizona Republic*. Dean made a phone call to
Chicago, then one to Rye, New York. When he finished he turned
to Jackson.

"Stonewall," he said, "you just won't believe this."

Jackson has a Mack truck hulk and a loud, gravelly voice that
one friend likens to "spring thunder down the Grand Canyon."

He boomed: "You kidding? After what I been through, I'll believe *anything*."

Dean smiled: "Even that you're now a stockholder in Sears, Roebuck? Someone's given you three shares. The $1.35 is a dividend check."

Jackson said: "I just might use them to start a proxy battle. It's the only kind of law trouble I haven't been in yet."

•   •   •

What happened to Clarence Jackson, among other things, was a sheriff's sale and a sly, unethical lawyer. The peculiarities and opportunities offered by the sheriff's sale of property to satisfy a court judgment sometimes tempt lawyers to become sly, unethical and, with a little luck, rich. The temptations and combinations do not exist only in Arizona. In February, 1968, there were more than 100 middle-class families in my own county, Nassau County, New York, who had been victimized gravely by such sales and their aftermath. And it's not as if they were done in by some archaic laws. They lost their homes and their equity because of new, modernized laws enacted in 1963—enacted, supposedly, to *help* middle-class homeowners caught in a jam. None of their tragedies are as total, as dramatic as Clarence Jackson's, but for each of these families deprived of their homes, the law has turned out to be a cunningly wicked oppressor.

In Black's *Law Dictionary*, a "sheriff's sale" is defined thus: "A sale of property, conducted by a sheriff, or sheriff's deputy, in virtue of his authority as officer holding process." (Holding process simply means that the sheriff is carrying out the orders of the court.) In Clarence Jackson's case, and in the others I shall describe, the court ordered the property sold to satisfy a judgment.

The means of collecting judgments from the poor wage-earner have been far better publicized. By now much of America has heard of the evils of wage garnishment and wage assignments that enable firms selling on installment to collect from a delinquent purchaser by getting hefty deductions from his wages. But the sheriff's sale has had far less publicity and cries of outrage. Thousands of workingmen have lost their jobs when their wages were garnisheed or attached—many employers don't like the extra bookkeeping involved—but victims of sheriff's sales have lost their homes and equity—quietly.

Clarence Jackson wasn't one of the quiet ones.

Now sixty-four, he came to Phoenix from Joplin, Missouri, in 1927. He was the son of a strawberry farmer. In Arizona he worked as a steeplejack and small-scale contractor. During World War II he built trailer camps and homes for the War Department. Then he got government contracts to supply meat to workers at Parker Dam in northern Arizona.

He did well, and by 1953 he was married, had a son and owned a 400-foot-long tract of land in northeast Phoenix. On the property were a shopping center, a gas station, some rental houses and some vacant land. His family had their own three-bedroom house on the property and were sitting pretty. The property was worth about $250,000 and there was only a small mortgage against it. He had a new Oldsmobile and $20,000 in savings. In all, their property was earning them about $36,000 a year.

Jackson decided to build eighteen motel-apartments on the remaining vacant lots of the tract. He planned to furnish the new apartments with original Western-style furniture made to his own design. He found a skilled furniture maker, and they decided to invest in a good set of power tools.

They ordered $1,500 worth of tools from Sears, Roebuck, but since Jackson knew he would need all the cash he had to help finance the motel, he made a small down payment of $75 and agreed to pay $75 a month. When the tools were delivered they were without motors. By this time Jackson had paid in $900, much of it before delivery of the tools.

When the wrangling with Sears got serious, Jackson asked his lawyer, Fred Wilson, a former state attorney general, for advice. Wilson advised him to stop further payments.

Sears, properly, came calling for the remaining payments or the tools. The demand was made by American Credit Bureau, the local Sears collection agency, represented by Paul H. Primock, a local attorney, and a former state assistant attorney general.

Primock took the claim to court. On May 19, 1955, a Superior Court judge ruled that Jackson must pay Sears. Jackson immediately appealed the verdict but he or his attorney failed to post two necessary bonds to cover the judgment of $625. A week later lawyer Primock obtained a writ to have the Maricopa County (Phoenix) sheriff sell the *entire* Jackson property in order to settle the $625 judgment.

In accordance with law, the impending sheriff's sale was advertised in small type in the local weekly legal journal, *The Chronicle*. Apparently neither Jackson nor his attorney saw the four required notices that appeared in June, 1955. On June 30, 1955, the $250,000 property was sold on the courthouse steps to "the highest bidder" for $647. The sheriff's deed showed the new owner to be "Sears, Roebuck and Company."

In Arizona, as in many other states, there is a redemption period of six months during which the sold property could be redeemed by the original owner. But since neither Jackson nor his attorney knew of the sale, they didn't redeem. On February 1, 1956, the unredeemed property was sold to Frank and Ethel Schwartz, the parents of the head of the American Credit Bureau, the Sears collection agency. Two months later the Schwartzes sold the property to the recently formed Pacific Investment Company, Inc.

This firm had been formed *two months before* the sheriff's sale in June, 1955. It had been incorporated by two legal secretaries and their employer, attorney Paul Primock. All of which would suggest that even back in April, 1955, Primock had had an idea about acquiring the Jackson property—one way or another. A corporate shell could hide his activities.

Primock's curious actions deserve a little special attention. He wasn't the first attorney with inside knowledge to pick up property for a fraction of its real value. Can lawyers do this? According to an opinion on legal ethics by the American Bar Association, rendered in 1931 in another related kind of situation, it was not ethical. The 1931 opinion went this way:

. . . certain lawyers make a practice of buying judgments, notes . . . from bankrupt estates for much less than their face value and of then collecting them at large profit to themselves. . . .

The Ethics Committee decided this practice was "improper":

It seems to us that such a course of conduct is violative of both the letter and spirit of Canon 28, which forbids lawyers to stir up strife and litigation. This opinion, it may be claimed, bars attorneys from entering a speculative field, which might be profitable and which is open to laymen; nevertheless we feel that the dignity of the profession as well as the ethics of the situation, are entirely consonant with the view herein expressed.

What attorney Primock did, of course, was far more serious, far more heinous. He had deliberately set up a dummy corporation to acquire a valuable property through a judgment he had obtained from a client, Sears, Roebuck.

Primock scented great opportunity here. He needed something to overcome the losses he had suffered when the Creole Club, a Phoenix night dive he headed, closed in March, 1955. Its license had been suspended after ten months of operation because disorderly persons had been allowed to frequent the place, and two ringleaders of a marijuana and heroin peddling gang had been found and arrested on the premises.

Having acquired the Jackson property quietly, Primock sat on it discreetly. He made no attempt to collect the rents from any of the tenants and certainly didn't inform Jackson he was now the owner.

Why such silence? Why pass up an opportunity to collect the $36,000 annually the Jacksons were making a year on the property? Primock was being cleverly patient. By doing nothing he would not alert Jackson that he no longer owned the property. By keeping quiet there was a chance that the statute of limitations would come into play, and Jackson wouldn't be able to do anything legally even if he discovered the truth. And finally there was always a chance Jackson would drop dead. It would be much tougher for his estate to try to upset Primock's ownership of the property.

So, in complete ignorance that he no longer owned his property, Jackson went about his business, collecting rents from his tenants and planning his new motel. He got a tentative mortgage commitment of $125,000 on the proposed project from an investment company, which naturally checked the title to the property. They now found that it was no longer owned by Clarence Jackson but some mysterious Pacific Investment Company.

With the news out, with concealment no longer necessary, lawyer Primock began trying to collect rents from the tenants on Jackson's property. Some paid him, others continued to give their monthly checks to Jackson. A few refused to pay until the question of ownership was settled.

Jackson's original attorney, Wilson, had moved to another part of the state, so Jackson now got two Phoenix attorneys, Otto Linsenmeyer and Stephen Connors, to fight for him. For a flat fee of $10,000 they agreed to fight to upset the sheriff's sale of the Jackson property.

On September 30, 1957, the Arizona Supreme Court, in the case of Clarence Jackson vs. Sears, Roebuck, held that the sheriff's sale **was** illegal on a technicality of timing. Now Jackson got his property back, but things were not the same as before.

His living expenses during this battle had eaten up his savings. He now owed attorney fees, and a life insurance company wanted $37,000 he owed them for the mortgage on the property plus interest and back payments.

The only way out was to sell his reclaimed property—under the gun of foreclosure by the insurance company. In that kind of sale, with the acrid smell of potential law trouble all around, property seldom fetches what it is really worth. So Jackson had to settle for a rough deal that brought him only $70,000—$54,000 in cash and $16,000 in the form of 160 acres of desert land, some 60 miles west of Phoenix. Jackson didn't get a dime of the cash after the mortgage was paid and the lawyers satisfied. The 160 acres? He mortgaged that for a few thousand to live on.

At the time of the sale of the property Jackson still hoped that he would come out ahead because of a damage suit he had pending against Sears for $220,000. After the sale he discovered that his lawyers had signed away his right to sue in connection with any of the previous land transactions. Jackson has sworn in court this was done by his attorneys without his consent.

Jackson's lawyer, Linsenmeyer, says the right to sue Sears had to be waived, else the $70,000 sale could never have gone through. He says these documents were signed in front of Mr. and Mrs. Jackson.

Jackson went to the bar association with a complaint against Linsenmeyer and Connors for conspiring to cheat him. The bar's grievance committee investigator said that "the charges were sour grapes . . . unfortunately this man's mind is filled with injustice, and my opinion is that the normal delay of litigation killed him."

Metaphorically, only. Jackson wasn't dead yet—in spite of further soul-killing troubles that might have caused even Biblical Job to follow his wife's advice: "Curse God and die." For example:

—Jackson couldn't find a job because he was nearly sixty.

—He was ineligible for welfare because he owned the desert land, even if it was nearly worthless.

—He worked on a construction job for his ex-lawyer Linsenmeyer for less than six months. Linsenmeyer refused to pay part of the wages Jackson thought he was due. Jackson sued the lawyer and his claim for $2,300 was upheld. But Linsenmeyer has appealed and refused to pay. "Why should I," he said. "This guy still owes me plenty in past attorney fees."

—Jackson is ineligible for unemployment insurance because he never made payments on himself. He might be eligible if he can *prove* he was once employed by Linsenmeyer.

—After forty years of marriage, Mrs. Billie Jackson left her husband. "We didn't have a fight or an argument or a dispute," Jackson explains listlessly. "I just couldn't feed her. I don't blame her. She could take the ups, but she couldn't take the downs."

—Jackson tried to interest the Maricopa County attorney, Robert K. Corbin, in reinvestigating the case against attorney Linsenmeyer. He left thirty-four legal folders of files—some twelve inches thick—with Corbin. They got lost. "And I have no idea where they could be," says Corbin. "I've torn this office apart trying to find them, and we will continue to look." Corbin's investigator did spend some five months checking out Jackson's claims. But no action could be taken, since fraud could not be proved and the statute of limitations had expired.

—He lived in his son's rundown, tiny little cottage on the northeast edge of the city. But it is eight miles to downtown Phoenix, and the pickup truck Jackson managed to retain from the once sizable property needs tires and a new engine. So he hitchhiked once a week downtown—for 100 successive weeks—just to keep his claim alive at the unemployment insurance office.

—He had a meager vegetable and fruit patch going on his son's small property that provided him with a bare and meatless diet—until the spring of 1967 when a lack of fertilizer and insecticide killed the patch's growth completely. Other anonymous enemies—Mexican fruit flies—devoured his grapes, peaches and figs.

Strangely enough this almost incredible legal tragedy was being played out privately until March 11, 1967. Until that time there hadn't been a line in any Phoenix paper—except the legal notices that attorney Primock had run in 1955.

It wasn't as if Jackson didn't try to get his story told. He wrote his state's senators in Washington: "The reason I am writing is because I'm going nuts trying to find someone who can help me." His letters rambled on about the power tools: "Experts say they were just new scrap iron, junk worth about $14 a ton. I had about $20 worth, which I bought for approximately half a million dollars."

He was told, of course, to get a good lawyer. In lawyers' offices he poured out his account, and invariably the aghast counselor led him to the door: "My God! Somebody owes you half a million dollars." But, personally, he wasn't in a position to take on a case so hopelessly involved.

Jackson went to two Phoenix newspapermen, one a columnist and the other a general assignment reporter. Another reporter who knows both men explains why nothing happened: "Unless you have four hours to spare, the Jackson story is difficult to understand, and his appearance, obsession and method of transmitting the details do go against him. . . ."

Finally on March 11, 1967, Jackson found a more receptive newspaperman in the shape of Jim Young, a Phoenix real estate broker who had once served as an Arizona legislator. His paper is a small, informal offset weekly called *The Arizona Spokesman* ("Speaking out for freedom, democracy, and better government, the foundations of the U.S.A., the World's Greatest Republic."). Young, a Democrat, told the story briefly in two issues. The Jackson tale was headlined "From Riches to Rags." The lead was:

> The County Attorney of Maricopa County and the Arizona Attorney General's office agree that "someone owes Clarence Jackson $500,000." But they refuse to move on the case in which Sears, Roebuck and Company seized property worth over $250,000 for the satisfaction of a $600 debt.

Still, the story remained a purely local matter. Then in its July, 1967, issue a new Arizona quarterly, *Reveille,* told in still more detail, "The Strange Unhappy Case of Clarence Jackson." The story was written by Paul Hughes, a local newsman and TV personality, who now runs the magazine in the absence of its publisher and founder, Robert B. Choate, Jr., now with the Ford Foundation. As a result of this story, Jackson did get back in the supermarket business—as a $1.40-an-hour carryout boy at El Rancho Supermarket, which is about two miles from where his former $250,000 property is located.

Now the story began to interest J. Edward Murray, managing editor of the daily *Arizona Republic.* He was particularly interested by the legal aspects because he is chairman of the press-bar committee of the American Society of Newspaper Editors. Murray assigned the story to one of his best reporters, Paul Dean, who proceeded to check out every aspect of it during the next four weeks.

On Sunday, August 27, 1967, Paul Dean's long, detailed account appeared. A few days later *Time* magazine had its own account in the issue of September 1—"The Luck of Clarence Jackson"—and Jackson's tale became known nationwide.

Most of the readers' letters that appeared referred, inevitably, to Dickens. How is it, asked one *Time* reader,

that Sears, Roebuck, having retained this scrofulous attorney [Primock] and empowered him to act in its name, does not have the same responsibility for his actions as it would if a clerk shortchanged a customer. . . . If it is possible for a lawyer to act "ostensibly" for a corporation while in fact pursuing private and nefarious interests, then we have some loose bricks in our legal structure—most of which seems to have fallen on Mr. Jackson's head.

Another reader was simply confirmed in his "suspicion about three sacred cows: the law, lawyers, and Sears, Roebuck."

The "scrofulous attorney," Paul H. Primock, died in April, 1963, of a heart attack. He was forty-nine. I asked a local investigator to check on Primock's will, to see if there was any clue as to Primock's profits by this kind of sharp practice. His report:

Attorney Primock left an estate of only $7,979. Not much there to indicate big profits from quick deals. Ironically, $2,500 went in attorney fees and another $2,500 to the will's executor.

I have tried to see if Primock was involved in other sheriff's sales. There is no cross-reference. Without checking every sheriff's deal for the past 15 years it would be impossible to come up with an answer on that.

Attorney Wilson, Jackson's original lawyer, who had, supposedly, advised him not to pay Sears, refused to talk to newsmen at all. Sears, of course, couldn't get away with *that*.

For one thing, several local prominent citizens wrote Sears' headquarters in Chicago expressing their ire at the situation.

Sears reacted in several ways. First, it issued a memorandum for its credit managers in its 785 stores urging them to exercise "much closer supervision" of the company-delegated collection agencies. The memo went on:

Customers who make verbal inquiries relative to this particular case should be informed that it was a very unusual case which involved many legal technicalities . . . they should be informed that most of Mr. Jackson's financial difficulties began after Sears had divested itself of the property.

In fact, Sears had begun questioning the Jackson mess back in 1956 when it sent a letter to attorney Primock asking him to "relate all of the facts" in the judgment he had secured against Jackson.

Primock in his reply in 1956, said that before the sheriff's sale he had contacted Jackson's attorney, Fred Wilson, for the $625 owing but received nothing. Primock further insisted that a sale notice of the property had been posted on Jackson's block-long development.

Sears is still conducting a long, intensive investigation of the entire matter. It naturally feels that it is getting the blame for something it had little to do with. As a Sears attorney put it: "As far as we can tell, all Sears got out of it was $312, representing half the money owed by Jackson, with the other half going to the American Credit Bureau."

Then in December, 1967, Sears acquired another reason to interest itself in the Jackson affair. The $1.35 check Jackson got at year-end was a dividend payment on three shares of Sears, Roebuck stock. Paul Dean found that the stock had been anonymously transferred to Jackson by a "wealthy old lady in Rye, New York," who had read of Jackson's monumental troubles. The three shares were then worth about $180.

There was another good thing that happened to Jackson as a result of the publicity. Someone sent him a check for $100 to repair his broken-down pickup truck. There was a proposal of marriage and a free, dues-paid membership in Losers, Incorporated, of La Crosse, Wisconsin.

The local and state bar associations, already uncomfortable at many of the disclosures in the entire affair, got another blow. In September, 1967, a Phoenix citizens' group moved to disband the State Bar of Arizona, an agency it claims is "a sanctuary to protect the dishonest acts of lawyers." The group hopes to get sufficient signatures on an initiative petition—about 38,000—to enable the voters in November, 1968, to repeal the law granting the State Bar broad disciplinary powers over its members. They feel the policing function should be handled by the Arizona Supreme Court. (Actually the Court now has the final say on disbarments, anyway.)

Among the charges the petition-gatherers level against the bar is that it allowed its members to "bankrupt" Clarence O. Jackson.

Several local lawyers were and are still appalled at the Jackson case, particularly the prime role of lawyer Paul Primock. Several feel that if Primock had been acting simply and ethically he would have first tried to secure a judgment against Jackson's new car, worth far more than the $625 sought, or even against his $20,000 savings account, rather than against his total property. Primock's having a handy, quiet little corporation ready, and then sitting still for months after he had acquired Jackson's property, makes some lawyers certain he was up to no good.

One of the lawyers called the situation "nightmare stuff." He added, "What happened to Jackson is one of the most terrible things I ever heard of happening to a man in this country."

But nothing has changed. It could happen again.

In lesser measure, it *is* happening again within a few miles of where I live in Nassau County, New York.

5 HOW TO GET KICKED OUT OF THE MIDDLE CLASS BY A LAW

Unnecessary laws are not good laws, but traps for money.
—THOMAS HOBBES, *Leviathan*

On February 9, 1967, Walter Byrd, a forty-year-old employe of the Department of the Army, was at the lowest point of his life: he was about to be kicked out of the middle class. He had just lost a corner brick Cape Cod home in New Cassel, Long Island, a neat neighborhood of one- and two-story private homes, not far from the original Levittown.

Byrd, a short, compact ex-sergeant major in the Army, bought the home with his wife, Dorothy, in 1958 by saving $2,600. With the $13,600 house they got an $11,000 mortgage. In 1967 the house was worth about $20,000, and the Byrds had paid off part of the mortgage so that it was down to $9,000. In all, then, they had had an $11,000 equity in the house.

At this moment in February they had already lost their house, their stake in suburbia. It was *not* because of some sly, scheming lawyer. They had lost it because a group of learned, very able law professors—financed by the New York State Legislature—had, in their wisdom, revised a set of New York State law practices dealing with the sheriff's sale of homes for debt. With their revisions —which they had innocently thought would *help* the strapped homeowner—they provided a cruel set of weapons for clever connivers.

For the Byrds, this private catastrophe was particularly grim and poignant. The loss of their home and the $11,000 equity in it was, in a sense, even greater than Clarence Jackson's endless tragedy in Phoenix. The Byrds have one disability that even Clarence Jackson, the victim of random misfortune and legal chicanery, didn't have to sustain: the Byrds are Negro.

Their route to the middle class hadn't been easy.

As a sixteen-year-old Pennsylvania lad, Walter Byrd entered the Army in 1942 ("My mother signed for me"). He was in Pacific combat, earned two battle stars, and after the war was over was assigned to West Point where he rose to become the sergeant major of the supply unit. There he met his wife, Dorothy, who was then working with the Quartermaster laundry unit. In 1953 he got his discharge and began working for the Department of the Army as a civilian. Now in 1967 he had risen to a GS-7 rating, earning $6,300 at Fort Hamilton, where he works for a unit that buys cobalt, mica and tungsten for national defense.

In New Cassel, Byrd was active as a lay minister in the local Pentecostal Church, to which the Byrds contributed $200 a year. As an active do-it-yourselfer, Byrd had built in many improvements in the house, including a ten-foot-long hi-fi unit for the living room.

Now at this tragic moment in February, 1967, the comforts, and friendships the Byrds had formed in New Cassel were at stake. In desperation, Walter went seeking a lawyer to see if anyone could get him out of the mess.

"Maybe I was too suspicious, but I had never used a lawyer in my life. Even at the home closing we used the bank lawyer. I asked around at my union if they had any kind of lawyer service but they didn't," he told me.

Somehow, he wandered into the second-floor office of the Nassau County Legal Aid office in Mineola. He got to see John C. Schaeffer, Jr., attorney in charge, who turned him over to Robert Akeson, six-three, lanky, gray eyed ex-Marine staff sergeant. Now 36, Akeson has been a Legal Aid lawyer six years. "I get a big kick out of it," he admits boyishly.

As with all applicants for legal aid, Walter Byrd had to establish that he was eligible. When he was asked how much he earned, he said $6,300 a year, his gross pay. Akeson grimaced faintly. With only one child the Byrds were over the earnings limit. Ordinarily Nassau Legal Aid would not take on a client with a wife and two children if he earned more than $125 a week, or $6,500 a year. Still, as Akeson puts it, "we're flexible. We have to consider a man's net or take-home pay, too. He was close to our limits, really. From the first sentence when he came in I knew what kind of trouble he was in. He said, 'Mr. Akeson, I don't own my home anymore.' He was in a sweat and I just sensed this was another Article 52 case. I figured that by this time I probably knew more about that damn article than any lawyer on the Island."

Always fearful of taking on clients who can afford private lawyers, Legal Aid men ask detailed income questions. Did Mrs. Byrd work outside? Byrd said she didn't. In his desperately frightened state he forgot that his wife did have an odd kind of income: she earned $5,000 a year for taking care of four Negro foster children in their home. The money is paid by a Nassau County welfare agency that tries to place as many homeless children as possible in private homes. Had Akeson known the Byrds had a joint income of $11,300 a year there would have been nothing he could have done for them; no way he could have taken on the case. As far as Legal Aid was concerned, they simply would have been earning too much money.

In all innocence the special question wasn't asked and that minor sin of omission turned out to be the luckiest break the Byrds could have gotten during their troubles.

It all started with an installment purchase of a three-piece living room set in 1958 from the Simon Furniture Company in Manhattan for $550. They made their monthly payments steadily and had paid off about $220 when Dorothy Byrd became very sick. She needed two operations. Even though the Byrds were covered by health insurance, including Blue Cross, they were still out more than $800, including $500 spent for blood. When several payments were missed, the Simon Furniture Company turned over the delinquent account to their attorney, who got a judgment against the Byrds in December, 1959. The facts of the judgment were filed in the basement of the County Clerk's office in Mineola, Long Island.

Simon Furniture turned the judgment over for collection to

Abbe Credit Corporation in New York City, and the Byrds made occasional payments of $10 or $20 whenever they could. Since they had gone heavily into debt to pay for Dorothy's four-month siege of illness there was almost nothing left over to pay for the furniture. (Mrs. Byrd didn't have the foster-child income then.)

Meanwhile the judgment against the Byrds and thousands of similar judgments were occupying the attention of the Advisory Committee on the Civil Practice Act. The Advisory Committee, consisting of a group of eminent and learned law professors, reported to the New York State Legislature, which financed their efforts.

Essentially, what they had to do was modernize and simplify the Civil Practice Act of 1920–21. This governed, among many other categories, the procedural law on debtor and creditor, installment sales, sheriff's sales, and the like. Since 1921 there had been many changes and amendments, and now an omnibus revision was needed. The job took nearly six years and covered six separate reports submitted to the legislature, which finally adopted the whole package—covering eight closely printed volumes—to take effect in September, 1963.

Under the old law, when the sheriff sold a home for debt the original owner had a year to redeem his property, if he could. Very few redeemed, according to Assistant Professor David A. Siegel of St. John's Law School in Brooklyn. Siegel, a specialist in the state law involving money judgments, had made a long study of the subject. He found that not only did few original owners redeem but hardly anybody would come to a sheriff's sale to buy the distressed property because the owner's right of redemption made it an unattractive purchase. Accordingly, he and the other law professors recommended the right of redemption be eliminated. "Its abolition is designed," he wrote, "to increase the price bid at the sale and the number of persons bidding." In short, if the highest bidder could get the auctioned property immediately, why, there would be more bidders for the home. Then, presumably, the auctioned home would fetch appropriate prices, since there would be active bidders, instead of the usual small clique of insiders specializing in distressed property.

Another change was introduced in 1963. In the past, a creditor with a judgment—say, a furniture installment firm that had a judgment against a defaulted buyer, as in the Byrd case—had to try to get its money first by trying to collect on personal property before it could move against a man's home. This would include a debtor's bank account or car. No longer. Now a creditor could move immediately to take over a man's home.

Both new provisions obviously made it easier for creditors to get their money by acting directly against the debtor's home. But the logical legal theory had ugly realities.

Before the new Civil Practice Law and Rules (CPLR) went into effect on September 1, 1963, whip-sharp characters studied it carefully and saw immense possibilities. Among them were some collection attorneys and a few realty companies that specialize in buying up distressed properties at sheriff's sales and tax sales.

One of the realty outfits was the Community Capital Corporation, Robert E. Blackman, president. The corporation was formed shortly after the present CPLR went into effect in 1963. Blackman is thirty-six, olive-skinned, and separated from his wife and three children. With some pride he showed me a *New York Times* clip for September 4, 1965, which listed his bankruptcy declaration. He was identified as a real estate broker and investor: Liabilities $480,573 and assets $10,541. Then he withdrew his bankruptcy declaration and determined to pay off "dollar for dollar." He told me he still owes $80,000 but hopes to pay that off in three or four years. "Most of the people I owed money to were local attorneys. Why should they be stuck?" (They had lent him the money to conduct his real estate speculations.)

Blackman dropped out of Cornell after two years and became a real estate salesman. A year later he had his own office and bought properties on foreclosure. "Things went great. I was borrowing money at two percent a month to buy property, but suddenly the market dropped and I was stuck with $250,000 worth of property. Also, my marriage collapsed then."

The office of Community Capital is a windowless basement in a modern two-story building in Mineola, the county seat of Nassau County. Blackman's office is across the street from the county building where he does his research. There in the basement of the county building he checks through the recorded judgments. One day while conducting such a search he found that Walter and Dorothy Byrd seemed to have several judgments against them.

"You gotta be careful," Blackman explained. "You can't tell which judgments are still valid. A man finishes paying a judgment, the lawyer involved should send a 'sat'—a satisfaction of judgment to the country records section. But it's a nuisance and a lot of lawyers don't do it."

One of the men in the Nassau County Sheriff's Office was more vehement. "You got these cheap lawyers. A judgment has been paid off in full, the lawyer comes along and says gimme another $25 or I don't put in a satisfaction of judgment. 'Clean' lawyers will do this without charge. What the hell, it only costs him $1.50 for the County Clerk fee to issue a certificate of satisfaction."

Clearly, then, many of the thousands of judgments entered with the County Clerk aren't valid. Many of them have been paid, but because some lawyer wouldn't issue a "sat" unless he got the extra $25 there are thousands of people in Nassau, as elsewhere, who have serious clouds on their home titles they don't know about. Only when they try to sell their home do they generally find out. Often such a suddenly discovered impediment to their ownership will kill the sale.

Blackman satisfied himself—he wouldn't tell me how—that the judgment the Simon Furniture Company had against Walter and Dorothy Byrd was valid. It had not been paid off. Then he drove to their home in New Cassel, gave it a long once-over and concluded that it was eminently salable. Now he was ready to move.

He phoned Simon Furniture and told them that Community Capital was ready to collect their judgment for them against the Byrds within six months. All he wanted was a 50 percent fee plus any attorney fees.

Admittedly, Simon Furniture had long before given this account to Abbe Credit, but it is customary to give "dead" accounts to collection agencies on a nonexclusive basis, for a limited period of time, pending results. Robert Rivkin of Simon Furniture consented. Later he was to say in an affidavit:

What was strange and what should have struck me at the time, but unfortunately did not, was why Community Capital Corp. was specifically interested only in the Walter and Dorothy Byrd account. . . . It was also strange that unlike other collection agencies that I had dealt with, who requested nothing in writing, Community Capital Corp. sent me two forms to sign.

One of the forms provided that Blackman's attorney, Mark S. Charwat, of Mineola, would be authorized to act for Simon Furniture in any legal matters connected with collecting the judgment. But unless Blackman did collect, neither he nor his attorney were to get anything. Charwat was to keep the furniture firm "fully advised of developments."

On October 8, 1966, Blackman had all the necessary authorizations from Simon Furniture. For a supposedly hustling collector he made no moves to collect: no calls to the Byrds, no threatening letters or ominous visits.

Meanwhile the Byrds, completely unaware the sky was about to fall, were still making payments from time to time to Abbe Credit on the old furniture bill.

As soon as Blackman had the necessary authorization to act for Simon Furniture, he moved through his attorney to have the sheriff of Nassau County prepare an execution sale against the Byrd home. To comply with the legal provisions, Blackman gave the sheriff $175 to cover his fees and the cost of the four legal notices that would be run in *Newsday*, a leading Long Island daily.

The sheriff prepared a notice of sale, which indicated that the Byrd house was going to be sold because of a judgment for $592.26. Actually, at this time the Byrds only owed the furniture company $371. Thus Blackman was spending $175 plus the cost of his attorney in order to get half of a $371 judgment, which would be $185.50. Obviously, it made no economic sense at all—unless there was a possibility of a much bigger payout.

The Byrds were sent a mimeographed notice of the proposed sheriff's sale. Walter Byrd doesn't recall getting it. But, he admits, "I was negligent. I knew I was paying Abbe on the furniture bill and I probably just figured this was legal rigmarole."

On December 10, 1966, Blackman visited the Byrd home and talked to Mrs. Byrd. According to her affidavit the following took place:

He told me he was a collector for Simon Furniture. He sat down in my living room and said we owed $900 to Simon. He read from a little card. I told him that the original furniture did not cost that much. He asked me if I wished to consolidate all my bills. He said he wished to speak to my husband to try to help us out. . . . I showed him the book from Abbe Credit and told him I was paying them. . . .

He never disclosed the fact that an execution against our home had already been issued on October 10th. He told me that I had a very nice home and asked whether I had given any thought to selling the house. He left and told me no one else would bother me about the bill.

The next day Dorothy Byrd called Simon Furniture and told them that a collector had come to her home but that he wasn't from Abbe Credit. She asked why two people were collecting this account and why the latest collector was asking for $900 when the Byrds only owed Simon $371. She said she would continue paying Abbe Credit as she had in the past. In December she tried phoning Blackman at his office, only to be told he was away on vacation.

The sheriff's sale took place on January 12, 1967, in a windowless conference room of the Sheriff's Office in the Nassau County Building in Mineola. Present besides the sheriff's office clerks were Blackman and a friend of his named Andy Libasci, who works for Regal Realty in Jamaica, New York. Regal Realty, which has been in business more than thirty years, specializes in buying up distressed properties at sheriff's and tax sales.

Libasci, a thin-faced, wiry ex-Navy veteran of about forty, made the only bid—of $100—on the Byrd home. In the absence of any other bids the sheriff sold the Byrd home to him, so that he now had a property with at least $11,000 equity in it for only $100. Shortly thereafter, Libasci turned over to Blackman the sheriff's deed to the Byrd home. He says now that he had only done it as an accommodation for his friend, Blackman, who didn't happen to have $100 with him. More practically, of course, it would have been most awkward in the eyes of the law if Blackman, just a temporary collector for Simon Furniture, were to acquire the deed directly as a result of a judgment won by his "employer." (In a vaguely similar spot in the Phoenix property of Clarence Jackson, attorney Paul Primock had some friendly dummies buy the Jackson property for him at the sheriff's sale.)

That same January 12—the grimmest Thursday the Byrds ever had—they got the first real warning that their home had been taken away when they received a telegram from Blackman: YOU HAVE TEN DAYS TO VACATE YOUR HOME.

Through all this, Simon Furniture, which had been the innocent vehicle Blackman used to get the Byrd home, never got a dollar out of Blackman, who was going to collect the judgment for them.

By late January, 1967, when Blackman legally owned the home, Walter Byrd decided he had better look for a lawyer. A fellow church member told him the Nassau Bar Association had a Legal Referral Service. He called and they suggested a law firm in Westbury. He went there and told the lawyer his trouble, and the latter, with Byrd, called on Robert E. Blackman. "But the way they talked—I kept hearing figures like $7,000–8,000 that Blackman insisted he had to get—I decided this wasn't for me. But the lawyer didn't charge me anything when I said I wouldn't hire him."

Then on February 9 he visited Bob Akeson at Nassau Legal Aid, and the Byrds became clients.

Their legal position was pretty hopeless. Blackman had been rigorously and meticulously legal in all his maneuvers. Akeson almost didn't have the heart to tell Walter Byrd that, bad as things seemed, they were actually much worse. Byrd knew he no longer owned his own home, knew that he was being threatened with eviction from the home by Blackman. What he didn't know is that even after losing his home and being kicked out, *he would still be liable to the bank on the unpaid balance of his mortgage*. Not only had he lost his $11,000 equity in his home, but he was still liable for the $9,000 that remained unpaid on his mortgage: a catastrophic $20,000 disaster because they owed a few hundred dollars on furniture bought eight years before. And, incidentally, he would still owe Simon Furniture for the unpaid balance, plus interest.

"Sure, you could say the Byrds *should* have taken steps earlier," Akeson told me. "But lots of people often act like ostriches when threatened by legal action. They're *afraid* of lawyers and they don't understand 'legalese.' "

There had been many others before the Byrds who had come to Legal Aid. In one case a doctor's $90 bill had led to the sale of a $19,000 house; in another case a couple lost their home as the result of an unpaid $147 dental bill.

The one remote hope Akeson saw for the Byrds was the fact that Abbe Credit had accepted one of their $10 monthly payments after they had already lost their house to Blackman. No doubt it was a minor clerical error, but still it should not have been accepted.

In his first talks Akeson found Blackman, the new owner of the Byrd house, insisting on getting at least $8,000 to let the Byrds have their house again. Blackman knew the equity in the house was about $11,000, so in a sense he was offering a kind of bargain. Not, of course, as great a bargain as he had obtained for $100 plus the $175 in sheriff's costs.

Now Akeson talked to Simon Furniture and their attorneys. For the first time the firm found out just what Blackman's Community Capital Corporation had been up to when it persuaded the credit-furniture company to let him try to collect their judgment from the Byrds. They were properly horrified—particularly when they discovered they and Abbe Credit were being sued for $20,000 damages by the Byrds.

As Simon Furniture was to say later, officially:

During fifty years in business, we have *never* requested or authorized an attorney or anyone acting on our behalf to levy against a debtor's home, in order to satisfy a debt owed to us! . . .

I must admit that we . . . were "duped" and taken for complete fools by the Community Capital Corp. . . . We never authorized Community Capital Corp. or their attorney to levy against the Byrd's property and they never consulted us. . . .

Now Simon Furniture joined Akeson in a move to upset the sale of the Byrd home to Blackman. They asked the court to set aside the sale on the ground that the court had the power to do this "where there exists hardship, mistake or unfair conduct." Their language was even stronger: "The payment of $100 at a sheriff's sale for a piece of property that can be resold, after satisfaction of mortgage, for a net profit of at least $10,000, is most unconscionable and most shocking."

Their court motion went on to urge the court to vacate the sale, "in the light of the 'duping' . . . by Community Capital Corp., and in the light of the fraud and misrepresentation and premeditated scheme of unjust enrichment practiced by the defendant Community Capital Corp. . . . ."

With Simon Furniture also arraigned against him, Blackman was in a weaker position. When the case came up in the Supreme Court in Mineola in August, 1967, the judge's sympathies were clearly with the Byrds. When he asked Akeson's and Blackman's lawyers if they couldn't get together on a settlement, the lawyers went out into the hall to talk it over again.

As Akeson recalls it: "We had the judge's sympathy, I'm sure, but they had the law on their side. By this time Blackman had gotten a title policy on the Byrd home, which meant that the title company thought his ownership was secure, too."

At first Blackman wanted $7,500. By gradual stages he was whittled down to $4,500, $2,500, and finally he remained adamant at $1,750. He was able to show that he had made three payments totaling $375 to the bank that held the mortgage on the house; $150 for a title policy; another $30 for a new fire insurance policy. What with one thing and another he insisted he had already paid out $730, not counting his lawyer fees. Finally, Akeson urged Walter Byrd to accept the settlement. Byrd agreed but asked for a few months to round up the money. By November 20, 1967, the Byrds, making enormous efforts—friends, family, credit union—were able to get their hands on $1,750, and reacquired their home.

The Byrds are enormously grateful to Bob Akeson and Nassau Legal Aid. "We pray for them at our church," the Byrds told me. "And to help the Lord help us," Walter Byrd went on, "the Byrd family no longer buys anything on time. When we want something we save for it. When all that mess was going on I slept pretty bad, kicking and cursing myself: after all our hard work and sweat to get the land and build this house and then lose it for $100 . . . . it was just killing me."

Ray Vietheer, the Nassau deputy sheriff, in charge of these home sales, was visibly pleased when I told him the Byrd case had a fairly happy ending after all. Vietheer, who looks like one of those heavy, obdurate, emotionless deputies out of Central Casting, was fairly vehement when we discussed the new law that made possible these sales of homes for small debts.

"I worry about these sales. They're *final*. A fellow volunteer fireman I know in my town on the south shore called me: 'Hey, Ray, what kind of racket you guys working?' He was also about to lose his home on a sheriff's sale, which meant I'd have to be in on it. I felt like hell. But he worked it out and saved his house. But a lot more didn't. We had about 150 homes sold on sheriff's sales in Nassau County in 1967. I'd sleep a lot better if there was at least a ninety-day grace period *after the sale* during which the original homeowner could redeem. Imagine losing a home for $100. It's just crazy."

Curiously enough, even Robert Blackman thinks the present law is too harsh. "There ought to be at least a thirty-day redemption period. And you know what else? Every lawyer handling collections or working for these installment houses should be required to provide a satisfaction of judgment free of charge when a man has paid up."

Blackman was moody because he thought, from something I'd said, that it seemed like a racket.

"You've no idea about how bad things are. Look at it from the side of the merchant or doctor. There are millions of dollars in unsatisfied judgments right here in Nassau County. You think I'm getting rich on this stuff?"

I asked him why he stayed in it if it wasn't lucrative. "I got a lot of creditors to pay off, and there are possibilities here. It's not too bad. You know, I'm living in one of the houses I took over."

In spite of the great human interest and curious perversion of the law that these home sales for small debt entail, the operations of the 1963 law change have not engendered any newspaper publicity, editorials or feature stories in any New York or Nassau County daily, even though hundreds of families have lost their homes this way in the past five years.

Bob Akeson denounced the "brutally harsh" results of new law changes in an article for the *New York Law Journal* of October 18, 1967.

In his research he found that New York in 1820 had given the homeowner the right to redeem his home after a sheriff's sale because of "so much oppressive speculation" attending these sales. Accordingly, the legislature 150 years ago provided some powerful but not unreasonable checks upon "the peremptory and sweeping desolation of an execution at law." All this was swept away with the severe 1963 changes in the law. Akeson went on to point out that the 1963 law was originally even tougher: at first it didn't require the sheriff to notify the family involved that he was going to sell their home for debt. That came in a minor 1965 legislative change.

Some twenty other states also have no right of redemption for the poor homeowner who has lost out to a sheriff's sale, Bob Akeson pointed out.* But states such as Connecticut, Delaware, Georgia, New Jersey, Ohio, Oklahoma and South Carolina provide that the sheriff first proceed against personal property—a car

---

* Connecticut, Delaware, Florida, Georgia, Louisiana, Maryland, Mississippi, Missouri, New Jersey, North Carolina, Ohio, Oklahoma, Pennsylvania, Rhode Island, South Carolina, Texas, West Virginia, District of Columbia, Hawaii and Puerto Rico.

or savings, for example. Then only, if he still hasn't got enough to satisfy the debt, can he proceed against the home. In several other states the law provides no redemption by the original owner but stipulates that the home cannot be sold unless it fetches at least two thirds of its appraised value. Such restrictions have obviously prevented the wholesale loss of homes through sheriff's sales as has taken place in New York State since the new law was passed.

Bob Akeson feels the law should be changed "in order to strike a more favorable balance between creditor and debtor." More specifically, he recommends the restoration of the right of the debtor to redeem his home after the sheriff's sale; that the minimum bid at the sheriff's sale should approximate the fair value of the property; and that such sales should each require the approval of the court and give the court authority to reject a low bid.

One day when I was discussing the role of collection attorneys in the Jackson case in Phoenix and in the Byrd matter with one of the officials in the Nassau County Sheriff's Office, he said: "The law doesn't look too closely, so a lot of stuff goes on that shouldn't. Most collection outfits are run by attorneys, and we're sure some of them are getting these homes through dummies at our sales. But it's all legal, so what can we do about it? Who's gonna pass a law saying lawyers can't make a fast buck when they see the chance?"

6 "STOP THE LAWYERS"

The one great principle of the English law is, to make business for itself. There is no other principle distinctly, certainly and consistently maintained through all its narrow turnings. Viewed in this light it becomes a coherent scheme, and not the monstrous maze the laity are apt to think it. Let them but once clearly perceive that its grand principle is to make business for itself at their expense, and surely they will cease to grumble.

— CHARLES DICKENS, in *Bleak House*, 1852

Then there are those who fear that aggressive bar action [against unauthorized practice] will further impair the bar's reputation with the public at large, a reputation they feel is always rather dubious. There is an unconcealable element of greed involved in lawyers attempting to further their monopoly, it is argued.

— PROFESSORS QUINTIN JOHNSTONE and DAN HOPSON, JR., *Lawyers and Their Work*, 1967

The grumbling Dickens mentioned hasn't stopped. Instead it grew and fulminated into a recent local revolution. Jack Cade's revolt in 1450 in England against the Lord Chancellor and all concerned with the law profession was bloodier and had an enduring recorder in William Shakespeare. His line, from *King Henry VI*, "The first thing we do, let's kill all the lawyers," has become the inevitable opening line of every antilawyer manifesto.

The most recent revolt against the lawyers took place in one of the unlikeliest places in America and was led by spiritual descendants of George Babbitt, Sinclair Lewis' back-slapping real estate man. That it was a ballot box rather than a blood revolt doesn't make it any less historic. Still the admixture does sound pretty preposterous: Arizona? *Revolutionary* real estate brokers?

In 1964 the American Bar Association in a syndicated column, "The Family Lawyer," told of a gamy Arizona lawyer named Major Hopkins who used to advertise back in the 1890s:

Come to Major Hopkins to get full satisfaction. I win nine-tenths of my cases. If you want to sue, if you have been sued, I am the man to take your case. Embezzlement, highway robbery, felonious assault, arson and horse stealing, don't amount to shucks if you have a good lawyer behind you. My strong point is weeping as I appeal to the jury, and I seldom fail to clear my man. Out of eleven murder cases last year I cleared nine of the murderers. Having been in jail no less than four times myself, my experience cannot fail to prove of value to my clients. Come early and avoid the rush.

Obviously the Major was a lawyer who knew his people. Only an inspired genius would have added that great line: "Having been in jail no less than four times myself . . ."

The ABA column went on to explain that "at last a scandalized profession determined to police itself." But the column didn't say anything about a different kind of police action by lawyers that brought on the Arizona revolution. The action was intended to make more money for lawyers.

It started with Ford Hoffman, a Phoenix real estate broker—a nonfirebrand and nonrevolutionary. In fact Hoffman still isn't mad at lawyers. He is still a bit incredulous that his little $4,000 routine real estate deal started the great battle.

Physically, Ford Hoffman is a cross between W. C. Fields and Babe Ruth. He is not much of a drinker but he has been a sports nut most of his life. He was a four-letter man in high school, played football three years at Arizona State College and was Arizona's commissioner for the national Amateur Softball Association for twenty-five years. During the Depression years he was state director of youth and recreational activities under the Federal Works Agency. He had also taught elementary school physical education in Phoenix. Now in his sixties he still manages the Sun City Saints, a women's softball team. In all, you could hardly get more American than Ford Hoffman.

The revolution began early in July, 1952, when Hoffman as a licensed broker drew up an agreement of sale, warranty deed, quitclaim deed and bill of sale on a property. They sound awfully impressive, but in fact they are just printed forms and filling them in took Hoffman less than fifteen minutes. He made no charge for the work, but he did get a broker's commission on the sale. It didn't even occur to Hoffman that he was guilty of one of the dirtiest phrases in the legal lexicon—"unauthorized practice of law." (UPL spewed out as initials at bar association meetings makes a sneering epithet.)

The bar has always been concerned with people who "practice law without a license," but the UPL committees of the state and local bar associations really didn't get under way effectively until 1933 when lawyers, along with the rest of us, were really hurting (1936 was the last recorded time an American lawyer wrote and had published a popular article soberly titled "Don't Be a Lawyer" *).

Since then, with increasing effectiveness at countering the invasion of law by accountants, real estate brokers, title insurance firms, insurance agents, banks, trust companies and notary publics, the unauthorized practice committees have earned the unkind nickname of "business agents of the lawyers union."

Among lawyers themselves there is considerable disagreement about these UPL committees. Former Supreme Court Justice Wiley Rutledge, a conservative, said in 1941:

> I do not like what I fear is becoming the bar's trade-union approach to the problem. . . . I doubt whether . . . it is necessary or desirable for bar associations to become closed shops, not only as to the business

---

*The author, J. L. Bernstein, who is now editor of the *New Jersey State Bar Journal,* isn't as pessimistic today. He thinks that things *have* changed for many lawyers today and opportunities are greater.

lawyers are now performing but as to a great deal of business which has always been done by other men, although lawyers may have been doing it for a long time.

The more orthodox view was expressed in 1951 by Edwin M. Otterbourg, a New York lawyer who was one of the pillars of the UPL committee:

> Actually, unauthorized practice of law is a swindle upon the public. Whenever it takes place, some person receives either incompetent or unqualified advice, or advice which cannot be honestly disinterested. . . . Reliance upon such advice may result in irreparable injury and loss. . . .

For several months I tried to find serious instances of such injury and loss suffered by the public. I couldn't. I finally stopped trying when Professor Quintin Johnstone, of the Yale University Law School, wrote in a 1967 book: "Nor are there many instances of persons being harmed from having laymen do their legal work." Further, he went on, there is a "public benefit from much of the lay competition that now exists. Lay legal services often are performed at lower cost than if the work were done by lawyers."

In fact Ford Hoffman was simply filling out forms without extra charge—which every real estate man in the state had been doing long before Arizona became a state.

It started friendly. Hoffman was told that it was going to be a test case when the State Bar of Arizona on October 30, 1953, filed its suit against him claiming that he had practiced law without a license. At the same time a similar action was brought against five title insurance companies, since they, too, often filled out these forms in cases where real estate purchasers bought title insurance.

Superior Court Judge Henry S. Stevens ruled in favor of Hoffman and the title companies. He said real estate brokers and title companies could continue to prepare certain legal documents and perform some other services incidental to their businesses without being guilty of unauthorized practice of law.

The State Bar now carried the case to the State Supreme Court, but Hoffman, who felt he had already spent too much in defending himself, dropped out of the case. On November 1, 1961, the Arizona Supreme Court unanimously overturned the lower court ruling. Neither real estate brokers nor title companies could prepare *any* of the documents, including even the simple printed preliminary purchase agreements.

The fact that the brokers didn't get paid for the work of filling out these printed forms didn't matter, said the court. That they had been doing it unhindered for many years also didn't count. But, the court admitted, "the record does not disclose any testimony regarding specific injury to the public from [these] practices."

The court was also out to close all loopholes, such as the possibility of the brokers and title companies getting legislation giving them the right to do what they had been doing all along: ". . . although the legislature may impose additional restrictions which affect the licensing of attorneys, it cannot infringe on the ultimate power of the court to determine who may practice law."

Now what had started out as "a friendly little test case" lost all cozy amicability. The Arizona Bar, which had been supported by the American Bar Association, rejoiced at a great victory. The Arizona Association of Realtors, of which Ford Hoffman was not a member, got into the battle. This was *serious*.

Why should real estate men think their very livelihood was affected by the Supreme Court ruling?

Robert E. Riggs, now a professor of political science at the University of Minnesota, but then a young lawyer in Arizona, analyzed the realtors' problem cogently:

Although loss of the right to prepare other documents might be an inconvenience to the real estate agent, the preliminary sales agreement was vital. By it the agent obtained the signatures of both parties, binding them to the sale. Sales could be lost if a prospective buyer or seller changed his mind while waiting for a lawyer to draft the sales contract. Cost was also a consideration, since the agent might have to pay the lawyer for filling the blanks on many sales agreement forms for sales that were never consummated.

Now, too, the newspapers of Arizona began to see some of the sweeping implications of the Supreme Court decision. The Tucson *Daily Citizen,* for example, saw it as

likely to hike the cost of the average real estate deal. What is more, the ruling will put more money in the pockets of the lawyers . . . the customers are now forced to retain attorneys to represent them. . . . One lawyer estimates that this could amount to anything from $25, the basic hourly charge for legal services, to $100. . . . Another lawyer contends that a projection of this type of reasoning by the court ultimately could affect the buying or selling of cars through an agent. . . .

But for the Arizona *Daily Star* there was an even more important issue involved: The Supreme Court, in denying the Legislature the right to determine what constitutes the practice of law, had

arrogated to itself and to members of the State Bar of Arizona a legalized special privilege that is denied all other professions. . . . Thus we see the court composed of lawyers settling it in favor of lawyers. . . . It would be just as sensible and justified if the medical doctors would demand that such specialized services as blood examinations, and microbiology, be done by licensed M.D.'s. It is now done by technicians. Nurses would be denied the right to take cardiograms, and so on. . . . It is adverse to the public interest in the additional cost it imposes on the average citizen.

Jim Cooper, a political reporter for the Tucson *Daily Citizen,* looked forward to a great battle. First, he established his amused neutrality:

In this business of reporting politics I've had many opportunities to get to know lawyers. And in my private life I've had several brushes with real estate people—so it is delightful to witness a battle between these two sharp and cagey classes of citizens.

But his neutrality was shaken after he talked to some lawyer friends: "Screams of anguish have been heard on several fronts, while the lawyers are chuckling with glee. Simply, they have provided themselves with more business. . . ."

As president of the 500-member Arizona Association of Realtors, Stewart M. Winter, a tall, slender, sandy-haired Tucson realtor, realized that his group's appeal to the Supreme Court for a rehearing might not be the most effective method of settling the problem. Several other realtors began thinking more boldly, too. One of them wrote:

I cannot see how we can win any battle where we have to fight in our opponent's back yard under rules they set forth, and with officials who have a natural affinity to our opponent. In my opinion the only way possible to settle this matter once and for all is to go to the people and have them vote for a Referendum which will permit us to live.

In Arizona, as in twelve other states, the people can institute a constitutional amendment. In order to place the amendment on the regular ballot, at least 15 percent of the registered voters have to sign the initiative petition. Some 60,000 signatures would be required for such an amendment to be voted on in the November, 1962, general election. And the petitions with the names would have to be filed not later than July 6. They had four months.

The realtors hesitated. They knew getting 60,000 names and the campaign after that would be expensive. It couldn't be done just by the state's 500 realtors or even some of the state's 10,000 other real estate brokers and salesmen who were not members of the Arizona Association of Realtors and thus didn't have the right to use the trademarked word, Realtor. The title companies were apparently going to be uncertain allies. Meanwhile some of the realtors who hoped that the Supreme Court might soften its original stand began to fear that the court wouldn't hand down its decision until it was too late to get the petitions under way.

In March, 1962, the realtors voted unanimously to circulate the initiative petitions. It wasn't an easy decision. They knew that if they didn't get the required signatures not only would their "image" suffer a great loss of prestige, but even if they got it, they would still be in for a bitter campaign in which their enemy, the State Bar, would be supported by the American Bar Association. As Stewart Winter warned his fellow realtors "the ABA could not afford to lose."

"Hell, man," another realtor said, "we can't either."

Like embattled small boys enlisting their fathers' help, the Arizona realtors sent a delegation to Chicago, to get the backing of the National Association of Real Estate Boards. NAREB promised to lend $25,000. They also agreed to give the Arizona group its mailing list of members.

The State Bar was much more complacent. First, several of their leaders thought it might be possible to get a court injunction to knock out the realtors' petition for a referendum. But many more felt they had an enemy who didn't know his own weakness. Later one lawyer analyzed the realtors' "vulnerability":

"These are sharp characters. They'll do anything for their commissions. And there are 10,000 of them. Figure on the average each of them has done dirt to at least five families. Say, 50,000 families or at least 100,000 votes against them right there.

"Then just on the money bit alone, they're vulnerable. They get 6 percent commission on a real estate deal: they sell a $30,000 house they get $1,800 from the seller. How can you compare that to the one- or two-hundred-buck fees some lawyers are going to make drawing up these real estate contracts and papers?"

The only trouble with his argument was the missing element of compulsion. You didn't *have* to get a real estate broker; you *could* sell your house yourself. Many people did. And even if you took on a broker, you knew you could bargain with him. Cutting his commission greatly to effect a sale was not uncommon.

Some lawyers looked forward to the realtors' victory. "Think of all the litigation that will come our way when some of these half-assed agreements lose their pants," one of them put it with inelegantly mixed metaphors.

The realtors hired a public relations firm, organized the state into precincts and assigned quotas of names to real estate offices. Then on May 31, 1962, the Supreme Court handed down a slightly modified decision. Now the real estate broker could draw up a listing agreement with the seller and present it to a buyer and have the buyer accept it by adding his signature. "The only problem," Stewart Winter pointed out, "is that listings are seldom, if ever, sold *exactly* as originally written. It is one of the prime functions of the broker to negotiate and bring about a meeting of the minds between buyer and seller."

And another, homelier problem: "Over 65 percent of the residential home sales are transacted in the evening. How much would a lawyer charge to fill in routine forms at night?"

The Supreme Court also ruled that by June 15 it would be illegal for a licensed broker or salesman to draft or prepare *any* document incident to a real estate transaction other than the listing agreement. In short, from June 15 on, the buyer and seller each would be forced to employ a lawyer to draft all documents necessary to the sale. And pay him, of course.

On July 6, 1962, the real estate men filed some 107,420 signatures on their petition with the Secretary of State of Arizona. This was nearly twice as much as the needed 60,000 and represented 28 percent of the electorate. It was also the largest number of signatures ever filed on an initiative measure in the state's history. The Secretary of State assigned it a number, and now the conflict was to become the Battle of Proposition 103.

That day the *Arizona News* of Phoenix declared editorially for the real estate men.

> The cost of an attorney's fee has been added to the rather heavy closing costs when a home or other piece of property changes hands. . . .
> The real estate men and title companies were expected to be content with this ruling—just pass it on to the customer as manufacturers do when the cost of a product goes up with wage or other production increases.
> In taking their case to the people, the realtors are warning the public that the legal fraternity is known to be eyeing other professions from

which they could collect a legal fee in every individual transaction. . . .
. . . . this appears to be a case in which, unless the people speak, their
rights will be submerged by the selfish demands of a profession which
has demonstrated throughout the contention on this issue, that it has
regard for no rights but its own.

Now for the first time the Arizona Bar became worried. Prom-
ises of help were sought at the American Bar Association convention in August. There the National Conference of Bar Presidents
urged the ABA to lend all possible assistance to the State Bar of
Arizona in its fight against the proposed amendment. In Arizona
two public relations firms and an advertising agency were taken
on for the campaign.

The campaign slogans emerged quickly. The realtors chose
"Protect Your Pocketbook" and "Protect Your Right to Choose,"
and the bar's was "Save Our Constitution." The realtors were in
a better position to spread the word: they had received nearly
$100,000 from real estate brokers outside of Arizona and another
$35,000 from brokers within the state. The lawyers were able to
raise $26,500, with comparatively little from outside the state.

The car-bumper stickers simply said: 103—Yes; the radio and
TV commercials were choruses chanting, "103—Yes, Yes, Yes,"
with the announcer coming over urging everyone to "protect his
pocketbook and his right to choose." In the last few days of the
campaign the slogan became rawer: *"Stop the Lawyers."* The realtors got an unexpected assist from a local law journal, the *Arizona Weekly Gazette,* which carries local court announcements
and news of pleadings. The *Gazette* had a long news item from
Salt Lake City where an unauthorized practice of law group had
cited the many professions and occupations that were currently
infringing on law practice. Included were architects, "who quite
generally draw construction contracts and notices of completion";
banks and trust companies, "when they go too far in estate planning"; claims adjusters, when they intervene between attorney
and client; CPAs, "when they give tax advice without limitation"; life insurance brokers and salesmen, "when they give estate

tax and estate planning advice"; and notaries public, who "prepare legal documents"; and, of course, real estate brokers.

The news story, widely reprinted in realtor ads, surely helped convince some of these groups that the lawyers would turn on them, too, when they had finished with the realtors.

"Our concern is for that bewildered, overtaxed and unorganized victim of the high cost of living—the Ultimate Consumer," editorialized the *Arizona News*.

For that reason we are obliged to pay tribute to the realtors of Arizona who are the advance troops for a host of other professions eyed by the legal fraternity to—and we quote—"raise the income of lawyers." . . . We don't want to see lawyers in want. But in comparison with their economic plight, the Ultimate Consumer will soon be in rags and tatters if he has to make an appointment with an attorney and pay a fee every time he has a Notary attest his signature. Leave us not be beastly to the Consumer.

The bar's ads stressed the theme: Do you really want a real estate salesman to make out your important legal papers? And, "You'll be sorry if you vote for special privileges for real estate brokers or salesmen." "The Arizona constitution is for all people. Keep it *intact*."

The last appeal was odd, considering that the Arizona constitution had been amended forty-eight times, with thirty-three of the amendments proposed by the legislature and fifteen by petition.

By November 2, Election Day, there was little doubt that the realtors would win. The only real question was by how much. Even the realtors were surprised by their majority; some 236,856 voters supported them, and only 64,507 were against the amendment, a majority of nearly 4 to 1.

The postmortems for the lawyers were sobering. They knew their profession had acquired a more tarnished image. In a letter to the *Journal of the American Bar Association* in May, 1963, an Oklahoma attorney spoke for many when he wrote: "In the Arizona case it was apparent that the bar was more concerned about its loss of business than it was about public welfare." A West Virginia attorney wrote that the Arizona Bar had missed the chance to turn the tables: the bar should have sponsored a constitutional amendment limiting commissions on a realty transaction to 0.5 percent instead of the prevailing 6 percent. "The people of Arizona would just as resoundingly vote their realtors out of the real estate business as they have voted the realtors into the practice of real estate law and the legal profession out of it."

An Arizona lawyer, Robert E. Riggs, a Mormon who had practiced in his father's law office in Tempe for a year before deciding that he would be happier teaching political science, did an analysis of the battle for the *Arizona Law Review.* "But," he told me recently, at the University of Minnesota where he is teaching, "they wouldn't print it. They felt I was too hard on the lawyers, too critical of the bar." The study, which appeared in the *Southern California Law Review,* actually was quite mild in its conclusions:

> This may be a time for reappraisal, as the *American Bar Association Journal* has suggested. If such it be, this essay is a plea that the reappraisal look beyond tactics and methods to the basic premises and concepts defining the role of the legal profession in society.

In looking back on the case, Dr. Riggs still feels that "the bar is very privileged and very protective of itself." He still finds it incredible that the Arizona Supreme Court had ruled as it did in outlawing the preparation of any contracts by realtors. "How can judges be impartial vis-à-vis lawyers in a matter such as this?"

During the contest a Tucson attorney offered a $100 prize to "the first Tucson real estate broker who can pass the examination on Real Property Law given at the University of Arizona College of Law." He got no takers but he did plant an idea in Stewart Winter, president of the Arizona realtors, who had put $10,000 of his own into the campaign which had taken eighteen months of his business time.

Winter knew that a lot of applicants who took the real estate license test in the state had not gone beyond high school. Under the statute a salesman is only required to have "a fair understanding of the rudimentary principles of real estate and conveyancing, the transfer of property." Nor are there any minimum educational requirements. After the 1962 victory the real estate brokers rapidly expanded their educational clinics and seminars. Now not only brokers but their salesmen must take a rather comprehensive course in real estate as a condition of membership.

The Real Estate Board went further and established a recovery fund which will reimburse clients of all brokers to the extent of $10,000 in the event they suffer a loss attributable to a broker who is unable to reimburse them. As of April, 1967, the fund, which has $300,000, hasn't had to pay out anything. The money is raised by voluntary increases in license fees from the brokers and salesmen.

I asked Winter if there had been, as the lawyers predicted, an upsurge in litigation over real estate contracts. "I haven't heard of a single case," he told me, "and I get around a lot all over the state. Actually, I have heard some grudging compliments from lawyers that many of our realtors have become as expert in the drafting of these documents as are most lawyers."

And Ford Hoffman, the man whose $4,000 real estate deal started the battle, thus making him a footnote in the unwritten history of the lawyers vs. the people:

"Sure, I'm proud of being in this. Most of the people we deal with are folk who are just getting by from one monthly payment to the next. They just can't afford these lawyers' fees on top of everything else. We saved them a lot of dough."

•   •   •

Elsewhere the more than 200 local unauthorized practice committees kept up their court actions against real estate brokers and even notaries. An Arkansas case was brought involving a rural notary, Alfred Creekmore, who filled out blank real estate forms and bills of sale because there wasn't a lawyer within twenty miles. A previous decision restricting the right of real estate brokers to fill out these forms brought out another consequence of letting only George, the lawyer, do it. In the old days, said an Arkansas Supreme Court justice,

> it took only a matter of four or five minutes to fill in the blanks on the necessary deed and mortgage forms to complete a real estate transaction . . . but since the [restrictive] decision it takes some three or four days to get a lawyer to prepare the necessary instruments; and occasionally a broker takes a blank form, fills in all the necessary information, transmits it to the office of the lawyer, who subsequently retypes the whole instrument, for which he is paid a fee. Testimony further shows that many mistakes result from passing the information necessary to preparing a deed from the broker to the lawyer.

In short, as long as the broker filled out the forms it was swift, cost-free and accurate. Once the lawyer forced his way into the act it became drawn-out, expensive and filled with dangerous errors.

The Arkansas court saw it sensibly and ruled that brokers could again fill out the forms as they had once been permitted to do. But not Creekmore, the notary, since he wasn't in the real estate business. However, he was allowed to fill out income tax forms.

In Illinois the brokers and the lawyers were embroiled in a ten-year court battle that was finally resolved in October, 1966. Here the bar won clearly: *only lawyers* could handle the completion of all real estate transactions, regardless of size. Both the buyers and sellers had to have attorneys, and the lawyers, of course, had to be paid.

For a time the Illinois brokers thought of getting a constitutional amendment along the Arizona lines, but in Illinois a two-thirds approval of each house of the legislature is required before the proposed amendment can go on the ballot. Presumably when the brokers took a head-count of the many lawyers in the legislature, they decided the idea wasn't too practical.

The Chicago *Daily News* interpreted the lawyers' victory this way on October 27, 1966:

Don't be surprised if the final cost of buying that new house you are buying is $200 more than you figured. . . . Sources within the legal profession told the *Daily News* the agreement would primarily affect the average home buyer, who previously did not hire an attorney. He could now pay as much as $325 extra on the purchase of a $30,000 home. . . .

Recently in Chicago I talked to an active real estate broker whose firm sells about 140 homes a year, new and used, with an average value of $20,000–$25,000. He said:

"I used to practice law before I went into real estate. But when the Chicago Bar went gunning for Quinlan & Tyson [a major North Shore real estate firm] on this unauthorized practice business, my sympathies were all with them. It's not just the $100,000 this battle cost the firm, but the way they stuck it out knowing in their heart of hearts that judges wouldn't turn against lawyers.

"You never know how things are going to work out. The lawyers won, the brokers lost—and as a result the lawyers are putting money in my pocket. How come? Well, I used to bring in lawyers to do the closings on these houses. None of that one-percent-of-the-house-value stuff, either. They knew I was a lawyer so I could get them to come in on a volume basis. Usually it would work out to about $50 per closing, which I paid. Now the buyer and seller have to bring in their own lawyer, and on a typical $25,000 house they're paying about $250 each, or one percent. That makes it $500 on a $25,000 house for which I used to pay the lawyer $50, or maybe $75 if the closing time was a little inconvenient for him. I figure my clients are now paying $50,000 more in legal fees than before the court decision. Found money for the lawyers. You know what they say: to develop an appetite you start eating. Now they're getting this extra-fat spread and what do they do? They also come in for a little extra graft. A lot of these lawyers get the mortgages for their clients and, of course, they pick up a nice finder's fee from the mortgage firm. I'll bet not one of them tells the client of this little gimmick. Not nice."

There are about a million new homes built in the United States each year and an estimated two to two and a half million existing homes sold—or a total of about three and a half million home sales. The increase in legal fees, if the Illinois verdict spreads, could be hefty. At a modest set of legal fees totaling only $200 per house, this would come to $700,000,000 a year added to the cost of living in a house of your own.

Fortunately, several State Supreme Courts have not seen fit to go along with the zealous unauthorized practice committees. In Michigan, Missouri, Wisconsin and Minnesota, real estate brokers are still permitted to fill in forms without the help of lawyers. These states, in effect, are following the reasoning set forth by the Minnesota Supreme Court in 1940:

> It is the duty of this court so to regulate the practice of law and restrain such practice by laymen in a common sense way in order to protect primarily the interest of the public and not to hamper and burden such interest with impractical technical restraints. . . .
>
> The rare instances of defective conveyances in such transactions are insufficient to outweigh the great public inconvenience which would follow if it were necessary to call in a lawyer to draft these simple documents.

Many lawyers would agree. Admittedly, most of them don't have to depend on closings for any important part of their income. Still a lot of lawyers would go along with M. David Stirling, a Whittier, California, attorney who wrote about attorney fees in general in a recent issue of the *California State Bar Journal:*

> Today many practitioners will agree, although perhaps with great reluctance, that there remains a deep-rooted distrust of the legal profession and the entire legal system by many laymen. . . . Some even believe that the legal system is constructed so as to enrich attorneys by compelling the layman to seek an attorney's services, or make it possible for attorneys to drag what should be simple matters out over a longer period of time by use of various legal devices.

7 *RULE 4: WHERE THE MONEY IS*

(From a shooting script of *The Fortune Cookie,* in which Jack Lemmon portrays Harry Hinkle, a TV cameraman injured slightly while filming a football game. His attorney, Walter Matthau, is his brother-in-law, Willie Gingrich, who has "a brain full of razor blades. He would have run afoul of the law a long time ago if he didn't have a slick lawyer—himself.")

WILLIE (*In hospital room.*) And what are you doing walking around?

HARRY I'm trying to get some circulation in my legs. Do you mind?

WILLIE Circulation? That's the last thing we want. Now why don't we just get back in bed . . .

HARRY What is this with the *we?*

WILLIE We're in this together—you and I—straight down the line—fifty-fifty.

HARRY Fifty-fifty?

WILLIE Don't you think that's fair? I'm devoting ninety percent of my time to this case. And if *you* louse it up, *we* lose the case, and *I* get nothing.

One of the few enduring and *continually profitable* sub-industries of our time has never been assessed by the security analysts of Wall Street. They are not interested because it is impossible to buy stock in the only consistently profitable part of the *injury industry.** The injured seldom come out ahead; the insurance companies did for a time, but now they survive mainly through an investment fluke. Only the lawyers have profited continually

*The term was coined in 1960 by University of Michigan law professor Alfred F. Conard.

and without exception. But so far you can't buy stock in any law firm.

We properly honor the founders of our great industries, the Edisons and Fords whose daring, ingenuity and hard work helped create a useful industry providing employment for thousands where only a vacuum existed before. But the founder of the still-growing American injury industry has been overlooked. The man who almost singlehandedly set the industry on its modern path and invented most of its illicit angles, the man who showed generations of American lawyers the road to its surest dollar, has never been honored. There are no laudatory biographies or films, no law school chairs named after him, no ABA prizes in his honor. Not even a footnote in any legal text. I would like now to give him a small measure of overdue recognition.

His name was Abraham Gatner, and in 1907 he was a fresh-faced hustling lad of eighteen who had two years of high school. But he looked at the future and sensed it could work well for him. He became our first ambulance chaser. The place was Manhattan, which then had only a few hundred automobiles—more than enough for a hustling chaser. (In 1905 there were just two automobiles in Kansas City, but through the operation of some unknown laws of magnetic attraction they managed to crash into each other.) The rare automobiles were then called "devil wagons" and you could discuss *all* the reported auto accident law cases in a four-page review. It had not begun to be an industry.

The industry started in New York in 1907 when founder Gatner persuaded a law firm to take him on to give his idea a chance. His self-made job was to hang around police headquarters at 9:00 A.M. and get a list of the previous day's accidents from a newspaper reporter, who was given one dollar. With the list, Gatner would run out to get the accident victims signed up on retainer agreements for the law firm.

Gatner named his work, proudly but incorrectly, "ambulance chasing." Actually, at first he didn't reach the injured until hours after the ambulance left.

Word got out, and soon Gatner was joined by two rivals, working for other law firms. They also had their pet reporters whom they paid for the accident lists. Being sensible, the three agreed to parcel out the city in special territories for each so that they wouldn't find themselves bidding for the same accident victim. But Gatner pulled a fast one: he got a partner who would get the accident list the same day—at 6:00 P.M. from a reporter for an afternoon paper. But in a few months his two rivals caught on, and there were harsh words, which didn't faze young Gatner. Instead he availed himself of a new service, the telephone, which he had installed in his apartment. It was the first phone on the block. He arranged to have a clerk in the police department phone him at 2:00 A.M. to give him the accident list. By 5:00 A.M. he was out hustling retainers. It was several months before his rivals caught on. By the time they did, he was another step ahead. In those days doctors were glad to take fifty-cent fees for examining an injured person. Gatner quickly saw possibilities here: soon he was able to persuade some physicians that a patient who had signed one of Gatner's retainer forms really needed three, four or five visits. The medical buildup was invented.

He prospered, as did his law firm; he got a commission on each case as well as his salary. In 1912 when he was twenty-three Gatner took a bold step. He quit his pioneering job as chaser and joined the enemy as an insurance company adjuster.

In those days, records insurance chronicler Robert Monaghan, "the adjuster was given a wad of dollar bills as he set out each day and instructed to make as quick and as cheap a settlement as he could."

With his alert mind for nuances and profitable possibilities, Gatner quickly saw the need for befriending chasers who were now following the occupation he had pioneered. He would give them cases from his insurance company list and in turn received a portion of their commissions for getting those victims signed up with the lawyers they were working for. Thus, fee-splitting in our injury industry was born.

Before long he had a hand in the first actually faked accident case, another moneymaking innovation. During his year as an adjuster he got a course in practical negligence law and made a lot of pliant friends inside insurance company offices.

With his probing insights into accident insurance, Gatner was now able to rationalize the awkwardly growing injury industry. He arranged a "partnership" with a rising lawyer. Gatner's salary was a $30-a-week drawing account against a commission of one third of what the lawyer got on cases Gatner brought in. He persuaded the lawyer to let him set up the first 24-hour-a-day law office in U.S. history. Into the day-and-night office Gatner's growing sources sent tips on accidents. By phone the office alerted free-lancers in the field who would rush out to sign up the victims.

The injured—mostly industrial accident victims at this time—were starting to develop a little sophistication about lawyers, and Gatner persuaded his lawyer-partner to offer them medical services for which the clients eventually paid, and even loans to poor clients, which they repaid with interest when the lawyer collected for them on his 50–50 contingent arrangement. The partnership had a good run of nearly six years, and it broke up only with the coming of workmen's compensation laws in 1916. Gatner now took a fresh look at the mounting number of trucks and autos and decided to give this aspect of the injury industry his concentrated attention.

The police telegraph bureau in New York had just been installed so that the various precincts could wire in details on local accidents to police headquarters. Many of the chasers were paying off a clerk in the headquarters telegraph office for their leads. Gatner, always the innovator, sought fresher information—from the policeman who was sent to the accident scene. Gatner got in touch with hundreds of them and promised each three dollars—a lot of money in those days—for every tip on an accident, provided the cop took care of one other small detail. When phoning in his report he would deliberately change some minor detail, such as the injured man's address. Thus not only would Gatner have an initial advantage, but his competition would waste their time trying to track down the right man at the wrong address carried on the police telegraph bureau line.

As other ambulance chasers started increasing the size of tips to accommodating cops, Gatner remained one step ahead. At the newly created New York Police Academy he told the cops-to-be of their opportunities to flesh out their pay by keeping Gatner's phone number with them at all times.

In those days liability insurance wasn't a commonplace, and Gatner had long ago realized that not all accidents could be profitable. How to find out quickly if a prosperous or insured individual was responsible for the accident? Simple. He would phone the parties responsible and, posing as the police lieutenant in the precinct where the accident happened, ask who carried the insurance. If there wasn't insurance he would find out what kind of business it was. From that he could tell to within $50 how much his lawyer-partner might be able to collect from them. Now he would phone the hospital, posing as a reporter, to find out the patient's condition and whether he was still there or was sent home. If the patient was still bed-ridden Gatner would manage to get in—he knew lots of hospital nurses and clerks—and get the victim to sign the retainer agreement.

In the early twenties, Gatner reached the peak of his profession. He was the manager of a 24-hour-a-day law office with eleven chasers on the payroll at $3,000 a week, exclusive of commissions. There were also two investigators, three attorneys on salary, several stenographers and clerks. The setup had been financed by a lawyer who as silent partner had put up the $31,000 to get it started. In its first year the office did a gross volume of $400,000, of which $165,000 was net profit. The original $31,000 had been earned back in the first four months alone.

Gatner was proud that his office was run fairly honestly. "We gave everybody a good shake," he used to say. But he was bitter about lawyers who, unhappy with a mere 50–50 deal, managed to find ways to get still more. Insurance historian Robert Monaghan tells how they did it:

The case over, the lawyer would call the client to his office and say: "Well, we won a verdict for $2,000. You get half and I get half. Right?"

The client would agree. Then the lawyer would give him a receipt for $1,000 and direct him to sign it, which he would do.

"Now let's see," the lawyer would say, jotting some figures on paper, "one thousand dollars. My court fee is so much and our expenses were so much. We had to pay the witnesses such and such a sum, etc., etc. That all comes to $500. Five hundred from a thousand is five hundred. Here's your money." And he would count out $500 and hand it to the client. If the client complained he was talked down—outbluffed. If the client took it up with the bar association or the authorities, the lawyer had the signed receipt.

Finally in 1928, when he was thirty-nine, Gatner came a cropper during one of New York's cyclical investigations into ambulance chasing. He was found guilty of defrauding one of his lawyer associates and served a brief jail term. No doubt the fact that he had been a willing witness for the investigation mitigated his sentence considerably.

With that Abraham Gatner, the founder of the great American injury industry, the innovator of nearly all the techniques used by modern ambulance chasers, disappeared from history, unsung, unhonored.

How little has changed is illustrated by the operations of an ambulance-chasing office uncovered during a recent (1966–67) investigation in Chicago. As the Chicago *American* said in its exposé series:

> Ambulance chasing is one of the safest and most lucrative rackets in America—netting profits equal to dope, gambling and prostitution, but unlike those crimes, it is all but unpunishable . . . the majority of personal injury cases here are handled by fewer than 100 lawyers. About 40 doctors appear in most cases . . . chasing down accidents for attorneys has become a full-time job for about 50 men in Chicago alone—using police radios, and dividing their territory into zones corresponding with the police department's six traffic areas. Policemen, firemen, insurance adjusters, nurses, interns, tow-truck drivers, and garages are on the payoff list.

In Chicago the chasers get a minimum of $100 "a head" by sending victims to a lawyer's office and as much as $1,500 if the victim has more serious injuries. And more: "For a badly injured person a chaser can command a percentage of the lawyer's fee— usually one third. In a prime case he might ask for bids."

Still, the chasers and the lawyers who employ them *do* serve a socially useful purpose of a kind. Listen to a retired bar association investigator of a large Midwest city.* He said in 1967, "We have 200 lawyers who are ambulance chasers and I'll say this for them. They may be as unethical as hell, but most of them'll sure get you more money than if you went to some of the big ethical firms." He is also disenchanted with the ethics of some of the auto insurance companies, partly as a result of an accident he and his wife were in not long ago in Missouri. Their new car was wrecked by a truck. They were injured but didn't require hospitalization. Then,

This adjuster came to our motel and told me to sign a paper. I told him I was in the business and wasn't going to sign anything. The adjuster got snotty: "You don't sign with me you don't get a dime out of my company." In the back of his so-called mind he probably was counting on that old casualty insurance company gimmick: don't be in a hurry to settle with injured parties who are over 65. Keep stalling and with a little luck they'll die on you.

The ex-bar association investigator relished his encounter with the aggressive adjuster.

He was pretty well-trained; knew all the cute tricks—except persuasion. But I knew he had given up on me signing when he asked if he could use our bathroom. I had all I could do not to bust out laughing. I said, sure. Well, maybe he did have to pee, but you know why he *really* wanted to go to the bathroom? He wanted to see what medicines we were taking for our injuries; take down the pharmacy names and the prescription numbers. Handy information if it came to trial.

He was going to hire a Kansas City lawyer to handle his case— until he discovered that the lawyers there got 50 percent of the

* We encounter him again in Chapter Eight.

settlement, plus their expenses. ("Hell, it could end up 60 for them and 40 for me with just a little fast shuffle on the 'expenses.' ") Through his connections he was able to find a firm that would take his case for a more normal third of the amount collected.

Those Kansas City lawyers are as bad as the Florida operators. Down there they also take 45–50 percent of the award. Yet whenever some law review youngsters do a survey on how much negligence firms take on these accident cases around the country, it always turns out that 25 percent or maybe a third is par. I guess they just ask the wrong lawyers. Now there's something bar associations ought to regulate.

They should but they don't. Fortunately, a few courts have taken a lead in this direction partly because one ranking New York State justice vividly remembered the time he had been in charge of a typical New York City ambulance-chasing investigation.

Ever since he was an assistant district attorney in charge of the 1937 New York City accident fraud investigation, Justice Bernard Botein has kept up a lively, perceptive interest in the continuing growth of our injury industry and the bar's growing dependence on it.

"The fastest way for a young, unscrupulous lawyer to clean up is to follow the ten-year rule," Justice Botein told me. "For some reason that perhaps the experts on cycles ought to look into, most large metropolitan areas seem to have ambulance-chasing investigations about every ten years. Suddenly there's a great hue and cry and investigation, and the papers are filled with details of lawyers and their chasers and accident faking and the padding of medical and hospital bills. A few lawyers are disbarred, several doctors get their wrists slapped, the bar issues an earnest statement and a month later—things are back to normal. Now all a lawyer would have to do to benefit from this cycle is come to a city that's just had an ambulance-chasing investigation and proceed to rip and tear for ten years and then leave in time. Then the next city that's just had an inquiry, and so on."

No one goes in for ambulance chasing or personal injury law practice because they like running or the smell of hospitals or payoffs to cops. They do it because, as Abraham Gatner began proving long ago, there is a lot of money in the business. Just how much?

In 1967 we had 102 million drivers licensed to operate the 96 million cars and trucks on our roads. That year we had 13.5 million accidents in which 53,000 of us were killed, 3.7 million hurt and 24.3 million cars damaged. Some 900 insurance companies took in $10 billion in auto insurance premiums in 1967. How much of this filtered down to the lawyers?

The figure used most often is $640 million, which was first mentioned in a 1965 issue of *Insurance Management Review,* a weekly. More recently Martin Mayer, in his book *The Lawyers*— an all-encompassing, quite friendly Baedeker of the profession— thought $650 million was closer to the mark.

My own estimates are considerably higher. In 1967 about $4 billion was paid out to auto accident victims for bodily injury and property damage liability. The best guess is that about a fifth of this went to people who didn't bother getting lawyers. That leaves some $3.2 billion that went to claimants who *did* have lawyers. How much did the lawyers get? Martin Mayer used a figure of 25 percent, but I think that's much too low.

In 1966 the Defense Research Institute, representing insurance lawyers, did the latest survey of contingent fee arrangements in the fifty states. In most of them lawyers were taking a minimum of 33.3 percent. Often the minimum fee schedules mentioned a lower figure of 25 percent, but this jumped promptly to 33.3 percent once suit was filed, so understandably lawyers filed suit almost immediately if for nothing more than to increase their share.

In addition some fourteen states reported contingent fees of 40 to 50 percent of the award. These included most of the Southern states (Alabama, Arkansas, Florida, Louisiana, Mississippi) but also included Pennsylvania (up to 40 percent permitted in Philadelphia and 50 percent in the rest of the state), California, Connecticut, Missouri, Oregon, Rhode Island, Nebraska, Oklahoma and Vermont.

No one knows how many cases were in the 33.3, 40 or even 50 percent category, but clearly to use a 25 percent contingent fee basis as representing the United States in 1968 is not reasonable. Let's take an intermediate figure of 36 percent, which is what was found to be the average in a study of 3,000 personal injury cases conducted by the Columbia University Project for Effective Justice in 1961. Now, 36 percent of $3.2 billion—paid out to claimants who had lawyers—comes to $1.15 billion. If we add to that the estimated $200 million earned by insurance company defense counsel for handling the more important auto cases that actually went to trial, and another $200 million that went to lawyers handling nonauto-accident victims, we have a marvelous lawyer's treasure trove of *more than $1.5 billion earned from contingent fees in accident cases.** If the total spent by the U.S. public on legal services is some $4 billion, the injury industry provides our lawyers with more than a third of their total income. This includes much more than a few thousand shysters working steadily with their ambulance chasers or even the rich, well-publicized negligence specialists who argue the blockbuster cases. Included here is a remarkably broad spectrum of the whole legal profession.

J. Harry LaBrum, a prominent Philadelphia lawyer who represents insurance companies in personal injury cases, estimates that "more than 50 percent of all private law practice, in terms of dollars, flows from automobile accident cases which involve liability insurance."

Another estimate of the importance of the average personal injury contingent fee case to *most* lawyers was presented by Maurice Rosenberg, a short, bright professor of law at Columbia. An infantry staff sergeant in World War II, Rosenberg has been studying the small, daily battles of auto accident victims and the courts for more than a decade. At a 1965 meeting of the Federa-

---

*In December, 1967, Professor Jeffrey O'Connell of the University of Illinois Law School estimated the figure at $1.3 billion. Close enough.

tion of Insurance Counsel, Rosenberg told about a lawyer friend who was familiar with upstate New York lawyers and their great dependence on personal injury cases and real estate for their living. He said that if some way were found of taking personal injury cases out of the courts

about two thirds of the bar in New York State would feel the pinch badly. Most of them are lawyers who have a big personal injury case or two a year, an automobile case or two a year, and make $5,000 to $10,000 on the cases they have. Otherwise, they would practice real estate law or contract law. . . . If you take the automobile cases out of their files, they may give up being lawyers and go over all the way to real estate brokerage or insurance brokerage and would stop trying to make a living practicing law.

Lewis C. Ryan, a past president of the American College of Trial Lawyers, saw the removal of accident cases from the courts not only ruining "50 percent of the legal profession" but it would also

adversely affect the other half because the industrious, imaginative and skillful trial lawyers who specialize in tort litigation would quickly invade and master the other fields of practice in which the other groups excel. . . . If automobile litigation is lost, the American trial lawyer is a dead duck, and the entire profession will suffer damage from which I don't think it will ever recover.

In order to prevent this dire prophecy from coming true, the December, 1967, meeting of the New Jersey State Bar Association had an extraordinary turnout at its traditional Atlantic City gathering. The most controversial speaker on the program was Professor Jeffrey O'Connell, who was there to tell the lawyers how he and his colleague—Professor Robert E. Keeton of Harvard Law School—proposed to take accident litigation out of the courtroom. Since 1965 the two young law professors have been ardent and imaginative advocates of a new approach they call "Basic Protection." Under it, all motorists would have to carry compulsory insurance that would pay victims immediately, *regardless of who was at fault.* (The most frequently used analogy is home fire insurance: if you have a fire, you get paid for loss by your own insurance company whether the fire was caused by lightning or your own carelessness with a cigarette.)

As the two professors explain it:

Claims would be submitted to one's own insurance company rather than to that of the other driver . . . payments would be made as loss occurs, month by month, rather than in one lump sum . . . payments would be for net loss; that is, no payment would be due for loss covered by other sources such as Blue Cross and sick leave pay . . . the claims would be for objectively measurable loss, no compensation being paid for pain and suffering.

What got the New Jersey lawyers aroused—and a lot of others, too—was the additional provision that would take most of the auto cases out of the courts:

Coupled with this new form of insurance would be a law doing away with injury claims based on negligence in traffic accidents, unless the damage were higher than $5,000 for pain and suffering, or $10,000 for other items such as medical expense and wage loss.

Since those limits would easily cover the overwhelming bulk of all auto cases there would be very few court cases or litigation. "The wasteful bickering over fault—with all the cost of investigators, lawyers and courts—would be eliminated in the great majority of the cases."

Speaking to a clearly hostile audience, Jeffrey O'Connell said that "the pocketbook of many lawyers" was a larger factor in the opposition to his proposal than moral considerations. A reporter noted that "the professor was the only one who could be heard voting in favor of the plan." The reporter went on:

Herbert E. Greenstone of Newark, speaking in behalf of the N.J. Trial Attorneys Association which mobilized the campaign here against the auto insurance plan, asserted that the trial lawyer is "champion of the consumer, and the public." To be accused of "feathering our own nest" is unfair.

In Massachusetts the Keeton-O'Connell plan had a much better run. There some 250 Boston lawyers supported it, and it unexpectedly swept past the lower house of the Massachusetts legislature before a fearful lobby of negligence lawyers killed it in the state senate.

In October, 1967, State Representative Michael S. Dukakis, a proponent of the measure, described the opposition as "tough, aggressive and, since the passage of the bill by the lower house, near hysteria":

There are attorneys in every city or town in Massachusetts. Many are well known and respected. . . . They have their champions—also lawyers—inside the legislative chamber. They usually know their stuff and they can be extremely adept at picking apart the language of a long and complex bill. They can often baffle a non-lawyer legislator with arguments about constitutionality and due process which sound plausible.

But as far as the public was concerned the factor of lawyers' fees in negligence cases was even more plausible:

. . . the majority of lawyers in Massachusetts strongly oppose the basic protection bill and will continue to do so . . . the public feels that the lawyers are doing well by the status quo and that their opposition to change is motivated primarily by a fear of what will happen to their fees . . . [there is] widespread public cynicism both in and out of state legislatures about the role of the lawyer in the present auto tort and insurance system.

At this writing the Keeton-O'Connell measure is due to be introduced in the legislatures of California, Connecticut, Illinois, Minnesota, Rhode Island and Wisconsin, but the panicky negligence lawyers are mobilizing their legislative friends and colleagues formidably. It doesn't sound as if the most imaginative attempt to replace our negligence mess is ever going to get a chance.

•   •   •

Like poker, the contingent fee is pretty much an American invention. In England and most of Europe, for example, a lawyer cannot become a partner in a lawsuit by taking a fee only if he wins for a client. The contingent fee first became accepted in the United States about 1848, mostly to help workers injured on jobs. Since they didn't have money to hire a lawyer, the contingent fee was the only way to get a civil suit under way. At first, lawyers limited their take to 15–20 percent. But by 1900 in the United States, lawyers were taking anywhere from 40 to 60 percent, and contingent fees started getting a shady reputation. During the 1928 New York ambulance-chasing investigation, U. S. Attorney Charles A. Tuttle pleaded with the New York State Bar Association to back regulation of the contingent fee, that "arch tempter to the ambulance chaser, and the greatest incubator for torts, false claims, witness fixing and perjury."

The only other places where contingent fees are permitted are Spain and the Canadian province of Manitoba. There a lawyer's fee in a typical $5,000 personal injury award would be fixed, not by the lawyer—as is true in the United States—but by the court's taxing officer at about $800 to $1,000, or between 16 and 20 percent.

Twenty percent also happens to be the upper limit permitted lawyers in actions undertaken for clients injured by U.S. government-owned vehicles. In many U.S. courts, lawyers cannot take more than 20 percent if the accident victim is a minor. And in most states, lawyers representing clients in workmen's compensation cases cannot get fees above 20 percent, and even that figure is usually applied only to the difference obtained above a settlement offer. (Case: Joe is injured on the job and is offered compensation of $2,000. He doesn't accept and gets a lawyer who gets him $3,000. The lawyer can only get 20 percent of the $1,000 he was able to add on—or $200.)

The federal government has also stepped in to limit lawyers' fees in social security benefit cases. Every year a number of elderly persons applying for the benefits are victimized by lawyers who charge them exorbitant fees to "help" them apply. In Chester, South Carolina, an attorney used to charge applicants $50–$200 without providing them any real services; occasionally he would get them copies of their birth certificates. In Iowa, one lawyer was forced to return $980 of a $1,000 fee he charged a farmer to get him on social security. In another case an attorney was forced to return $2,612 of a $2,662 fee.

With all these limitations it would seem that the law or the courts would also have stepped in with restrictions on how much contingent fees lawyers could get in personal injury cases. In theory, there is Canon 13 of the ABA's Canons of Professional Ethics which says the contingent fee "should always be subject to the supervision of the court, as to its reasonableness."

"Supervision" and "reasonableness" have reassuring rings. But what protection for the public does Canon 13 *really* provide? asked Lester P. Dodd, a former president of the Michigan Bar Association:

Is the [contingent fee] contract approved by a court when made? No. Is it automatically brought to the attention of the court when settlement is made under its terms? No. . . . When his claim is settled or his judgment paid, a check is issued jointly to the attorney and the client . . . the client has the option of paying the agreed fee or of retaining another attorney to ascertain his rights and test the fairness of the fee agreement. A right, perhaps, but a rather naked right to one who may desperately need his money.

Dodd, writing in *The Detroit Lawyer* for August, 1961, saw some other strange aspects of the contingent fee agreement, which is always

drawn by the lawyer. He is a party to it and necessarily represents himself in its negotiation. Can he also represent fairly the other contracting party? . . . we take in stride and accept as routine a practice which permits the lawyer to enter into contracts with his own client under which he acquires a direct personal interest in his lawsuit.

Not only does the lawyer have a direct personal interest, but *often his interest conflicts with the interest of the client:*

A settlement offer may to one seem reasonable—to the other unreasonable. One may need money more desperately than the other . . . lawyers have been known to refuse to discuss settlement of a case—"until next year because, for tax reasons, I can't afford another large fee this year."

Long ago the idea that the contingent fee is only for the poor unable to hire a lawyer was abandoned. I once interviewed a wealthy widow living in an expensive duplex apartment on Fifth Avenue in New York. Her broker husband had been killed in a railroad accident. She had tentatively suggested to her lawyer that perhaps she could pay him his regular hourly fees to pursue her claim. He said, no, he preferred to handle it in his customary way—the contingent fee. The railroad settled long before trial and paid the widow $200,000 of which the lawyer got $50,000. I called the lawyer and asked him if he knew how much time he had put in on the case. He said, about 400 hours—50 full eight-hour days—which seemed rather excessive since his pretrial preparation had been quite limited. But even if his 400-hour figure was accurate, he was being paid at the rate of $125 an hour, an incredibly high figure for nontrial work.

In 1959 the editors of the *Ohio State Law Journal* tackled the problem through a questionnaire mailed to some 1,300 lawyer-readers of the *Journal*. One statement was: "Lawyer C signs a ⅓ contingent fee agreement with a client who has a personal injury claim. The client can pay for counsel, win or lose." Then followed this question: "Did lawyer C's conduct involve unethical practice?" Of the 578 who responded to the questionnaire some 184 thought C's conduct was unethical or probably so; but 363 disagreed. There was nothing unethical about taking a case contingently even if the client could afford to pay. But an astounding majority, 454 lawyers felt that even if the conduct was ethical, it was not "desirable as a practical matter." The final and payoff question went: "Will an attorney using a ⅓ contingent fee, on winning a case, get a larger or smaller fee than if he had taken the case on retainer? What percentage larger or smaller?"

Of those answering, the overwhelming majority, 90 percent, felt that lucky lawyer C would indeed get a larger fee this way. How much larger? They divided nearly evenly here: a little more than half thought the increase would be up to 25 percent; but the rest could foresee increases anywhere from 26 percent to 300 percent higher.

I talked to about a dozen leading personal injury lawyers, and none of them would take a case on anything other than a contingent fee basis. But all of them had also stressed the "great risks" they took on these cases in defense of their taking a third to a half of the amount recovered. "After all, if I lose the case I get nothing for the time and effort I've invested." Were they all gamblers at heart or was there another, more plausible reason?

"There is almost no risk," explains Presiding Justice Bernard Botein of the Appellate Division, First Department of New York:

> There is very little that is contingent about the contingent fee. Recoveries are obtained, mostly through the medium of settlements, in over 90 percent of the claims handled by lawyers, so that the dread contingency of no recovery and therefore no fee is pretty remote.

Actually the 90 percent figure is too conservative. According to a Columbia University survey, points out Justice Botein,

> 97 percent of the money recovered for accident claims does not involve the wringing, grueling ordeal of a completed trial, yet lawyers are entitled to be paid the full scheduled fee in these cases.

Still, there *are* lost cases, there *is* office overhead. Is the profit picture quite so fabulous as Judge Botein would have it?

I talked recently to a prosperous northern New Jersey attorney who specializes in personal injury cases. He is self-confident, very competent and handles about 400 cases a year, all contingent. Of these only 38 or so actually go to trial, and in that group he loses about 4 cases or 1 percent of all the cases he has. He has a staff of five including an investigator and his office overhead is about $92,000 a year. About 65 percent of his cases come in cold—he has several relatives who are doctors and a brother who is an orthopedic surgeon at a leading Catholic hospital. His brother *is* a great source of cases, but 35 percent of this lawyer's cases are fed him by other lawyers to whom he gives a third of his fee.

"My average case is a $5,000–$7,000 recovery. I just don't touch any likely to bring less than $3,000. I figure each case I get costs me about $200 for an initial investigation. In addition to those four or so cases I actually lose a year, I guess wrong once or twice a year. The insurance people offer, say, $30,000 to settle and I say, not enough. So we go to court and I get a verdict of only $10,000, say. It happens."

In 1966 he had another untoward happening. He won a $165,-000 award for a boy badly injured in an accident. His contingent fee contract called for a third, but since a minor was involved, the New Jersey court reviewed his fee and knocked it down to 27 percent. "I was going to appeal but we finally worked out a compromise at 30 percent. Not bad."

On the basis of his figures, his yearly balance sheet might look something like this for 400 cases (average of, say, $6,000 recovery):

	$2,400,000
Office overhead . . . . $	92,000
400 case investigations @ $200 each . . .	80,000
Payments to lawyers referring cases . . .	280,000
Payments to clients figured at a 33.3% contingent fee (although he does often get more)	1,600,000
Total paid out	2,052,000
Total net profit (for the lawyer) . . . . $	348,000

The remarkable thing about this lawyer, who has been in practice eighteen years, is that he isn't at all well known outside Essex County, New Jersey. He isn't an officer of the trade association of personal injury lawyers, The American Trial Lawyers Association; he doesn't get interviewed the way Melvin Belli does; he doesn't have the fame among other lawyers that Jacob Fuchsberg and Harry Gair of New York do in this field. In fact, I'm certain the vast majority of the lawyers in the New York metropolitan area have never heard of this forty-two-year-old attorney. Yet year in and year out he is good for a *net* of nearly $350,000 a year from contingent fees. And even more—if he had not paid out some $280,000 to other lawyers for referring cases to him. Is this ethical?

Canon 34 of the American Bar Association's Code of Ethics flatly prohibits a division of fees between lawyers where there is no division of service or responsibility. A prominent Washington attorney, who is outraged by the situation, writes:

> The practice of dividing fees with another lawyer, who has done no more than refer a client, is so widespread among certain segments of the bar that the phrase "the usual forwarding fee" is commonly employed, and there are many members of the bar who are altogether unaware that they are following a practice which may subject them to disbarment.

I asked my prospering New Jersey personal injury specialist about this:

> A man is hurt in an accident. He goes to his family lawyer or more likely just the lawyer who handled his home closing or a relative's divorce. Most people don't *have* lawyers. They *go* to someone. The case sounds pretty good and the lawyer, who wouldn't know a sacroiliac from a sacred fount—and *knows* he doesn't know—calls me because he's done business with me before. And that's *all* he does. *I* want it that way. I got my methods and forms; I don't want him sticking his two cents in and lousing me up. Oh, maybe if it's one of those rare cases that actually goes to trial he comes around one day and sits at counsel table. It looks good, you know. He knows I'm on the up-and-up. He's going to get his

check for a third of my fee the day after the insurance company check is in my office.

Obviously the lawyers who send him cases aren't *ethically* entitled to a third of his fee, which would be, in a typical $6,000 award, about $650 for making a phone call and listening to the client for maybe a half hour.

Understandably lawyers love these referral fees that entail almost no work. Occasionally downright embarrassing situations come about, as one did in Miami in 1961 when lawyer Edwin L. Strickland got a "forwarding fee" of $25,333 from prominent negligence attorney Perry Nichols. "The mere referral of the case on the telephone did not take one minute," Strickland insisted. "I played no part in the case, gave no advice, prepared no pleadings."

Strickland was insisting on how little he did because he was also Judge Strickland, and Miami has an ordinance prohibiting judges from practicing law on the side. The twelve-man Metro Commission that ran the city decided not to discipline the Judge even though the County Attorney told them that acceptance of a referral fee *did* constitute the practice of law. (Nichols had won a $190,000 judgment for the client, a widow whose husband had been killed in an auto accident and took the standard 40 percent, or $76,000. Strickland got the usual third of that for making the happy phone call.)

The case caused one letter-writer to the *Miami News* to come up with an interesting idea:

> Now that $25,000 referrals for judges are approved, I have a suggestion. Let each Metro judge and each circuit court judge have one referral a year in lieu of their salaries. Think of the money the taxpayers would save.

Since there is so much money for lawyers who do nothing but make the providential phone call to the lawyers who will actually handle the case, it didn't take long before some attorneys decided the ideal way to "practice law" was to be the prosperous middle-man who just made the phone calls. The word, in the trade, is "brokering" or "farming out."

How much "brokering" can go on in a large city was disclosed in April, 1967, when John S. Boyle, Chief Judge of the Circuit Court of Cook County (Chicago), testified before the U. S. Senate Committee on the Judiciary. Judge Boyle was responsible for installing a computer system to keep track of the personal injury suits filed in the county. As a result he found that 36 Chicago lawyers were largely responsible for the great logjam of personal injury cases. These 36 lawyers were attorneys of record in almost 18,000 pending personal injury cases—more than a third of the county's backlog of 50,000 cases. It appears, said the Chicago *American* editorially on April 24, 1967, that

these lawyers—none of whom is considered prominent in the personal injury field—have been hustling personal injury cases, then farming them out to other lawyers for a percentage of the fee. The obvious result of having so few attorneys grab off so many cases is that trials and settlements are slowed to a trickle. . . . It is ambulance chasing on a huge scale, presumably with a well organized system of contacts and communications, that enables a handful of lawyers to grab many more cases than they can handle. The damage to the county's judicial system is clear, and we believe the bar association should make it priority business to stop this greedy industry.

One of the few lawyers I could find who had been disciplined for brokering personal injury cases was a New Yorker, Louis Kaye, who on January 13, 1966, was disbarred for "farming out" 50 accident cases in a 15-month period. Kaye, now in his mid-sixties, made his living mostly by representing defendants in New York's Gamblers' Court. He would sell a batch of negligence cases for 50 percent of what the other lawyer would collect as his fee. Only Kaye wanted his money in *advance*. He would ask for and get $6,000–$7,000 for a small batch of cases. Obviously the lawyers buying these were so certain they would pay off well, they were willing to make the substantial advance payments. Kaye had been disbarred once before—in 1928 after he pleaded guilty to a felony count when he was accused of using the mails to cheat insurance companies with fraudulent accident claimants. But he got back again in 1935 after he managed to get a Presidential pardon for his crime. (There were curious ways then, as well as in some subsequent administrations, of getting Presidential pardons.) Kaye is a battler, and in March, 1968, even though he had been formally disbarred two years before, he was still practicing law; he never stopped. He appealed the disbarment decision, and in New York as in many other states, an appeal can prevent the disbarment order from taking effect.

With so much money to be made out of the contingent fees in personal injury cases—even if you didn't work on the case at all—it was inevitable that even sharper practices would come into play.

A New York attorney who served a long apprenticeship with one of the old-time giants of the PI business talked recently of the newer development. I know him quite well:

"You're always telling me how lousy lawyer ethics are. All right, tell me what you would do. The lawyer who just walked out came here with a proposition. It went something like this: he had 'ins' with five insurance companies. He mentioned a specific case I have pending with one of them. The case is worth maybe $15,000, but I'd gladly settle it tomorrow for $12,000, even $11,000. It would be a good settlement. Now the lawyer comes out with the dirty words: 'Listen, counselor, I can get you $22,000 for it. But I need 10 percent for my man.' "

He explained: "This lawyer has a deal with key characters in the adjustment departments of those insurance companies. When he says 'my man' he means one of the officials in the company, someone who can approve a large settlement. Now tell me, what would you do? Take him on, get more money for my injured client and for myself or blow the whistle on him at 44th Street [the New York Bar Association grievance offices]?"

He paused. *"You'd* hop over to the bar association, right?"

I nodded, and asked, "And you?"

"That's the difference. You're not trying to make a living out of the law business. I am. Sure, I was tempted but one thing held me back: I couldn't *trust* this guy; I didn't know him well enough. So I said, no thanks. And now I keep wondering: did I do right by my client? I could have added another $5,000 for her injuries by playing along quietly, even after giving $2,000 to the fixer and his friend in the insurance office." He laughed mirthlessly. "With my luck, all I'd need now is for her to get wind of what she missed here and come out and sue me for malpractice for not having gotten her *more.*"

The lawyer who came in to suggest the 10 percent arrangement is one of a growing number found in New York and other large metropolitan areas. They're called "point men" in the trade, and while most of them are lawyers some are retired adjusters. (The name "point men" arises because they ask for "10 points" rather than 10 percent of the total recovery.)

Another lawyer who has been approached by "point men" added some details. "When a man's power is not commensurate with his earnings there's a great temptation to turn his power to personal profit: cops, building inspectors, etc. Most mutual insurance companies don't pay decent salaries to their claims department heads. Stock companies aren't so bad.* You might have a man making $10,000–$12,000 a year and in charge of approving millions in payouts every year for a mutual casualty company. It's *unreasonable,* so he cheats, and this new system comes into operation. He uses a trusted intermediary, who only goes to men he feels he can *talk* to, and he can easily double or triple his salary. Just like the rest of us who aren't above getting the garage to pad our car repair bill to cover the $50 deductible, he figures, what the hell, it's only the company's money."

The enormous lure of the contingent fee for lawyers has recently attracted the attention of insurance company defense attorneys. Usually they represent the insurers, the defendants, in

*A stock insurance company is one owned by stockholders who aren't necessarily policyholders. A mutual company is "owned" by its policyholders, even though they have little real control over management.

trials for anywhere from $200 to $400 a day in court. Some lawyers, such as Emile Zola Berman of New York, are switch-hitters
who might be representing a plaintiff one week and an insurance
company the next. But John D. Phelan, president of the American States Insurance Company in Indianapolis, is unhappy about
the practice. In a talk before insurance counsel in March, 1965,
he warned:

> . . . we in the insurance business are forced to choose more carefully
> where our business shall go . . . it would be stupid for us to pay the
> rent and light bill of the attorney who has helped change the claims
> climate by a dramatic verdict dramatically obtained.

In terms that made many of his listeners distinctly uncomfortable, he stressed that too few insurance attorneys speak out
against the evils of contingent fees:

> Let's recognize that the defense attorney presently may feel he has a
> great economic stake in the continuance of the contingent fee. Contin-
> gent fees exist and are continued because of the active or passive sup-
> port of defense attorneys and the rest of the bar. The bar, if it chose,
> could have brought unlimited contingent fees under control—through
> judicial rule or legislation. Generally it has not chosen to do so.

Then he got his audience of leading defense lawyers really
squirming:

> Unlimited contingent fees have seemed good to the business side of
> the practice of defense law. The economic theory is simple. Unlimited
> contingent fees generate suits in quantity. Suits in quantity require de-
> fense law in quantity.

Phelan's naked exposition of the enormous stake *all* lawyers
have in the contingent fee seems to have aroused other like souls
in the industry, and in October, 1965, the National Association of
Mutual Insurance Companies, which has 1,100 member compa-

nies, became the first insurance trade group to speak out against the excesses of contingent fees:

. . . if contingent fees were reasonably limited, the savings to the public on last year's losses in automobile liability alone would be approximately $250,000,000 thereby allowing sizeable premium rate reductions to the insurance buying public.

Now therefore be it resolved we hereby request the various state bar associations to draft, introduce and sponsor model legislation for the proper limitation of plaintiff lawyers' contingent fees.

Earlier that year the Defense Research Institute, which has 4,000 insurance lawyer-members—as opposed to the 24,000 plaintiff lawyers who belong to the belligerent Trial Lawyers Association—also urged control of the contingent fee. But a more realistic DRI, knowing of the great influence the prospering personal injury lawyers have in many state legislatures, urged that the control should be imposed by another agency:

The judiciary, upon whom the duty of supervising the profession rests, should assume the responsibility for protecting the public from every form of overreaching by attorneys, including protection from unreasonable charges, whether by way of retainer or contingent fees.

Lawyers may quite properly be required to furnish the courts with appropriate information concerning fee arrangements and performance in accordance with such contracts, and to answer complaints by clients with regard to fees charged.

In short, the DRI lawyers felt it was time the rest of the nation copied what two New York counties, Manhattan and the Bronx, had been doing since January 1, 1957, under a court-imposed regulation known as Rule 4.

In 1953 Presiding Justice David W. Peck of New York's Appellate Division, the state's second highest ranking court, had his clerks examine more than 150,000 contingency fee agreements filed by lawyers in Manhattan and the Bronx, his court's territory. Some 62 percent of all the agreements permitted the lawyers to take half the amount recovered. It seemed to Justice Peck that when the contingent fee approaches the 50 percent level, "it ceases to be a measure of the due compensation for professional services and makes a lawyer a partner or proprietor in the lawsuit."

So he and his fellow justices in the Appellate Division of the First Judicial Department (Manhattan and the Bronx) instituted for the first time in U.S. court history a maximum scale of fees that attorneys could collect in contingency personal injury cases. The scale, Rule 4, permits attorneys either to take a flat third or submit to a sliding scale allowing them 50 percent of the first $1,000 recovered, down to 25 percent of any amount over $25,000.

In order to permit the court to check on obedience to the rule, the court requires attorneys to file a signed statement with the court showing just how the award was divided and how much was spent on medical and investigatory expenses. Failure to file these statements leads to disciplinary action.

Rule 4 brought forth anguished cries from the city's leading negligence lawyers and from every bar association in the city except one. A group of prosperous personal injury lawyers fought the rule to the state's highest court, the Court of Appeals. In May, 1959, that court upheld the right of the Appellate Division to regulate attorney fees. Court of Appeals Justice John Van Voorhis, writing the majority opinion, pointed out that in the United States "the risk of the lawyer under contingent fee agreements has been reduced and his remuneration magnified." He also warned of "growing public resentment" against contingent fee lawyers "who are trying to sail too close to the wind."

After the U. S. Supreme Court refused to hear the case, the personal injury lawyers tried another tack—a windward course through the smoother waters of the state legislature. A 1960 bill to overturn Rule 4 passed the Assembly, whose biggest single bloc of members were lawyers. In an editorial calling on the upper house, the Senate, to defeat the bill, *The New York Times* said: ". . . excessive contingent fees are far too common . . . from everyone's point of view except those lawyers who seek to exploit their clients' misfortunes [Rule 4] must seem fair and badly needed." The New York *Herald-Tribune* called the legislative attempt to override the courts here "shameful stuff." Perhaps as a result the bill did not pass the Senate, and Rule 4 has since spread to much of the rest of New York State.*

The lawyers opposing Rule 4 said they were fighting it on principle—that the courts *shouldn't* have the right to set the level of contingent fees. They were only slightly embarrassed when it was pointed out that the Canons of Ethics of the ABA itself provides that the contingent fee "should always be subject to the supervision of the court as to its reasonableness."

The New York decision called forth some bitter comments from Orville Richardson, president of the Missouri Bar Association, about the *ingratitude* of the New York judges:

> For years the bar has fought furiously to preserve the independence of the judiciary, to increase salaries of judges, to give them more assistance, better quarters, earlier retirement on adequate pensions and so on. Now, ironically enough, it is the judiciary which has turned upon and which threatens our own independence.

Mr. Richardson may have been particularly sensitive to the judicial stab-in-the-back because Kansas City, Missouri, is generally considered to have the highest contingent fee arrangement—a flat 50 percent—for all personal injury cases.

Another judge Mr. Richardson must feel is a double ingrate is U. S. District Court Judge Gerald J. Weber, of Pittsburgh, who as an attorney had profited from contingent fee cases. On September 20, 1967, Judge Weber handed down an opinion that must have made the negligence lawyers of Pennsylvania acutely uncomfortable.

A fifty-one-year-old railroad fireman was killed in January, 1965, in a collision of two trains. He left a wife and two teen-age

*Since January 1, 1965, all contingent fee agreements in Massachusetts are subject to Rule 14, imposed by the state's highest court. It is not as specific as New York's Rule 4, but it clearly brought the question of the reasonableness of the fee under court supervision.

children. Long before trial or even pretrial hearings, a settlement of $85,000 was agreed on by the two railroads involved in the collision. The victim's wife had hired a lawyer to prosecute the action for her on a flat one-third contingent fee basis. Accordingly he wanted $28,333 as his fee, plus an additional $2,193 for expenses he had advanced. The case came to Judge Weber because the interests of the two children were involved.

Judge Weber thought the lawyer was getting too much, that flat contingent fees regardless of circumstance were unfair. As a lawyer, Judge Weber wrote, he had also handled many contingent fee cases: "I lived with and to an extent upon the very system for many years before coming to the bench." But now as a judge he was seeing some of the real dangers of the contingent fee system:

> An inflexible contingent fee agreement may operate as a block to early settlement in those cases which ought to be settled. Both parties feel forced to protect their bargaining position. The litigation drags on and the beneficiaries are deprived of their damages during the time when their loss is most critical. . . . To what extent did the inflexible contingent fee agreement operate to delay a settlement which would otherwise adequately compensate the beneficiaries, reduce the expenses and provide a reasonable counsel fee?

He felt that the courts and lawyers were only paying lip service to the idea that contingent fees are always subject to the control of the court according to Canon 12 of the Code of Professional Ethics. Too few of these cases actually came to the courts to determine just how "reasonable" the contingent fees were. As far as he was concerned, ". . . a flat fixed percentage for all cases at all stages and in all circumstances does not meet the test of reasonableness. This becomes more obvious as the amount of recovery rises."

Accordingly, he cut the lawyer's fee from $28,333 to $19,583, using a scale that must have aged every PI lawyer who saw Judge Weber's opinion: he allowed 33.3 percent on the first $10,000 of recovery; 25 percent on the next $50,000 and *only 15 percent on everything over $60,000.* In addition he knocked out the $1,642 for "investigation and preparation" of the case by the lawyer. In all, then, Judge Weber saved the widow an additional $10,392, a sum that could give her two children a fine edge on their college educations.

Unfortunately, Judge Weber's action is all too rare in either federal or state courts. As a result I found it easy to collect horrible examples of lawyers' overreaching in contingent fee cases— without judicial intervention. I had some incredible cases:

A Gary, Indiana, railroad worker who, after a six-year legal battle, won a $25,000 award for serious injuries, took home only $4,166. At last report the lawyers were battling over the remaining $20,834.

A ten-year-old Miami boy who got only $661 out of a $2,578 verdict for auto accident injuries. The boy's attorney took $1,260 as his fee, and the rest went for expenses. To correct this staggering injustice the boy's father had to hire another lawyer, for $190, and sued to recover. The court forced the original overreaching lawyer to pay the boy another $666, so that in the end, after expensive litigation the lad ended up with *half* of what he had been awarded.

A Virginia salesman got only $15,000 of a $33,000 court award for serious accident injuries.

A Los Angeles woman, the mother of ten, was awarded $90,000 for the "wrongful death" of her husband in an auto accident. The lawyer took 40 percent, or $36,000—for which he had actually put in less than two weeks' work.

But even when the lawyers hold their take to a third of the award, what emerges may be legal but hardly fair. Consider this example of the new arithmetic at work:

Boni Buehler, an attractive airline stewardess, lost an arm and a leg in a 1953 Lake Arrowhead, California, motorboat accident and won $265,000 in court actions. She agreed to pay her lawyer one third.

Question: How much did the lawyers get? How much did Boni

get? The first answer is easy. The lawyers got $88,000, just about a third. The second answer is stranger: Boni got $100,000. How come? Well, the lawyers took their third right off the top—before any expenses were deducted. Boni, the victim who was minus an arm and a leg, wasn't so privileged. She had to pay out nearly $80,000 in medical and hospital bills; Boni said one doctor charged her $1,500 for testifying twenty minutes, and she insisted others doubled and tripled their fees when they learned how much she was suing for. And there was other legal fees, investigations and the like. If she had been permitted to deduct these items first, her lawyers would only have been entitled to $62,000 instead of $88,000.

And there were other instances of the horrible arithmetic the victims had been subjected to. But the classic case I uncovered right in New York City which, after all, does have a control of the contingent fee and has demonstrated sharp interest in protecting the accident victim.

Item: A man is badly injured in an accident. He wins a court verdict of $53,544. Court expenses reduces it to $52,069. The lawyer takes a third or $17,356. *Problem:* How much did the injured man take home? *Answer:* $3,215, or only one fifth of what the lawyer got. Is this outrageous? Well . . . Is it legal? Yes.

In 1960 Gustav Mortensen, a $4-an-hour ship painter, was working on a steamship smokestack in New York harbor. When the scaffold caved in he fell to the deck. His arm was broken and he required bone grafts calling for five operations in seven years. During that time his arm was in a cast three and a half years. He and his wife used up their $6,000 savings, since he couldn't work at all during that time. His case was taken by a well-known personal injury lawyer, David Fink, who agreed to do it for a third contingency. In Brooklyn Federal Court, Fink won his client an award of $53,544. Fink took $17,356 as his third—after expenses of $1,475 had been deducted—which left, theoretically, $34,713 for Mortensen, a slight, grizzled gray-haired man of fifty-one at the time.

During the period of his disability, Mortensen received $54 a week as workmen's compensation and got many checks from the city's welfare department. All this, some $22,818, had to be repaid.* So did a preexisting claim from welfare for an older obligation: the support of his three children by a previous marriage. Another $8,680 here. Then there were court expenses and medical witnesses and such, which came to $1,475. When it was all over, Mortensen got a check for $3,215 on April 21, 1964. Quite legal. Certainly no overreaching by his lawyer, who stuck scrupulously to his one-third fee.

Inevitably, the final ironic goal—the elimination of the extraneous victim—had to be attained. The historic day was August 20, 1964. On that day, some 116 years after the contingent fee became an accepted part of American life, 57 years after founder Abraham Gatner created the basic underpinnings for our growing injury industry, the ultimate was attained. On that day the victim of a Brooklyn auto accident, whose case was settled for $8,600, ended up, quite legally, with exactly nothing. His lawyers got $3,232.

His name was Tom Hall and in the fall of 1960 he was injured in an auto accident. Four years later his lawyers won $8,600 for him—technically, anyway. In fact, the biggest winner was the New York City Welfare Department, which had given Tom Hall and his family $3,243 in relief payments. Then some $975 in disability payments he had received had to be repaid. There were hospital payments of $724 and doctor payments and various court charges. So when it was all paid out Tom Hall was left with zero. His lawyers got a legally permitted $3,232 or about 37 percent. (Instead of a flat one-third fee they opted for an alternate method of fixing their fee: half of the first $1,000; 40 percent of the next two thousand and 35 percent of the remainder, up to $22,000.)

Obviously, there's no lurking villain in these cases. The injured men *did* owe welfare and workmen's compensation carriers a

*In all, some thirty-two states have such recovery statutes. In 1966, New York State was able to recover $5.6 million from welfare recipients who had won accident awards, inherited money or had insurance policies mature.

good deal of money that rightfully should have been repaid. But both cases raise an interesting question. For *whose benefit* were these lawsuits instituted? The victims who got comparatively little or nothing? Not likely. The only real private beneficiaries were, of course, the lawyers.

•   •   •

Talking about the shortcomings of our contingent fee system often brings glinting reactions from some lawyers: "Ah. You're *against* contingent fees." I'm not. I think the system is useful and probably necessary. Without it our courts wouldn't be nearly as slow and overcrowded as they are; and the contingent fee does generate a considerable amount of nuisance and unmeritorious litigation. Still, on balance, it has enabled the poor and considerable portions of the middle class to have ready access to civil justice.

I feel about the contingent fee pretty much as did the late Max Radin, a great law professor:

> Contingent fees are good when they assist an otherwise helpless litigant secure his right against a powerful antagonist. They are bad when they deprive this litigant of a substantial part of the compensation for his injury.

I would go further. I feel that the leading negligence attorneys and their trade guilds such as the American Trial Lawyers Association have, on the whole, benefitted the American people. They pioneered imaginative courtroom tactics and legal approaches that make it easier for the injured to collect more reasonable damages in an increasing variety of cases that have nothing to do with autos. Admittedly their zest stems at least as much from selfish reasons as it does from a desire to advance the public weal.

What *is* needed—long overdue—is firm control by the courts over the contingent fee lawyer's percentages and his conduct. Most negligence lawyers still consider such a mild reform not only unreasonable but even dangerous to what is the most profitable and fastest growing form of legal practice today.

8 WHO'S WATCHING?

Bar associations are notoriously reluctant to disbar or even suspend a member unless he has murdered a judge downtown at high noon, in the presence of the entire Committee on Ethical Practices.
—SYDNEY J. HARRIS

I have found, far and wide, a growing dissatisfaction with the adequacy of the discipline maintained by our profession. . . . this dissatisfaction is justified. It is found among thoughtful lawyers . . . and it is widely prevalent among laymen.
LEWIS F. POWELL, JR.
President, American Bar Association, 1965

When I was a boy in Brooklyn a favorite Friday night diversion was listening to street-corner speakers. Generally, there were two programs: we could listen to a huckster hawking the health-making qualities of psyllium seed, or we could cross to the diagonal corner and hear a sibilant Socialist denounce the iniquities of capitalism. After his one-hour peroration he would have a question period. Most questions got the same answer: "Comrade, we'll change all that when we get rid of capitalism."

I was reminded of him in 1965 during a visit to San Francisco. The *Chronicle* carried an interview with Vincent Hallinan, a prospering sixty-year-old lawyer who denounced his fellow attorneys as "liars, hypocrites, servants to the capitalistic establishment." Hallinan, who ran as the radical Progressive Party candidate for President of the United States in 1952, admitted there were a few honest men among the judges and lawyers, but they were only "like clear puddles in an ocean of vile mud. . . . The only answer is to change the system from capitalism to socialism."

Not long ago a friend sent me a translation of an article that appeared in a 1961 issue of *Sovetskaya yustitsia* (Soviet Justice). The article was: "Eliminate Shortcomings in the Work of the Lawyers' Collegiums." (A rough equivalent of these collegiums here would be bar associations.) In many cases, the article said:

> . . . large fees have been set in the lawyers' collegiums without valid grounds, and this naturally has given rise to numerous complaints from citizens. But almost all of these complaints have been left unsatisfied. . . . There are still disgraceful cases of drunkenness, excessive zeal and other unethical acts in the collegium. Yet in some cases *the presidium has an irresponsible attitude toward warnings about the unworthy conduct of lawyers and has tried in every way to shield them and help them evade responsibility.*
>
> The presidium is not waging a proper struggle against lawyers who are discrediting justice by their conduct. It is not mere chance that out of 34 court rulings concerning the incorrect conduct of lawyers received by the presidium, it recognized only 19 as confirmed and punished only 3 lawyers on the basis of them. . . .

With a few exceptions the Soviet author of the article could have written an almost identical article about the disciplinary shortcomings of any one of hundreds of U.S., city, county or state bar associations. All of which would indicate that when it comes to lawyers, state socialism changes nothing. (Did lawyer-revolutionaries Robespierre, Danton, Lenin, Lassalle or DeLeon switch careers because they *knew* this?)

What it *does* show, said social critic Ferdinand Lundberg in 1938, is that the legal profession

> constitutes a body of men with other fish to fry than those having any connection with conservatism, radicalism or anything else. It exists for itself, for its own interests, not answerable to anybody outside the profession.

Nor would it appear is the average lawyer often answerable to anybody *inside* the profession. Denunciation of the bar's loose state of discipline goes back decades in the United States and centuries in England and Europe.

Roman commentators attacked rapacious and unscrupulous lawyers. Titus Maccius Plautus, the Roman comic dramatist, said that rascals never want an advocate as rascally as themselves to sustain their perjuries, that lawyers instigate the litigation by which they live.

In the eighteenth century, Oliver Goldsmith, describing a visit to the London law courts, commented sarcastically:

> "But bless me! What numbers do I see here—all in black! How is it so possible that half this multitude can find employment?"—"Nothing so easily conceived," returned my companion; "they live by watching each other."

But for centuries the trouble has been that for all the watching of lawyers' unethical, dishonest or blatantly criminal activities, very little has been done about them.

How *little* and the handicaps in the way of increasing effective discipline of lawyers were discussed at a remarkably candid seminar of bar association officials at the August, 1967, meeting of the American Bar Association in Honolulu's Hotel Illikai. (I felt there was a certain innocent insensitivity by the ABA officials who chose the Cutter and Clipper rooms for this meeting.) Present were some forty bar association executives and presidents and members of grievance committees, plus two nonlawyers: Adam A. Smyser, editor of the Honolulu *Star Bulletin,* who was there as a speaker, and myself.

All agreed with the comment of Blythe Stason, former Dean of the Michigan University Law School, that in a country with nearly 300,000 lawyers, "the number subjected to discipline is remarkably small."

Why it was so small was explained in different ways by the speakers. Among the reasons:

Money. "We have a $16,000 annual grievance budget for the whole state of Texas, which has 16,392 lawyers," complained Davis Grant, staff counsel of the State Bar. "You can't do much on that. We have thirty-five grievance committees, all unpaid, which sounds fine, but often some of these lawyers don't even know what misconduct is."

"We've been doing an inadequate job of policing the profession because we've been penny-pinching," said Russell N. Sullivan, past president of the Illinois State Bar. "We have to proceed more aggressively, which means spending more money."

Delay. "Some of these grievance hearings run for years," confessed J. Russell Christiansen, general counsel of the Chicago Bar Association. "There are too many hearings, too much delay. You can't blame the public for being skeptical of our intent." Delay is even against the interest of the lawyers accused, pointed out Vincent Cullinan, president of the San Francisco Bar. "The lawyer involved is under a cloud for months and even years before a case is resolved."

Rignal W. Baldwin, president of the Maryland Bar, described a new delay gimmick that was spreading. "We now have four cases where lawyers who have stolen from clients have pleaded insanity and put themselves in institutions, very expensive institutions. They can't be tried until they're released and presumably are 'sane' again. One of the lawyers involved took $43,000 from eleven people. Another fleeced an eighty-five-year-old woman of all she had: $10,000. We have a Client Security Fund with $140,-000, but we can't repay her until the lawyer is tried and found guilty. God knows when that will happen."

Suspended Punishments. "There's just no reason why an attorney once convicted should be permitted to practice law," said Sidney S. Feinberg, president of the Minnesota State Bar. "It happens too often. In 1962, when I was president of the Hennepin County Bar, a lawyer pleaded guilty to a felony. He was sentenced to the state penitentiary, but the court gave him a stay of sentence during appeal so that he could practice for months afterwards. Another lawyer convicted of a felony took an appeal and was also allowed to practice 'to settle his affairs.' Finally in 1964 the Minnesota Supreme Court amended its rules and provided that whenever a lawyer is convicted of a felony he is immediately suspended from the practice of law."

Feinberg explained his particular interest in the subject: "When I was in law school I worked for an ambulance chaser as an office boy. Naturally when I passed my bar exam and came up before the Committee on Character I was quizzed with particular intensity on legal ethics because of my past connection. I'll never forget *that* session."

In Texas, the bar was embarrassed when, in 1966, it emerged that three penitentiary inmates were still licensed to practice law. They were Clem McClelland, Houston's first full-time probate judge, who is serving ten years for stealing from estates; lawyer James Martin, doing four years for bribing McClelland; and Sam Hoover, former mayor of Pasadena, Texas, serving a sixty-year sentence for masterminding the crimes of some of his criminal clients. In Texas, as in many other states, a convicted lawyer is not disbarred until he has exhausted *every* avenue of appeal.

Ready Forgiveness. Disbarment is almost never forever. In most states a lawyer can apply for readmission from two to five years after he has been disbarred. In some areas lawyers can avoid the stigma of disbarment by "voluntarily withdrawing" from the bar, then reapplying later. Julius L. Echeles, a well-known Chicago criminal lawyer, who was sentenced to twenty-two months for peddling post office jobs, withdrew from legal practice. When he got out of prison he was readmitted to practice by the Illinois Supreme Court. And suspension of a lawyer for lesser infractions is usually only a matter of months. In a 1952 study of bar discipline, Judges Orie L. Phillips and Philbrick McCoy told of a California lawyer named Cedric Petersen who was suspended from practice after stealing a client's money. Soon after, he was reinstated and he stole again. And again he was suspended. A third time he was restored to active practice, and once again he embezzled client money. Only then was he finally disbarred.

In a 1967 survey, retired U. S. Supreme Court Justice Tom Clark found that in one state "out of thirty disbarments in a period of thirty years, twelve were reinstated, ten of the reinstatements being in the last ten years."

Secrecy. In Buffalo, New York, said John B. Walsh, executive secretary of the Erie County Bar Association, "We have two lawyers we suspect are grossly incompetent. God knows the damage they do their clients. But there is no way for us to tell the public. I'm sure every city has a similar problem. We had a case of a lawyer we were trying for thefts from his clients. We couldn't let the public know, of course, so he just kept stealing from new clients who came to him. It was eighteen months before we could disbar him."

Secrecy about discipline can be frustrating even within the profession, said Vincent Cullinan, president of the San Francisco Bar:

"Practicing attorneys often tell us: why don't you get so-and-so, the big guys, the big publicity seekers, the big chasers. . . . But they tell us this in private, on golf courses or at cocktail parties. Often, however, they don't know that even as they're complaining, the man has been disciplined or chastised."

In a Minneapolis case I had investigated I had come up against the bar's secrecy provisions on disciplinary matters. After the Honolulu discipline meeting I enlisted the help of Sidney S. Feinberg, president of the Minnesota State Bar. He promised to see what he could do.

The case involved a Minneapolis lawyer who was the defendant in a civil action in which he and an associate were accused of taking unwarranted fees of $245,000 from the estate of an elderly incompetent for whom he was legal guardian. Judge James Montague found that the "grossly excessive" fees constituted "a fraud" upon the estate and on the probate court itself. He ordered the lawyers to repay more than $139,000 of the fees. In a final settlement some $70,000 was repaid. The matter was studied by the Ethics Committee of the Hennepin County (Minneapolis) Bar. In spite of several requests I made, the committee refused to reveal what action, if any, was taken against the lawyer. The committee's secretary, attorney Ralph Parker, spent most of the time during our talk warning me of the dangers of a libel suit if I wrote about the case. The lawyer is still practicing law today. At this writing—six months after Mr. Feinberg's promise to see what he could do to find out what had happened in the case—I have yet to hear from him.*

Warning of "a storm ahead" for the profession, Adam A. Smyser, editor of the Honolulu *Star Bulletin,* urged them to publicize *all* disciplinary cases. "Here in Hawaii, bar discipline, unfortunately, is often aborted because the bar is afraid of the public's reaction if details of the accused lawyer's activities get out. Not only do you lawyers need more publicity in this area, but I think it might be a good idea if you allowed us laymen to participate in the proceedings of bar disciplinary groups."

Judicial Blocks. "I've been amazed that the courts in disciplinary cases often attack the bar counsel rather than the accused attorney," complained Russell N. Sullivan, of the Illinois State Bar. "In 1957 our State Supreme Court said the canons of ethics governing solicitation of cases by lawyers were outmoded and unfair. So we haven't been able to discipline any lawyers we know are guilty of ambulance chasing in mass accidents."

Another Illinois Bar official said that when bar disciplinary cases were reviewed by successively higher courts, the punishment tended to get reduced—"just as in military court-martials," he said. Time and appeal apparently always work in the accused lawyer's favor.

He didn't mention the case of attorney Thomas Hart Fisher of Chicago, but he was surely thinking of him. Fisher was then very much in the news as the missing attorney in the Alice Byron Atwood estate. Miss Atwood, who died in 1965 at age sixty-five, was the granddaughter of the founder of the great King Ranch of Texas. She left more than $10 million to a friendly policeman, Michael De Bella. Fisher, who had been handling Miss Atwood's affairs for nearly forty years, promptly left the state to avoid producing the mysteriously missing assets of the estate. A probate court judge found him in contempt. An early examination of the Atwood estate indicated that at least $6 million was missing.

Fisher, whose father had been Secretary of the Interior in the administration of President Taft, had had other well-publicized

*See Chapter Twelve for more on this case.

difficulties with clients and the bar association. For example, in 1948 he was found guilty of unprofessional conduct and disbarred for three years by a federal judge. The decision was appealed and reversed three years later. In 1958 Fisher, a thin-faced, thinning-haired socialite, was censured by the Illinois Supreme Court for actions against clients—but the Chicago Bar Association had asked that he be barred from practice for *five years*.

Recently Ohio also had a case of a lawyer who was shown a surprising degree of judicial tolerance. In 1965 Louis R. Mayer, a forty-four-year-old lawyer of Pepper Pike, Ohio—a Cleveland suburb—was found guilty of embezzling $22,000 from three estates and the account of a World War I veteran. He got a remarkably light sentence of five years on probation with the proviso that he make restitution. He got a job and after several months was fired when a $1,300 "bookkeeping discrepancy" was found by the firm. He then moved to Akron, Ohio, and wrote some large checks against a too-small bank balance. As a probation violator, Mayer was given a one-to-twenty-year sentence. Less than two months later the judge who had so sentenced him, Common Pleas Judge Thomas W. Mitchell, quietly ordered Mayer's release from prison. At this writing Mayer is still on probation—and still hasn't made restitution to his victims.

Some of the bar executives complained of a recent U. S. Supreme Court decision in the matter of a Brooklyn lawyer named Samuel Spevack who was disbarred after pleading the Fifth Amendment about his role in an ambulance-chasing ring.

Spevack had refused to produce his records, saying that they might tend to incriminate him. He was disbarred. But on January 16, 1967, the Supreme Court in a 5–4 decision ruled that a lawyer cannot be disciplined for refusing to testify about his professional conduct. In his dissent, Justice John M. Harlan said: "What is done today will be disheartening and frustrating to courts and bar associations throughout the country in their efforts to maintain high standards at the bar." He foresaw the "possible indignity" of such a lawyer coming to practice before the U. S. Supreme Court itself, since he was in good standing only because he had blocked an investigation into charges about his professional conduct.

Russell Niles, Dean of the New York University Law School, didn't think the Spevack decision by itself would tie the hands of disciplinary committees. "All the Supreme Court decided was that silence by a lawyer was not enough to disbar him. There are other ways of building a case against a dishonest or unethical lawyer." But you have to *want* to do it. The desire is not always present.

Confusion over Ethics. Paragraph 28 of the Chicago Bar Association's Code of Ethics says it is "unprofessional" for a lawyer

to breed litigation by seeking out those with claims for personal injuries . . . or to employ agents or runners . . . or to pay or reward, directly or indirectly, those who bring or influence the bringing of such cases to his office . . . every member of the Bar, having knowledge of such practices . . . [must] immediately inform [the Bar] to the end that the offender may be disbarred.

In 1966 Federal Judge Richard B. Austin, a member of the bar in good standing, took Canon 28 of the Code of Ethics seriously. He was considering sentences for two Chicago ambulance chasers who had pleaded guilty to evasion of income taxes.

David E. Vogele and Paul Skidmore pleaded guilty in the hope that the names of the thirty lawyers who had paid them wouldn't be made public. But Judge Austin wouldn't go along. "If anyone thinks a plea of guilty can keep the names of the lawyers from the public they are wrong." Vogele had failed to report $55,688 of some $146,000 of income. Skidmore held out on Uncle Sam some $91,000 out of known canceled checks totaling $201,482. The names of the offending lawyers were studied by the Chicago Bar Association. But as one bar spokesman told a reporter, "After all, I don't think a man's career should be destroyed because he simply violates a code of conduct he imposes on himself." In short, a self-imposed code must not be taken too seriously. Or as Dr. Corinne Lathrop Gilb, an attractive dark-haired University of California researcher into the professions, puts it:

Not all planks of a professional association's code of ethics are meant to be taken in the same spirit. Some are merely costumes the profession puts on to impress outsiders. Some are preachments to be honored but not necessarily obeyed. Some are guides but permissive ones. Some are tactical moves in controversies with outside groups.

As a result of the Chicago chaser's incriminating checks, one lawyer was disbarred. Another, Frank J. Mackey, Jr., who paid about $62,000 to both chasers, was given a six months' suspension. Another was suspended for a year, two for three months, and several were "censured." But most of the other lawyers involved seem to have come out of the experience with nothing more than a bit of embarrassment, including George M. Schatz, who had paid $1,605 to one of the chasers and had risen to the municipal court bench by the time of the investigation. Another was David E. Bradshaw, who had paid chaser Skidmore $4,016 in twenty-seven checks. He said they were investigatory fees. At the time of the bar investigation, Bradshaw was a member of the Illinois Crime Investigating Commission. Presumably he was busy investigating *other* crimes, since soliciting accident cases was not a state or federal crime.

In some cities the bar's refusal to act firmly might stem from strong sympathies by the grievance committee. In the past decade in at least two large U.S. cities the chairmen of the local bar grievance committees have been ex-ambulance-chasing lawyers grown wealthy and respectable.

The general difficulties of lawyers trying to police their ranks made me yearn for a specific state or city bar association that was doing an effective job. I made some inquiries among informed friends, and two specific state bars were recommended for my attention. I spent more time checking out both states, which had integrated bars. (Twenty-seven states have integrated bars.)*

Logically such integrated-bar states should have better disciplinary structures, since they control *all* lawyers in the state. But

---

*Nothing to do with racial relations. All lawyers in these integrated-bar states have to be members of the bar association in order to practice.

neither of the recommended states impressed me. I mentioned my disappointment to Glenn Winters, executive director of the American Judicature Society. Since 1913 the society has been primarily concerned with the quality of our courts. It also initiated the concept of the integrated bar.

He nodded sadly. "I know. The trouble is the executive director of the bar in _____ is just too old. The other man, in ———, is a friend but he's past his prime and has lost his zip."

I kept looking for a state bar with a model disciplinary organization I could write about. During my search, a cynical lawyer-friend phoned: "I have the guy you ought to see if you want to find out why bar discipline is so lousy." He gave me a phone number, and that led to my meeting "Tommy."

Tommy—which isn't his real name—talked freely for several hours. The only condition he imposed is that I not identify him or the bar association he worked for. I pointed out that any informed Midwest lawyer reading my account would identify him quickly, false name and all. Tommy agreed I was probably right but he insisted. "No logic," he said. "Call it leftover loyalty to an ex-client."

Tommy is now about seventy and has had more than forty-five years of intensive investigative experience—most recently in this Midwest city in which he worked as the bar association investigator for the disciplinary committee. He was a U. S. Treasury investigator for sixteen years and during World War II handled special investigations for the Air Force. After the war he joined one of the nation's largest law firms as its full-time investigator.

He recalled one of the firm's great successes. A client, a prominent foreign insurance company, had striven for years to be permitted to sell insurance in this Midwest state. Its applications were always successfully blocked by lobbyists for domestic insurers who didn't want further competition. Finally, the permission was granted largely, it seemed, through the intervention of a lawyer working for the State Attorney. The lawyer was suitably rewarded and made a partner in the firm, earning at least $100,000 a year. "Now I want to be fair about it," Tommy grinned. "He did the firm a helluva big favor, but he was also related to one of the partners, so I don't know which came first: blood or gratitude."

Tommy was there fifteen years, and although he was proud of the connection, he has an offhand irreverence about lawyers, legislatures and courts that I've often found in experienced investigators. "It was a pretty honest firm," he recalls. "They gave good service and charged like the dickens. They kept me busy and I liked working there."

In 1962 Tommy decided to retire. He had saved his money, had had some luck in the stock market. He and his wife—they have no children—had picked out a comfortable ranch house in California. After a few months there he got a phone call from one of the senior partners of the law firm he had worked for. The city's bar association had finally been persuaded to set up a full-time investigator at $10,000 a year. They wanted an experienced man who had a legal background and great discretion. The senior partner, a power in the local association, had recommended Tommy strongly. In fact the job was Tommy's if he wanted it. The senior partner hoped very much that Tommy would want it.

"I liked the old gent," Tommy says. "They were paying me a generous pension above my federal one, and I was kind of grateful to him for the fifteen good years I had with his firm. They took me on when I was past fifty, you know. So I talked it over with my wife and she said, if that's what I wanted, OK. Anyway, I was getting a little restless."

When he took the job, Tommy found it was even worse than he anticipated. "They never had an investigating department before, which meant I could set things up the way I liked. Fine. It also meant they didn't have the faintest idea what the hell was involved. They were getting about five thousand complaints a year, and about half of them were serious; worth looking into. And I was the only staffer. I could have used six other experienced investigators and believe me not one of them would have had enough goof-off time to develop a beer belly.

"Okay, I was all alone, which meant I had to concentrate on

the serious cases. Then I discovered that I didn't have any secretary, so I had to type my own reports and letters, which cut down
my available time for investigation by about a third."

In the state Tommy worked in, the bar association is charged by
the State Supreme Court with the maintenance of discipline.
The bar in turn had a large committee on inquiry. The secretary
of the committee, another full-time employee, did the initial
screening. If the case had substance and the complaint seemed
valid, the case was filed with the grievance committee, twenty-five
lawyers who volunteered their time once a week. The committee
was divided into four panels of six lawyers and one alternate.
Two panels met one afternoon a week and two one evening.
Then the full grievance committee would meet once a week to
hear recommendations of the panel. All members of the grievance
committee were automatically commissioners of the State Supreme Court.

The grievance committee, after holding hearings on a case and
studying Tommy's investigatory report, would make a recommendation in the case to the bar's top committee, its board of
managers.

The board could uphold the recommendation for discipline,
amend it or decide to drop it. If they decided to go ahead, the
case would then be presented to the State Supreme Court. At
this point the case against the accused lawyer would first be
made public.

"You don't have to be a genius to see that with this kind of a
setup, delay is your silent partner," Tommy said. "It could be
years before some of these cases would actually go to the court."

There were also other factors that created great delays:

"You needed a quorum of six members of the grievance committee to hear a case, and a lot of times you couldn't get six. You
know, busy lawyers and all that. A lot of them would come running in for a quick ten-fifteen minutes and then hop out. They
had signed in, so for the record it looked as if they had been there
through the whole session when they weren't. They were out for
the prestige of being on the committee."

The bar association Tommy worked for had a client security

fund.* "It sounded good on paper. The only trouble was no one knew it existed. They wouldn't publicize it so I wasn't surprised that in the three years I was there, there wasn't a single payout to any client who had been taken by a crooked lawyer. In fact there had been several embezzlements from widows and orphans while I was there, but no disbarments resulted. And no restitution. The main attitude was: 'Let's wait until the appeal is heard before we act,' and that could take, easy, two-three years. Cases had a habit of getting continued endlessly. Naturally the witnesses wore out and they just didn't come back.

"I remember one case really disgusted me. A negligence lawyer took $1,000—a lousy thousand bucks—from a widow with three small kids. He admitted to the bar committee that he had collected the money and spent it. When she had asked for payment he gave her a bum check. She asked again—and got another bum check. This went on five times. The sixth time the check cleared. I remember when the case was being considered, one of the lawyers on the grievance panel said, 'What the hell, she got her money back. What do we want to push him around for?' "

Tommy says most lawyers are not like that. "I'd say 85 percent of all lawyers around here are legit and okay. But that other 15 percent—maybe 1,100, 1,200 lawyers—you got to watch them around the clock. The trouble is they get away with so much, so easy, some of the other 85 percent get tempted to cut corners, too."

Like all good investigators Tommy had friends in the local police, the Treasury and the FBI. "This really got me. I had once studied law and got my degree, but I knew I wasn't going to practice, so I didn't bother taking the bar exam or coming up before the character committee. Now I discovered that at least five lawyers practicing in the city—men in good standing—had criminal records. They studied law and passed the bar after coming out of prison, where they had served time for major crimes, felonies. The bar association here had never even checked police records of applicants. They just sent out letters to the references

*See Chapter 1.

the bar applicant submitted. Hell, if you were applying for a license to serve liquor here they'd check you out six ways from Sunday, but a *lawyer? Anyone* could practice. How's that? *

"One of the last cases I looked into was a lawyer here who handles a lot of workmen's comp [compensation] cases. Does a great business. He's an ex-con. I turned over a copy of his record, but they still haven't done anything about him."

As an investigator for a law firm that handled a lot of insurance defense work in accident cases, Tommy was particularly interested in what the bar association was doing about solicitation of cases and ambulance chasing.

"Now *that's* a business," he said admiringly. "We have two PI [personal injury] outfits here that gross $2,000,000 a year each. One of them has a day and night shift, with eight on each shift. They handle 500–600 cases a year, mostly brought in by 12 chasers. The chasers here get $50–$75 a case if there isn't any hospitalization of the injured; $250 if the victim is in the hospital at least two nights and $750 if he's in two weeks or more. A few chasers are averaging $20,000–$25,000 a year. In addition to their 'finder fee,' the top chasers get a percentage of the entire award, even before the lawyer deducts his third or half. Less experienced chasers get a percentage of the lawyer's take only.

"Pretty soon I lost my enthusiasm for getting after the chasers. One case I helped develop, a man who had chased 300 cases, was finally indicted. His case was continued by the judge fourteen times. Finally, when it was getting too obvious that someone liked the chaser, the judge threw a little $300 fine at him."

After six months with the bar association, Tommy prepared a detailed blueprint of the way his department should be operating and the people it needed. The plan was politely turned down. One of the committee chairmen said: "What do you know of our problems? You're not a lawyer."

In June, 1966, Tommy resigned from his job. "I quit be-

---

*A situation surprisingly common in many other U.S. cities. For example, in 1966 the *Washington Post* reported that convicted felons were practicing law in many of the District of Columbia's local courts.

cause I wasn't earning the $10,000 a year they were paying me. And they wouldn't let me earn it by following my recommendations." Considerable pressure was brought to bear, and he went back. Finally, in December, 1966, he quit for good. In his letter of resignation—which he let me read, but not copy—he denounced the bar association's whole system of discipline, the incredible delays, the enormous disinterest of most committeemen and the frequent difficulty of getting a bare quorum of six to hear a case. It was a very strong letter, and this time there was no pressure on him to reconsider.

"You know how I feel *now*," Tommy said. "I wouldn't trust a lawyer any further than I could push this room. You can say I'm sick and fed up with lawyers. I'm sick to my stomach."

•   •   •

Soon after I talked to Tommy, I visited Bernard Botein, an old friend in New York City. As Presiding Justice—the PJ—of the Appellate Division of the First Judicial Department, New York Supreme Court, Bernard Botein is one of our boldest and most forward-looking jurists. As PJ he rules some 311 judges in 26 courthouses staffed by more than 6,500 nonjudicial employes—a far larger court empire than most of our states have.

Several of Justice Botein's pioneering innovations are described in other parts of this book. He is widely admired among his fellow judges, respected by thousands of New York's more responsible lawyers—and thoroughly hated by a certain small segment of the bar. With his luxuriously curly white hair, dark bushy eyebrows, olive skin and direct gaze, Judge Botein reminds one lawyer I know of "an implacable Old Testament judge. If he had a white beard I bet some of us would look around twice in Appellate Division to make sure we're in the right century." Another lawyer I had once asked about Judge Botein said, "Maybe he was a DA too long, but no one ever heard from Bernie Botein those mournful words: 'Sorry, counselor. *I've been talked to.*'" He was referring to the euphemism often used by a now dead State Supreme Court judge who was widely reputed to arrange his decisions in accordance with political influence brought to bear—or, more often, on the size of unexpected legal fees suddenly thrust on one of his relatives, a young lawyer.

I told Judge Botein of my inability to find anywhere in the United States a state bar that had done an outstanding job in lawyer discipline. "You looked in the wrong places," he said. "We're doing a pretty good job right here in Manhattan and the Bronx."

As a native New Yorker I had a memory of montaged headlines heralding one court scandal after another. As far back as I could remember there had been "probes" of crooked lawyers and ambulance-chasing and judges on the take. These had become a staple of metropolitan life. Judge Botein, who had conducted one of the city's many ambulance-chasing investigations during the thirties, smiled as he sensed my barely suppressed incredulity. "Things have changed around here. Go talk to John Bonomi."

In April, 1967, Orison S. Marden, president of the American Bar Association, asked Supreme Court Justice Tom C. Clark to chair a special committee to evaluate disciplinary procedures all over the United States and to recommend improvements. Marden, a Wall Street lawyer and former president of the New York City Bar Association, appointed to the seven-man committee a forty-three-year-old New York lawyer, John G. Bonomi. He probably knows more about what's wrong with U. S. Bar discipline—and what can be done about it—than any other of the nation's 317,000 lawyers. Since 1963 Bonomi, who has graying curly hair, a square face and a hefty build, has run what Judge Botein and several other knowledgeable lawyers consider the most effective and most comprehensive bar disciplinary organization in U.S. history. As attorney-in-chief for the Grievance Committee of the Association of the Bar of New York, Bonomi supervises discipline among the 22,000 lawyers who practice in Manhattan and the Bronx—the greatest concentration of attorneys to be found on earth.

I talked to Bonomi in his office in the Bar Association Building on West 44th Street in Manhattan. At one time he had thought of going into journalism, but after a little newspaper work he went to Cornell Law School instead. He practiced law briefly and then went to work for the New York County District Attorney Frank Hogan. During the six years there, Bonomi successfully prosecuted several Mafia overlords such as Frankie Carbo, Johnny Dio and Gabe Genovese. This led to his becoming chief counsel for the Kefauver Committee on Monopoly in Professional Boxing in 1960–61. From there he became chief counsel for the Fair Campaign Practices Committee during the 1961 New York election campaign. In January, 1963, he assumed his present post.

"I didn't know too much about it," Bonomi recalls. "In fact, there wasn't even a course in legal ethics at Cornell Law School." As a former journalist he knew the way to find out was to talk to others who were doing what he had been hired to do. He talked to other men with similar jobs in various parts of the country, and he visited several upstate county bar associations.

"When I was with Hogan's office there were some cute little tricks that some lawyers tried to pull on me that were unethical, but you couldn't *prove* it," Bonomi said. "Oh, say you're trying a criminal case. You're making a point and the defense lawyer approaches and indicates he wants a word with the judge out of earshot of the jury and the court steno. He comes up alongside and puts his arm around my shoulder, buddy-buddy, as he says something inconsequential to the judge during the huddle. Then he goes back to his client and winks: 'You saw me put my arm around the DA.' When I saw that little byplay I knew damn well what had happened. This attorney had told his client a fix was in, either with the judge or with the DA, which was why he needed a whole lot bigger fee. To show this 'in' with me he went through the arm business. When I found out what they were up to, I just used to remove the arm quietly and quickly.

"I just mentioned that to show I wasn't a wide-eyed innocent. I knew there were a lot of things lawyers did that they didn't learn in law school and were never sanctioned by any code of ethics. But what I found out in my researching days on bar discipline really threw me."

Among his first disillusioning discoveries was that very often the local bar discipline or grievance committee had almost nothing to do with the derelictions of lawyers.

"A lot of these committees spent almost all their time battling what the bar calls 'unauthorized practice of law.' You know, accountants, real estate brokers or estate planners who may or may not be doing legal work incidental to their regular job.

"Well, these committees may have been mislabeled a little—after all, they were trying to *discipline* a bunch of others even if they weren't lawyers. But in a lot of places there was no pretense at all: the grievance committee was frankly a lawyers' protective guild. And the chairman had a private barony. He could protect his lawyer friends, and harass his enemies if he wanted to, the first time they stepped out of line ethically.

"The chairmanship would be rotated every two years, and when a new man came in he'd find that the outgoing grievance chairman had taken all the records with him. Not only wasn't there any continuity, but the incoming chairman wouldn't have the foggiest idea of which lawyer had pulled a fast one before."

Sometimes Bonomi found an earnest, well-intentioned lawyer in the job as chairman. But too often he had an accompanying handicap. "Grievance work is often the last stop on the line for an aging lawyer. He'd be discreet and know every lawyer in the county and everyone would respect him, but to do a good job in grievance work you need the same kind of zeal and energy called for in a full-time prosecutor."

Bonomi knew that most of the grievance committees were run by purely voluntary efforts. To get good, full-time help to run them you need money. And for New York and the Bronx and its 22,000 lawyers you need a *lot* of money. At the time, Bonomi had a budget of $75,000 a year, but with the inspired help of Judge Botein he was able to double it.

Ever since he was an assistant district attorney in charge of the 1937 accident fraud investigation in New York, Judge Botein has maintained a vigorous interest in the dangerous temptations that accident cases provide some lawyers.*

* He became a State Supreme Court Judge in 1953 and Presiding Justice of its Appellate Division in 1958.

In his report back in the 1937 accident fraud investigation Judge Botein urged a *permanent* body of investigation to end the cyclic sweeps:

Sporadic investigations at best only exercise temporary restraining effect. They uncover a small fraction of the great volume of accumulated misdeeds. Only sustained perennial surveillance can discourage their continuance.

It took twenty-one years for Bernard Botein's good idea to be put into effect. And then he was able to achieve it only because he was Presiding Justice of the Appellate Division of the State Supreme Court, which is charged with the supervision of lawyer conduct in its area. In 1958 he created the Coordinating Committee on Discipline, responsible for a continuing investigation of attorneys in personal injury cases. With his backing and promoting, New York City became the first area in the country to adopt purposeful restrictions on the amount lawyers could take as a share in contingent fees in accident cases.*

In addition, PI (personal injury) lawyers also have to file with the court how they got the case; how much they paid out, and other details that could be monitored to unearth ambulance chasing, fee splitting, accident faking and the rest of the front-page family.

But to do any kind of purposeful job with the information and spot the derelictions would take money *every* year. A great persuader, Justice Botein invited Mayor Robert Wagner to a cozy luncheon at the Lawyers Club to convince the Mayor that for a mere $75,000 a year the city could have a permanent investigatory agency to police negligent bar members and protect all New Yorkers against overreaching and dishonesty by lawyers.

"I had along Orison Marden, who was then president of the local bar association, to show I wasn't riding a personal hobby horse. The bar was with me on this. I told the Mayor the city had been giving us $30,000 a year to pay for the actual trials and

*See Chapter 7.

hearings of lawyers up on charges in PI cases. But we still had no money for the necessary investigatory work. For the forty or so cases that came to trial, we had the money, but not for the nineteen hundred cases we had to check out."

The Mayor, a lawyer, was persuaded, and New York threw in another $45,000, so that the city's contribution was $75,000 a year. "The bar was putting up $75,000 for grievance work, so we had a good-sized budget of $150,000. With that kind of money we could do a good job."

New York now has a two-pronged disciplinary organization: the Coordinating Committee, which oversees all negligence practice, and the Regular Committee on Grievances, which checks out complaints in all other areas. The two teams are headed by John Bonomi. All nine lawyers on his staff are full-time and are well paid: the salary range is from $10,000 to $15,000. Most of them have had some prosecutorial experience. One of the two women lawyers, Barbara Lee, used to check out financial misdeeds for the Securities and Exchange Commission.

How effective has it been? In 1966 there were 15 disbarments among the 22,000 lawyers who practice in Manhattan and the Bronx. In California, which has nearly 29,000 lawyers, only six lawyers were thrown out that year.* In recent years the nationwide disbarment rate has run between 70 and 80. New York City's rate is about three times the average.

I threw at John Bonomi the obvious comment, which he had fielded many times before. "No, we don't have a higher proportion of dishonest lawyers here; nor are there more temptations here. I think we have a much higher disbarment rate because we're looking harder than elsewhere and we check out *every* complaint, even the ones that sound pretty whacky. A lot of times you just can't tell at first."

There was the Italian barber who came in to complain about a lawyer. "He had several strikes against him right off: first, he

---

*Thrown out is exactly right, historically. In England centuries ago, a lawyer was disbarred physically. He was thrown over a wooden barrier that separated the court and the official staff from the litigants and onlookers.

wasn't too coherent. Then the lawyer he accused was, as far as we knew, a reputable downtown lawyer who had once been a fairly prominent Ivy League athlete. And what was involved was a few thousand bucks. This was a man who, if he was going to be dishonest, might go for $50,000, $100,000, but a *couple of thousand!* And finally, it turned out that the barber with his wild story had just spent three years in a mental hospital. Every grievance committee gets it share of cranks, sore losers and plain nuts. And paranoids will talk forever. I have a hunch the barber would have been eased out of a lot of grievance offices as soon as he mentioned having come out of an asylum."

The barber had retained the lawyer to probate his wife's estate of $4,700. Soon after, the barber was hospitalized for a breakdown, partly brought on by his wife's tragic death. When he came out of the hospital three years later, he went to the lawyer to ask for the money.

There wasn't any, the lawyer told him: in fact, the barber owed the attorney some money. How come? Well, said the lawyer, "I paid out $2,724 for funeral and other expenses, which left a balance of $1,984. My legal fees and expenses came to $2,050 which adds up to $4,774, so that you still owe me $74."

The staff attorney got the barber's bank records and the estate file from the surrogate court. Now he knew there was *something* here. The lawyer was asked to submit a written statement about the complaint made or come in for a conference.

The lawyer came in and said he was well within his rights, that he had done his work faithfully for the estate. True, his fee was a bit high, but then he was a high-priced lawyer. Now the staff attorney, after reviewing the details, recommended that appropriate disciplinary action be instituted. The recommendation was supported by John Bonomi and one of the twenty-five members of the bar's grievance committee, which meets in three separate panels on Tuesdays, Wednesdays and Thursdays.

The case was considered by one of the panels, which voted that disciplinary action be instituted, that a full-scale hearing before an Appellate Division referee be arranged. The lawyer was told that he could have legal counsel to appear with him. Although the lawyer was subjected to severe discipline, there was no repayment to the barber, mainly because the lawyer was heavily in debt and probably judgment-proof. A client security fund—New York didn't have one then—wouldn't consider such a case, since there was no clear-cut case of theft here.

"The barber didn't get his money back," Bonomi admitted. "But we did take effective action against a lawyer who was over-reaching. If he had not been disciplined, I'm sure there would have been other temptations coming his way."

Bonomi's group doesn't depend just on complaints from the public—or other lawyers. They keep up an effective liaison with the police, the U. S. Attorney and other bar disciplinary groups in the New York metropolitan area. They also keep in touch with other agencies that might have occasion to discipline lawyers, such as the Securities and Exchange Commission in Washington. Bonomi's committee feels a lawyer guilty of having helped write and approve a dishonest stock prospectus that led to the bilking of innocent investors deserves to be disciplined by the bar, just as much as an embezzling lawyer.* Recently another lawyer was dis-barred for issuing worthless checks, even though none of them were given to clients. A six-month suspension was given an attor-ney who was a traffic ticket scofflaw. A slumlord-lawyer was dis-barred for deliberately using evasive corporate devices to conceal ownership of his buildings.

Most bar disciplinary committees are generally composed of lawyers from the city's leading firms. It is not just that these men are among the most respected, but as important is the fact that they have the *time* to sit on the committee and take an active

---

*A view not widely shared by other bar disciplinary committees. Recently, I checked out what happened to fourteen lawyers who had been disqualified by the SEC from appearing before that body again. Most of the fourteen had deliberately allowed dishonest or misleading prospectuses to be put out by their clients seeking investors. Only in New York and Washington had the bar associations—notified by the SEC—taken public action. Yet it is obvious that violations of the federal securities laws by lawyers are potentially far more serious and generally involve far greater financial losses for the public than run-of-the-mill lawyer embezzlement cases.

part. Understandably our 113,000 single practitioners—more than half the 212,000 U.S. lawyers in private practice—often feel that the disciplinary committee not only doesn't understand their problem but is stacked against them. (They might not be able to serve even if they were asked to, but at least *ask,* is their attitude.)

In New York, the bar has recently begun asking: "We now have a few men on the committee from small to medium-sized firms and two Negroes: Andrew Tyler, president of the Harlem Bar Association, and Hope Stevens, a single practitioner," Bonomi said. "It's a beginning, anyway."

The 2,000 or so calls that came into the office in the period from July 1, 1966, to June 1, 1967, looked something like this: First, the biggest single bunch, some 651, were not really complaints. Mostly, these were people wanting to get legal assistance or advice—minor fee disputes between lawyer and client ("He's charging me $6 for some kind of a cockamamie court paper. Do I hafta pay this?"); disagreements between attorneys which didn't involve any serious misconduct or even a breach of ethics. Another 240 complaints were about matters outside the jurisdiction of Bonomi's committee, which is restricted to actions of attorneys in Manhattan and the Bronx. So right there are nearly 900 calls that didn't take too much time of any of the nine lawyers in the office. But there are still some 1,143 complaints that called for some degree of checking.

Naturally, the biggest single category was "offenses against clients," which accounted for 589 complaints, and of these more than half, 359, were labeled "neglect." I asked John Bonomi about this:

"Neglect calls are what we get most of. The client calls us. He can't find out from his lawyer where his case stands. When he phones the call isn't returned, and so on. We get the lawyer on the phone: 'What goes?' What goes is that he's still dickering with the insurance company; he's waiting for a pretrial examination, or maybe even he's waiting for the client to give him the advance payment he requested. It could be anything. We ask the lawyer to send the client a letter saying exactly what he told us and what he's doing about it. We ask that he send us a carbon, too. The carbon goes into a tickler file, and a few weeks later we phone the client: 'How are things going?' The chances are very good that after our little reminder the lawyer is keeping in closer touch with his client."

The next single biggest category of offenses against clients is "conversion," which is simply stealing clients' money. The lawyer has cashed the insurance check and doesn't bother to send the client his share; or a relative in Mexico who was supposed to get $2,800 under the client's will somehow doesn't get the money. A related complaint is "commingling": instead of keeping client money in separate accounts, as he is required to, the lawyer has put it into his own checking account. He doesn't necessarily have larceny in mind, but the grievance committee knows that a lawyer who does this regularly can be tempted more easily than a lawyer who keeps separate accounts.

In the 1966–67 period the committee got 57 complaints from lawyers against other lawyers—a lawyer was soliciting cases; a lawyer had persuaded a client to drop his original attorney (the complainant) and take on the other man; a lawyer down the block was advertising, or he was splitting fees, which is theoretically forbidden but takes place every day in one guise or another.

There were another 73 complaints against lawyers that came from other lawyers, from the District Attorney's office, or just from items that some of the grievance committee had heard about. These involved lawyers who perjured themselves, were getting too many delays in a case or were concealing evidence; or they had claimed they had—and possibly did have—a fix in, with either a judge or some prosecutor.

Some 25 complaints had to do with the lawyer's conduct outside of client relationships: the lawyer was evading his income tax or simply failed to file; he had forged a check; he had perjured himself or was involved in bribery.

Of the more serious complaints alleging misconduct about 18 percent "warrant committee action" after the investigation by one of the staff attorneys. Nearly all of these cases resulted in an "admonition" or the beginning of formal disciplinary proceedings.

"In an 'admonition,' " explains Bonomi, "we tell the lawyer that what he did was wrong, and if he does it again he's going to be in real trouble."

A typical case was that of a prosperous lawyer who kept stalling a client on the settlement of a personal injury case. The lawyer was called in and admitted he was stalling: he had "made enough" this year and, for tax reasons, wanted his third of the settlement to be part of his next year's income.

"Now that's all right for a self-employed writer," Bonomi smiled, "—or a businessman. But a lawyer's first consideration has to be the client. The lawyer's tax problem shouldn't affect the client adversely. So we sent him a letter of admonition—after which he got busy and settled the case quickly—and we sent a copy of the letter to the client so he knew that we did something in the matter." In the 1966–67 period 82 attorneys received admonition letters.

Five attorneys who had eleven complaints against them resigned from the bar—after they signed affidavits that they could not successfully defend the charges made against them. Nine lawyers were convicted and formally disbarred. Eight were suspended for varying periods. They were censured, which meant, in effect, they were on "probation" from then on; another violation would lead to a long suspension or possibly disbarment proceedings. Only two lawyers won dismissals after trial of charges against them, which would indicate that Bonomi's staff is pretty sure of its facts when it recommends a trial for an accused lawyer.

Some lawyers were taken off the rolls for varying reasons: they were drinking heavily and neglecting their clients, or they were insane or, in one case, had been convicted of a sex offense in another state. One had lied to the Massachusetts Racing Commission, and another had bribed an official of the New York State Liquor Authority.

The actions of the committee in the more serious cases involving disbarments or suspensions are placed in the *New York Law Journal,* a daily legal journal, in a front-page box headed "Disciplinary." For the public and the daily papers the committee issues an annual report which generally makes one of the back pages of *The New York Times* like this:

City Bar Group Reports a Rise
in Cases of Lawyer Misconduct

I told John Bonomi that he didn't seem to go out of his way to publicize the work of his committee—no newspaper features urging people to come forward with complaints, no public service announcements on television to publicize the work of the grievance committee.

He admitted this, somewhat glumly. "We're frankly afraid of getting this on radio and TV. I figure we'd start attracting a bunch of crackpots and nuts. Two thousand of them a year and we'd have a helluva traffic jam in the office. I don't know the answer on this."

Another problem for which he admitted he didn't have an answer was what he called the "nonvisible offense."

"Say a large law firm has done something unethical or even downright crooked. If the information of what has taken place is limited to the lawyer and the client, we're up against a wall. The involved client isn't likely to come forward. Sometimes it starts with instructions to a private detective: 'Joe, we want you to investigate this case but *don't tell us how you did it.*' They know damn well he's going to wiretap and maybe send someone into the office after-hours to rifle someone's files for papers and things like that, but we're unlikely to ever hear of these cases. Or, there's been a lot of medical bill-padding in an accident case. The client who benefited won't come forward; and, of course, the other beneficiaries, the lawyer and the doctor, won't either. What do you do?"

John Bonomi doesn't allow himself to get too moodily introspective about the comparatively minor shortcomings of what is almost surely the most effective bar disciplinary organization in the country. "We just try to do a better job every year," he said.

I asked him to summarize his main advice to other bar disciplinary groups, recommendations that he will probably be submitting at meetings of the ABA's Committee of Evaluation of Bar Discipline around the country.

"First, money. No bar association can do the job by itself with dues or even special assessments. They must get city, county or state money. Two, you need large full-time staffs. Three, you've got to cut out interminable delays and stretched-out hearings on cases. A serious misconduct case can be heard in two actual hearings. When there's a long gap between misconduct and discipline, the complainant will become disillusioned. And worse, you're going to lose public confidence. When you lose it—or never earn it—you've got a downright impossible job on your hands."

Later, I asked Justice Botein about this. "The public's traditional attitude has been that the bar will always protect its own. In a lot of places that's been true. It still is in many parts of the country. The only way to overcome this attitude is by deeds. We have to show the reasonable complainant that he'll get serious attention from us; and get it quickly. Then the bar has a chance to solve this problem."

Bless those men in black robes. They're in the same union with us.

—MELVIN BELLI
In a talk in Washington, D.C.,
November, 1966

If it isn't easy to punish the evil or negligent members of the lawyers' union, naturally it is much harder catching up with the special card-carriers, the judges.

There are some 3,700 major trial judges in the more important federal, state and county courts, and another 5,000 judges in lower courts. In addition there are some 7,000 part-time justices of the peace and police court judges, most of whom are not lawyers.

No one has the remotest idea of the quality of our judges in the higher or lower courts. One of the few newspapermen ever given the assignment of just visiting courtrooms all around the nation and listening is Howard James of the *Christian Science Monitor*. He got the assignment early in 1967 and sat in on several dozen courtrooms. He later wrote: "If my sampling is a fair indicator . . . perhaps half these judges are, for one reason or another, unfit to sit on the bench. This is the same percentage given by several leading lawyers and judges interviewed."

In most cities I visited, leading lawyers usually had a considerable consensus on which judges could be "talked to" or "reached." They were fairly matter-of-fact about it, and if you were representing a client before such a judge—and you suspected the other attorney had some kind of edge with the judge— you took steps.

In Milwaukee one day I visited Richard H. Leonard, the editor of the *Milwaukee Journal*. We were talking about judges when Leonard repeated a conversation he'd had that morning with a lawyer he knew.

He had come in to tell Leonard of going into a judge's chambers to discuss an upcoming negligence case. Coming out just then was the lawyer for the other side. The lawyer in Leonard's office then said:

"Now I knew this other lawyer had made a $450 contribution to the judge's election campaign fund. So the first thing I did was ask the judge for a change of venue—another judge. The judge looked at me and asked: 'Don't you think I can be fair?' 'Judge,' I said, 'I don't even want you to *think* about it.' "

In New York an elderly attorney who has been one of the stalwarts of the New York County Lawyers Association has what he calls a "macabre hobby"—he keeps tabs on what happens to the judges' bagmen. A bagman is the intermediary who actually collects the bribe for the official.

"It's really pretty moral," he said. "Most of the bagmen come to a bad end—even if anything seldom happens to the judge, no matter how big a crook he was. We had this federal judge in New York in the late twenties, Francis A. Winslow. He was up to his ears in the bankruptcy racket, and his bagman was a fellow I knew slightly. His name was Helphand. He had a face like a fat frog—but, damn it, he always had beautiful women around him. Well, Winslow had to resign and I lost track of Helphand. Then one day in Seattle I stepped out of my hotel and there was Helphand, just this side of panhandling. He was down and out—he had to resign from the bar in New York when Judge Winslow resigned from the bench—and, in all, a living proof that the wages of helping bribe judges aren't good. I bought him a dinner and he was grateful. He died later; drank himself to death.

"Another New York judge, who came under scrutiny and re-signed, had as his bagman a man who ran a surety company. If you wanted a favorable decision from the judge the thing to do was buy a lot of insurance from the bagman."

The hobbyist recalled a more recent New York Supreme Court justice, X, "who screwed us badly on a lot of cases." As it happened, I had once known this judge: before he went on the bench we had been neighbors in the same building. I remember him as a very sharp Tammany wheelhorse who was then confidential secretary to a sitting judge. When he got the judgeship the stories about him became part of the folklore of the New York bar. The way to influence this judge was to retain his son-in-law, an attorney. The judge is now dead and I asked my informant if he had any follow-up information on the son-in-law. "The easy money days stopped when the judge died. Now the son-in-law has to look around for other gimmicks since he's not that smart a lawyer. He got involved in a zoning-case mess recently, and sooner or later they'll have him before the bar disciplinary committee. You'll see."

Recently I talked about Judge X with an old friend, a retired ranking justice in New York who is widely respected among the bar and judiciary alike.

He, too, had heard the stories about Judge X.

"I knew X pretty well, and I'd hate to have to give an attestation of complete honesty. What made him dangerous was the fact that he was such an *able* man. He could have been a great judge, but instead, I'm afraid, he used his great ability to disguise the fact that he was rendering decisions often paid for or otherwise influenced." The obituaries on Judge X were quite respectful. Very properly obituary writers don't allow common trade gossip to influence their evaluations.

One of the reasons judges are rarely disciplined is the archaic and large unworkable procedures. The main way is impeachment and then trial by the state legislature. (Impeachment is rather like a grand jury indictment—only much rarer, of course.) In the past 180 years in the United States, eight federal judges have been impeached—but only four were convicted. In all, fifty-five federal judges have been the subject of congressional inquiry, including the eight who were impeached. Another seventeen resigned during the investigation, and eight were censured. The rest were absolved.

On the state judge level, the available figures are far vaguer. In 1960 George E. Brand, former president of the Michigan Bar Association, checked court records of forty-five states as far back as possible and found legislative attempts to invoke impeachment proceedings against judges had been made in only seventeen states. As a result, nineteen judges were removed and three resigned—out of fifty-two impeachments.

Since 1960 the figure on sudden resignations of judges has risen sharply, owing almost solely to the influence of the California Commission on Judicial Qualifications. The commission got its start through a long investigation made by a state legislative committee on the judiciary. Its 1959 report summarized the commonest faults found among a number of state judges:

Some delayed decisions for months or even years . . . took long vacations and worked short hours, despite backlogs . . . refused to accept assignment to cases they found unpleasant or dull . . . interrupted court sessions to perform numerous marriages, which they made a profitable sideline by illegally extracting fees for the ceremonies . . . tolerated petty rackets in and around their courts, often involving "kickbacks" to court attachés . . . failed to appear for scheduled trials because they were intoxicated—or they took the bench while obviously under the influence of liquor . . . clung doggedly to their positions and salaries for months and years after they had been disabled by sickness or age.

California didn't have a lock on the jaundiced judges of the nation. Once during an American Bar Association convention in San Francisco I informally polled trial judges from ten different states, plus court administrative officers from four other states. Each of the fourteen knew of at least one judge in their state who was unfit to sit on the bench because of drinking, unjudicial conduct, senility, incompetence or plain corruption.

One of the administrative officers of an Eastern state was particularly concerned. "This judge is just crazy. Not eccentric or strange: I mean *crazy*. So far nothing's broken into the papers, but sooner or later he's going to make headlines and then we'll have a *public* problem. But under our state constitution only the legislature can remove a judge, and so far they never have."

Crooked judges are particularly tenacious in their hold on the bench. A prominent Illinois attorney recalled for me a state judge everyone *knew* was crooked. "Syndicate man, of course," he said. "Not even subtle about it. Every now and then he would openly admit to a lawyer in a case that 'he had been talked to' about a certain case and that he wouldn't be able 'to follow the law' in that case. He took long vacations, had extensive outside business interests and sat on the bench forever—until he died. Only the legislature can remove a judge, and it almost never happens."

In desperation, lawyers sometimes try to get rid of a bad judge politically. A county bar president in California told me how he and several other lawyers got up their courage to buck a senile but politically powerful judge.

"We got a good lawyer to agree to run for the nomination if we raised a war chest of $35,000. We did, and our man squeaked through, but if the old man had won, a lot of us could just as well have started building a law practice elsewhere. There has to be an easier way."

The easier way began on March 24, 1961, when the nine members of the California Commission on Judicial Qualifications took their oath of office. The commission idea was passed by the legislature and then approved overwhemingly by the voters as a constitutional amendment.

The commission's nine members include five judges appointed by the State Supreme Court; two experienced attorneys selected by the State Bar; and two citizens named by the governor. Their first complaint was against a "habitually drunken judge." The commission investigators found the charges true. The judge was told the commission would recommend his removal by the State Supreme Court. Late in May, 1961, the judge resigned rather than face public charges.

In its first year the commission got 127 complaints against judges—from the public, from lawyers and from other judges. "Of these 127," Jack E. Frankel, the tall forty-two-year-old attorney who is the commission's executive secretary, said, "some 36 on the face seemed to merit further serious investigation. In some cases, I investigated, and in others we called on state agents. The findings were presented to the full commission during their regular monthly meetings. In nine cases the judges accused resigned when they were told the commission would recommend their removal." At the time California had nearly 900 judges. It now has 965.

Since then some 30 judges under investigation have chosen to retire or resign. Only one judge decided to fight the charges—that he constantly berated prosecutors—and was upheld by the State Supreme Court. In 1966 the California voters gave the commission even broader powers.

As a result of the success of the California commission method, Florida, Maryland, Nebraska and Colorado have adopted somewhat similar systems of getting rid of unsuitable judges without going through the almost impossible legislative impeachment procedure.

In New York State, which has had a Court on the Judiciary

since 1947, only one Supreme Court judge has been removed—for being a key part of an ambulance-chasing ring—mainly because the procedure is much more elaborate and cumbersome than the comparatively simple California arrangement.

I asked my friend, the retired ranking New York justice, about the state of the judiciary in New York City:

"When I came to the bar a sizable number of magistrates here in New York were on the take. In the thirties here, justice was for sale and often for surprisingly minimal prices. No one gave a damn. Things got cleaned up, of course. Today? Well, I know most of the fifty or so Supreme Court justices in and around New York City and three, maybe four, are suspect. No, it's not the old crude bagman setup. But what happens is that certain attorneys consistently get remarkable favors from these suspect judges. When I knew key motions on impending trials were coming up before these judges, I used to shudder. You get the right ruling on motions before trial, and you could win the case even before the trial began."

He talked about the lesser judiciary—the judges in special sessions who handled criminal cases. "Oh, I hear rumors about a couple of judges in Brooklyn."

Things are much subtler today, he went on, than when he first came on the bench. Influence is exercised in more devious fashion, for one thing. He discussed a current battle, almost totally unreported in the press, between an enormously powerful real estate combine and another large corporation over the ground rental the corporation was paying on a prominent New York building. Several millions were involved. The combine had lost its case in the New York Supreme Court and the case was now going up on appeal before the Appellate Division. For its counsel the real estate combine hired a very young and rather inexperienced lawyer. It seemed a remarkable choice until you learned that the young lawyer happened to be the son of a powerful political judge who had enormous powers of patronage.

"If you had a real efficient, all-wise judicial disciplinary organization, the lawyers who hired the young man just to get his name on the appeal papers would be called in: 'Now tell us, just what did you gentlemen have in mind?' Well, maybe it was perfectly innocent—no sophisticated lawyer in New York would think so— but if attorneys got used to having such dodges questioned by a state judicial organization, they'd think a long time before trying that route again," he continued.

"But we don't have that. We don't even have a judicial disciplinary setup remotely as efficient as California's. I think that there is a relationship between bar and judiciary discipline. If lawyers can get away with murder, judges surely will. If lawyers start getting disciplined sharply and often, they'll be the first to bring pressure to get the judges in line, too."

It doesn't look too good. In February, 1968, former Supreme Court Justice Tom Clark, reporting to the midyear meeting of the American Bar Association in Chicago, sorrowfully told the legal profession he just wasn't getting its cooperation on his committee's survey of disciplinary procedures. He warned that the study could founder because only 106 of the country's 495 state and local bar associations had deigned to respond to his committee's questionnaires.

"We assume a lot of bar groups aren't answering," said one committee member, "because the discipline is so bad out their way there's just nothing to report."

Obviously if we can't do much about disciplining lawyers—we can't even get figures on *how many* are disciplined—we're a dismally long way from doing anything effective about judges who get drunk, out of line or fixed.

9 FEES: "COME RIGHT OUT AT THE BEGINNING AND SOCK HIM HARD"

. . . an essential profession is in a healthy state and growing at a healthy rate.
—REGINALD HEBERT SMITH
In *Law Office Economics & Management,* February, 1965

These are prosperous times for lawyers. The average income for those in private practice is $5,000 a year greater than for income earners in general, and top bracket lawyers are earning far in excess of the lawyer's dream of yesterday. The whirlwind which has blown the law helter-skelter has shaken the trees and when the trees shake the plums fall and are easily gathered.
—BURTON R. LOUB
Dean of Dickinson Law School, in a speech at Bench-Bar Conference, September 10, 1966

Reginald Smith and Dean Loub represent a new trend in discussions of how lawyers are doing. Until recently the poor-mouth criers led the chorus. Nearly every mournful voice wailed lawyers were not only below the salt but so far down the income table they only got cold scraps. Now, belatedly, comes some self-congratulatory frankness among lawyers. True, the old reflexes persist and you find atavists even among those who should know better. For example, late in 1965 N. Samuel Clifton, an ABA expert on lawyer earnings, was still pushing the old line when he addressed a bar conference in St. Paul, Minnesota: "Instead of the lawyer being at the very top of the economic structure—where he belongs—*he is far down on the economic scale.*"

Mr. Clifton was being carried away by his rhetoric of legal poverty. Or he may have missed a little item carried in the May, 1964, issue of the *Missouri Bar Journal:* "A Census Bureau economist recently reported that the lifetime earnings of a doctor is $717,-000; of a lawyer $621,000; of a manager and proprietor $593,000; and of a dentist, $589,000."*

Other more recent census figures also support the fact that lawyers' incomes have moved up sharply since the end of World War II. For example, in 1950 the nation spent only $1.3 billion on legal services; in 1955 it had risen to $2 billion and in 1966 to more than $4 billion. In short, we spent over three times more on legal services in 1966 than in 1950. True there are more of us to spend in hiring lawyers, and the value of the dollar has declined somewhat. Yet the enormous rise in what we spend for legal services is real and it means our lawyers are more prosperous than they have ever been.

What has been responsible for this great increase in legal income? More corporate work? More business clients? Nonsense, said Reginald Smith of Boston, considered by many authorities the dean of legal economists. Shortly before his death in 1966, he said, "The backbone of a law practice for most lawyers is made up of their individual clients, the human beings with their human problems." In short, us, the American middle class.

We are paying more for legal services *not* because lawyers are lovable good fellows we want to help out so they can become more active in the life of the community and run for office. We are paying more *and more* because legal services have become immune to the workings of one of our greatest American commandments: Thou Shalt Not Fix Prices. Price-fixing of legal service takes place every day by lawyers and bar associations who are sworn to uphold the law. Still, they are not lawbreakers. As lawyers point out with the sweet reason you use on a stubborn child, their kind of price-fixing isn't illegal at all. Most judges—who

*In 1964 the Brookings Institute did a field survey of the "investment and working behavior" of a nationwide sample of 957 individuals with yearly incomes of $10,000 or more. There were some thirty-eight lawyers in the group and five of them had incomes of over $300,000 in 1963; there were no doctors in the high category.

are, after all, only lawyers interpreting our laws—are generally in favor of this kind of price-fixing, which is called "minimum fee schedules." In the 1966 Survey of the Economics of Florida Law Practice, 75 percent of the state judges queried said they believed lawyers would benefit from a statewide minimum fee schedule. And about the same percentage of lawyers went along, too. The state, which has 8,000 lawyers, has clearly come a long way since 1921 when a Florida legislator introduced a bill to limit the income of lawyers. It didn't pass.

The survey, which was conducted by the unique Philadelphia legal-economics consultant firm of Daniel J. Cantor & Co., also drew a number of pro and con comments on the whole business of bar associations setting up minimum fee schedules: "The only way to improve the overall economic status of the bar is to raise the minimum fee schedule and castigate all attorneys who depart from it. . . ."

Lawyers opposed to these price-fixing schedules commented harshly: "It is deplorable that the bar is being dragged towards the gutters of a trade organization, whose prime interest is the dollars to be extracted from a client. Real lawyers were never more prosperous. It is the incompetent who think the world owes them a living, and the law schools are turning them out by the hundreds." And, "I believe suggested minimum fee schedules are unwise, unethical, and, depending on their use, potential violations of the antitrust laws."

More than half of our states now have statewide schedules of minimum fees suggested by their bar associations. In addition, some 800 local bar associations have similar schedules of fees.

Before much longer every U.S. county and state bar will have these price-fixing arrangements. They are spreading, say Quintin Johnstone, of Yale Law School, and Dan Hopson, Jr., of the University of Kansas Law School, because

the major attraction of minimum fee schedules for many lawyers is that they help keep fees up and reduce competition based on the price of services. As most schedules are periodically revised upwards, they are means for raising fees.

Some lawyers are opposed to the principle. The *Journal of the American Bar Association* carried an article in its March, 1962, issue, "Let's Throw Out the Reasonable Fee Schedules," by Jackson L. Boughner, a Chicago lawyer:

> A fee schedule promulgated by a bar association is nothing more than price-fixing [which] is illegal in interstate commerce and is frowned upon generally in the business world as an attempt to stifle competition. It has no higher standing in the practice of law.

Harry S. Gleick, a St. Louis attorney, went on to add that the word "minimum" on these fee schedules was quite misleading:

> I am sure many of us have noted the fact that in many instances minimum fees suggested by bar associations are rather high. Those charges must be tailored to the demands of the higher priced lawyers of the community, and the imposition of such schedules upon all lawyers will result in tyranny by the majority. . . . The lawyer who consistently charges small fees merely to entice business poses no real problem to the profession, but a group of lawyers who seek to dictate the fees of the entire bar of a community will bring criticism upon all.

But attorneys Boughner and Gleick are a minority. America's lawyers generally love the minimum or "reasonable" fee schedules, and for most of them the only regret is that they haven't been in effect longer.

The idea wasn't new. Back in 1872 the Bar of Sedgwick County (Wichita), Kansas adopted a schedule of minimum fees. (Drawing wills: $10; Divorce, uncontested, $25; contested, $50.) They could charge more, of course, but never less.

Legal price-fixing didn't go too well among the pioneers of Kansas, and in 1889 the state legislature decided that an agreement to fix attorneys' fees is against public policy and unlawful.

But other state bars, unhindered by such legislative restriction, were soon faced with the problem: what do you do if a fellow lawyer consistently undercut the bar minimum fees? What did you do with a rate-buster, a discounter, in your midst?

In October, 1961, the ABA's Committee on Professional Ethics and Grievances nailed that down with Opinion 302:

The habitual charging of fees less than those established by a minimum fee schedule, or the charging of such fees without proper justification, may be evidence of unethical conduct.

So far as I could find out, no lawyer has yet been bounced for charging less than the minimum fee schedule rates, but it shouldn't be long in coming. Judge Frederick Woleslagel of Lyons, Kansas, said in the spring, 1966, issue of the *Kansas State Bar Journal:*

As various state committees take similar positions and as bar associations increase their membership and become more effective, we might expect a trend toward greater professional censure to discourage lawyers from setting fees below applicable schedules.

Since Kansas didn't have a statewide minimum fee schedule—there was that state law passed in 1889—the State Bar invited Philip Habermann, executive director of the Wisconsin State Bar, to tell about the great things a minimum fee schedule had done for his state's lawyers.

Habermann, a chunky fifty-four-year-old attorney of Scotch-Swiss ancestry, practiced briefly before taking on his present job in 1948. In his high-pitched voice that tends to rise with vehemence, Habermann gave the Kansas lawyers the good tidings in the spring of 1965: ". . . obviously and desirably a fee schedule will tend to increase the income of lawyers. This is amply demonstrated in numerous states." How much would it increase their incomes? Nothing piddling: "Would you invest a dime if you knew you'd get $20 back within a few years? That is what we did in Wisconsin."

This marvelous investment, which yielded a 2000 fold return, was accomplished simply by spending $11,000:

We purchased 5,500 very attractive loose-leaf six-by-nine binders. . . . We reprinted our fee schedule on loose-leaf sheets of heavy paper.

Each item or each class of fees such as contingent fees, real estate, estate planning, divorce, bankruptcy, collections and so forth has a separate divider and a separate sheet. Now this binder, the printing and the mailing, cost us two dollars each.

I can't tell you how important the impact of this was. It was mailed out without any advance notice and within a matter of days, this schedule became the standard of fair compensation for lawyers in Wisconsin.

(A minor detail that Mr. Habermann didn't touch on was, just how businesslike had he been? Had he sensibly gotten bids from several printing firms and then selected the one that had the best price? Hadn't he shopped around for a printer who would turn out the very volumes that would make shopping around impossible for ordinary people in need of legal services?)

The Schedule of Minimum Fees for Attorneys in Wisconsin [he continued], overnight became the standard of fair fees throughout Wisconsin . . . it gave courage to many lawyers who had never had courage enough to charge a reasonable and adequate fee before. When they saw how simple it was to apply the recommended schedule and how easy it was to make these charges salable to their clients, in other words there was virtually no client resistance, they tended then to adhere very closely to the schedule.

There may have been no client resistance but there were some minatory growls from the *Milwaukee Journal,* the state's most influential daily. On February 21, 1960, shortly after the State Bar's first fee schedule was published, the *Journal* commented:

Positive genius for antagonizing the public seems to have seized the State Bar of Wisconsin* . . . in its loud talk of discipline for lawyers who undercut the recommended—and newly increased—minimum fees.

Insisting that lawyers must charge $18 an hour in order to aim at $14,500 a year net before taxes, the new fee schedule says that "the

---

*There must be *something* about Wisconsin lawyers. The late Professor Herbert Page, of the University of Wisconsin Law School, used to say, "One lawyer in town will starve to death; two lawyers will soon own the town." He believed this rule had nationwide application.

public is entitled to expect every licensed lawyer to be competent, and to be able to serve effectively." The public should indeed be entitled to expect this, but would be a sucker to assume that it is so . . . to lay down an axiom that *every* lawyer is worth and therefore must get at least the schedule is ridiculous. . . . If the state bar governors now propose to make the minimum fee schedule holy writ, it would be interesting to hear them defend clients accused of collusive price-fixing.

The *Journal* also found a few lawyers to attack the schedule. They quoted one who derided it as "a price catalog." Another called the bar's expense on the book "ridiculous. . . . If I have to show a schedule of minimum fees to my client in order to justify my bill for services, there's something wrong with me as a lawyer. Price fixing in any field is not right."

But most Wisconsin lawyers thought the schedule was great. "You would incite mutiny if you tried to abolish our schedule," Habermann reported. In the first eighteen months after the schedule was mailed, he said, "the overall net take-home pay of our lawyers in Wisconsin went up in excess of 10 percent." And a whole lot more as the years passed. Not automatically, of course. You simply ran off new fee schedule increases which could be inserted in the loose-leaf binder to replace the old fees. In 1963, for example, the hourly fee was jumped to $20 minimum to help lawyers maintain "their place in society." Lawyers in rural areas had to charge the same minimums as in large cities. Then in November, 1966, there was another jump to $25 an hour minimum.

The fee could be reduced if the client "is genuinely financially unable to pay." But don't take the client's word for it, the bar warned:

> Outward trappings of the client, such as newness and quality of his automobile, should be considered, and all financial resources and sources of funds available to the client should be weighed before concluding he is unable to pay minimum compensation.

(But no instructions about how to find out if the new car was bought on time or if the shiny new wristwatch the client wore wasn't just goldplated.)

A Madison *Capital-Times* editorial was written by Miles Mc-Millin, a peppery, handsome lawyer who hasn't practiced since 1945. He not only castigated the bar for raising its minimum fees without consulting the public but also touched on a more delicate problem:

> The public must not only pay the rates the lawyers decree from their privileged closed shop, it must take the word of the lawyers on how much work they put in. If the lawyer says he put in an hour's work on a case there is nothing the client can do but pay the $25. How can he prove the work wasn't done?
>
> But the lawyer is urged by the bar to snoop into the client's status . . . the lawyer is told that he should check what kind of car the client is driving to help determine whether he can pay the charges—in this case literally what the traffic will bear.
>
> The new fee schedule does not suggest that the lawyer also check the client's liquor cabinet, deep freeze, refrigerator and wardrobe but the lawyers have a Latin expression that covers the situation: *Expressio unius est non exclusio alterius.* (The inclusion of one does not mean the exclusion of others.)
>
> It's a pity the public doesn't have some rules in Latin or otherwise to protect its interests.

I asked Miles McMillin what happened after the editorial appeared. "Oh, they're always murmuring about disbarring me. They've become the new American priesthood: no one dare question their motives or conduct."

One lawyer McMillin knew actually protested to the probate judge about the size of his $8,000 fee in a large estate case: he wanted the fee cut, felt it was too much for the little work he did. The judge said it would be unethical to cut the fee, so the lawyer made a $5,000 contribution to a memorial foundation set up for the dead man.

When the *Capital-Times* ran the entire Minimum Fee Schedule on page 2 with the headline, PEOPLE: THESE ARE THE CHARGES YOU ARE GOING TO HAVE TO PAY YOUR LAWYERS FROM NOW ON, Philip Habermann was "flabbergasted. My first reaction was

'They printed our copyrighted schedule; we are going to sue this paper.' " He was soon convinced by several lawyers that it was marvelous free publicity for the bar's schedule. The page would have cost $800 as an ad.

The Wisconsin State Bar increased the earnings of its 5,600 members by at least $22,000,000 in just five years after it had introduced its first statewide minimum schedule. (This is what Habermann had meant about investing a dime if you knew you'd get back $20 within a few years.)

Some of the results of the fee schedule were even more salutary, even if you couldn't put a dollar figure on them. For one thing that old American custom, shopping around, was ended as far as Wisconsin legal services went. As Habermann explained:

> You can't get rid of shopping entirely, but certainly shoppers do get discouraged when they go from office to office. Lawyers who have the schedule available can smell a shopper the moment he walks in the door, and the way to treat them is to say: "Well, in this case we have a minimum schedule and I am sure that it will cost you that much and probably not much more." If you get rid of them, you probably haven't lost a very good client anyway, but after they hit a few offices and get the same answer, they usually light somewhere and stay.

Judges and the very courtrooms of the State also helped discourage shoppers, Habermann reported exultantly. Not only do judges there *respect* the schedule but they

> back up the bar in making these charges. Now you can go into some courthouses in Wisconsin and you will find notices posted on the courtroom bulletin board that "On all matters coming before this court, the court will in ordinary circumstances apply the standard schedule of charges prescribed in the Minimum Fee Schedule of the State Bar of Wisconsin." That is wonderful, when the judges cooperate with you that way. It gives the schedule official status.

The name may change from state to state but the effect is the same. In Idaho it is called the advisory fee schedule. Blaine Anderson of Blackfoot, Idaho, who had been president of his state bar association, talked at the ABA annual meeting in Montreal in August, 1966. The session was "The Anatomy of Fee Determination and Satisfied Clients," but the thrust of the meeting, it seemed to me, was rather more on satisfied *lawyers*.

"We prefer to call it an advisory fee schedule," said Mr. Anderson, "for the reason that in fixing the fee you usually charge somewhat higher than would be charged according to the minimum fee schedule. Too often the minimum tends to be the maximum."

Idaho has its stubborn legal-service shoppers, too, but they are brought around. Mr. Anderson told how:

> I practice in a town of 10,000 people and a county with a population of about 27,000. We have eight lawyers in the entire county. We have an understanding among ourselves that these obvious shoppers get nowhere. . . . It works very well for us. I would suggest if your local bar gets along, well, you get together and discuss it openly and frankly. . . .

The fee schedule also works fine in large cities, reported William J. Fuchs, a young, aggressive attorney from Philadelphia, that traditional source of our sharpest lawyers:

> . . . there has been a tremendous increase in net income of lawyers. We believe the minimum fee schedule was the largest single thing in improving the income of lawyers.

Earlier in the Montreal session, John D. Conner of Washington, D.C., a former chairman of the ABA Committee on Economics of Law, opened the meeting on "How to Improve the Fee" by asking a question that, somehow, never got answered: "Have we priced ourselves out of the market?" Instead of answering, he promptly went on to say, "We would all admit—possibly to ourselves if not to anyone else—that by nature we lawyers are inefficient." But the speakers who stressed the efficacy of minimum fee schedules seemed to negate the possibility that lawyers were inefficient when it came to setting fees.

William Fuchs, discussing the psychology of how to bill a client, quoted a Phoenix lawyer: "Make the first bill a good one." Then Mr. Fuchs added:

Come out and hit the client hard at the beginning. Get the air cleared. It's now or never. If you're going to bill a half-way rate on your first bill, you'll be at half-way rates for the rest of your career with that client. Come right out at the beginning and sock him hard.

There are subtler approaches. One of the most persuasive advocates of the gentler means of extracting a fee via the minimum fee schedule is Albert A. DuPont, a red-haired Jamaica, New York, lawyer and former president of the Queens Bar Association. In a talk not long ago before the Economics Institute of the New York State Bar he gave his formula:

Suppose you get a new client in the office. He has one of those routine matters covered by the minimum fee schedule. This enables you to be a good fellow and say, "Well, now, Mr. Jones, I've known your sister Ruth for a long time, and I admire her. Now I'd like to help you as much as I can." With an impressive manner, you reach into your desk drawer, where the schedule should be kept, you open it up and say, "I'll do it for the very, very minimum that the bar association says I can do it for, without practically getting disbarred." And you point out the item. "Now, you see the bar association says that the very, very minimum that I can charge in this instance, and Mr. Jones, if I thought you were a substantial man, it would be much more than that—here, is X dollars." And make sure you show it to him.

That stops most arguments right then and there, because it gives validity, it gives sanctification to the fee.

There's a little throwaway line in Mr. DuPont's account that deserves another look: "and Mr. Jones, if I thought you were a *substantial* man. . . ." Who wants to be thought of as *insubstantial?* Most of us, of course, if the lawyer's fee is going to be fixed according to whether we pay $75 for a suit of clothes or $150. But there are some clients who are *insulted* with minimum fees. William J. Palmer, a former California Superior Court Judge, who has written widely on legal matters, tells of such a splendid woman client visiting a lawyer friend of his:

She refused to be seated and talk about her case until I had quoted her a fee, saying that she had never been so insulted in her life as she had been by a dozen other attorneys she had consulted and who had quoted her a fee $450 to $500, thus making it clear to her that they did not realize her prominent social position and importance. Although I was confident $500 was a reasonable fee for the contemplated service, I promptly responded that my charge would be $5,000.

"At last," she commented, "I have found the attorney I want." She immediately employed me. . . . She paid my fee before I had rendered any bill and expressed her great pleasure. She told me she would refer any friends to me who might need legal services and did so in several instances. To this day, many years later, the incident has continued to bother me from an ethical standpoint, and I seriously question whether I would act the same way a second time. From every standpoint but one, the fee was excessive for the service rendered.

Judge Palmer was more philosophical: "For this particular woman, did not this service have the value that she was willing to pay?" But then he goes on to add that after a careful study he could find no authority "in judicial precedent or in professional ethics for the idea that mere ability to pay, however ample, adds to or is even a factor in the value of the service performed in a given assignment."

One of the reasons lawyers love probate work is that the problem of "ability to pay" never figures. They find out quickly how much money there is in the estate, and their percentage cut is assured. No probate judge would allow an estate to be settled until the lawyer has gotten his sizable fee. Not today, anyway.

As a result, one of the inside smile-provokers I heard most often from lawyers all around the nation was, "A lawyer with an extensive probate practice is known as a lawyer with a very good practice."

In 1966 Richard B. Bauer, a round-faced, bespectacled Denver lawyer—he is counsel for the National City Bank of Denver—undertook a nationwide survey of what attorneys' fees were in probate proceedings. It was an enormous and long-overdue task. Mr. Bauer undertook it because he felt probate law fees were getting an unfavorable press. He took as his standard a $100,000 estate and working from the highest cost to the lowest, the breakdown of fees went something like this:

$5,000 or More

New Mexico	$5,150
New Jersey	5,000
Alabama	5,000
Dist. of Colum.	5,000
Kansas	5,000

$4,000 or More

Alaska	$4,760
Louisiana	4,500
Indiana	4,325
Colorado	4,300
Vermont	4,300
New York	4,250
Arizona	4,120
Oklahoma	4,100
Illinois	4,000

$3,000 or More

Utah	$3,800
Pennsylvania	3,775
Virginia	3,750
Michigan	3,663
Massachusetts	3,600
Minnesota	3,500
Oregon	3,480
Montana	3,400
No. Carolina	3,350
Rhode Island	3,350

Arkansas	3,300
Missouri	3,300
No. Dakota	3,250
So. Dakota	3,175
Idaho	3,170
Tennessee	3,165
Washington	3,075
Wisconsin	3,050
Kentucky	3,030
Mississippi	3,025
Maine	3,000
Texas	3,000
West Virginia	3,000

$2,000 or More

Connecticut	$2,950
Ohio	2,800
Nebraska	2,675
California	2,630
Maryland	2,600
Florida	2,595
New Hampshire	2,500
Wyoming	2,350
Hawaii	2,310
Nevada	2,120
Delaware	2,000

Less Than $2,000

So. Carolina	$1,900
Georgia	1,800

The original Bauer survey appeared in the September, 1966, issue of *Trusts and Estates,* the monthly guide for bank trust officers. The heading was: "Survey Shows that Attorneys' Fees in Probate Proceedings Vary State to State but are Generally Reasonable."

There were some mistakes in Mr. Bauer's original computations, and bank trust officers were quick to pick him up. For example, a Phoenix, Arizona, trust officer found a $630 mistake in the Bauer figures: Arizona should be placed at $4,120, not $4,750. As he pointed out, the difference was important: "We receive many inquiries from attorneys and trust officers from all over the U.S. concerning probate costs in Arizona. Clearly this is a factor to people contemplating retirement in our sunny southwest."

But the enormous spread from $5,150 in New Mexico down to $1,800 in Georgia, for the same-sized estate and generally involving just about the same amount of work, aroused considerable interest among probate lawyers. Some were disturbed: "What would happen to the new automobile business if a Cadillac cost $5,000 in New Mexico but only $1,800 in Georgia? Georgia dealers would become the greatest Cadillac sellers in the world."

Of course, there's a great difference: you can't arrange your estate and your death to suit the lowest cost factor. But why should a Georgia lawyer and an Alabama lawyer only a few miles apart have such remarkably different evaluations of what their services were worth in probating an estate of $100,000? Were Georgia lawyers so much more efficient, or had the Alabama lawyers simply plucked a nice high percentage figure out of the air? Why did New Jersey lawyers ask $5000 when their equally well trained colleagues across the river in Delaware would only ask $2000? A lawyer friend said: "Now there's a research job. Is it possible that the Du Pont family, the richest and most powerful in the state, has been influential in keeping bar minimum fee schedules down on probate because it would be their estates that would be hardest hit?"

By his same cynical reasoning the wealthy retirees of New Mexico presumably have no influence on bar minimum fees in that state, and thus New Mexico lawyers have been able to establish and maintain the highest probate percentage rates in the country.

Another lawyer commented: "That list of Bauer's is going to be on the table every time state bar minimum fees are up for revision. You can bet your bottom dollar the revisions will be up. They'll always be able to say to critics: 'Hell, we're reasonable. New Mexico and New Jersey are much higher.' "

Until quite recently the effectiveness of such probate rate raises could have been thwarted by "misguided" probate judges, a lot of whom were not lawyers. Many of these nonlawyer probate judges were anxious to be helpful to the voters who elected them. They not only encouraged the executor of the estate to prepare the forms himself, but some of them even went further: *they* would do the forms. Apparently this was a problem even in 1872 in Sedgwick County, Kansas, when its pioneering bar minimum fee schedule was published. That early schedule contained, in italicized type, a warning to such well-meaning meddlers:

. . . it shall be unlawful for the Probate Judges . . . to write any petition or answer, or other pleadings in any proceedings, or perform any service as attorney or counsellor at law, in any case or cases pending before them . . .

Admittedly, certain self-interest was sometimes involved. In Colorado where nonlawyer probate judges were permitted until the reorganization of the state's courts in January, 1965, at least one probate judge was also an undertaker. He used to offer a very reasonable will-probate-funeral package that infuriated many lawyers in the county. But since he was the probate judge, the bar only cleared its throat nervously from time to time. What hurt the lawyers was that it was a flat-fee deal rather than a percentage fee, and the local bar knew it would have to do a lot of "reeducation" to offset the no-longer-available bargain.

In Idaho where only four of sixty probate judges were lawyers, many of them also offered the funeral-probate package. A similar system was found in southern Illinois until recently.

There used to be a nonlawyer probate judge in Hillsdale, Michigan, whom Bill Pierce remembers fondly. Pierce, an apple-cheeked professor of law at the University of Michigan, was recently appointed to the President's Consumer Advisory Council. In addition, he is president of the National Conference of Commissioners on Uniform State Laws. Even before he was appointed to these eminent posts, Bill Pierce had an amused, earthy interest in how the law and the courts *really* work. From time to time I visit him in Ann Arbor to draw on his remarkable memory and his unerring ability to cut through the legal thickets.

"Oh, he was a fine probate judge," Pierce recalls. "People would come in and ask him which lawyer they should go to for probate. He would look at them as if they had asked about hiring a butler. 'What do you need a lawyer for?' he'd ask. 'Anyone can file a petition. Here, let me show you how to do it.' And he would. Lawyers were very unhappy in that county."

Bill Pierce's interest in the probate courts goes back a long time. "I always used to be appalled: here are the courts that handle more money than any courts in the country, and there wasn't anyone looking on or yelling, hey, what goes on here! Every lawyer and judge I ever talked to said these courts needed basic reform, but damn few of them were willing to speak out. Things were going along too profitably."

The National Conference of Commissioners on Uniform State Laws and the probate section of the American Bar Association have been working for years trying to draw a newer and simplified probate code for the states. Bill Pierce did a lot of the work on the code before he recently became president of the National Conference. He thinks the code will be submitted to state legislatures for enactment late in 1968 or 1969. "Don't hold your breath. The adoption record on these uniform legal codes is spotty. So far only nine uniform codes have been adopted by as many as forty-five states, and an average of twenty-six years was required to complete action.

"The uniform probate code will especially bring out a lot of resistance. There's always general inertia, of course, but a lot of lawyers will battle it because when you propose changed ways of handling probate you're *repealing* their knowledge. A lot of probate judges won't like it either. The changes will be in the direction of what we call 'independent administration,' which means you don't have to go running to the probate judge for every little item. Cutting down trips to the courthouse by the heirs to the estate won't be popular with some probate judges, who have to be elected. They're afraid if you cut down the required visits you'll be cutting down on their exposure to the public, and that's very important in a small county."

The proposed code doesn't touch on the key items of whether or not the executor of an estate has to hire a lawyer—"it's neutral on that"—or on the percentage fees lawyers get in probate work. Pierce, like most of the lawyers who have worked on the new model code, thinks that the present percentage fee arrangement is "totally unrealistic," but they are doubtful any changes will take place here unless there is an enormous and sustained public outcry.

Bill Pierce wonders if there will ever be such an outcry. "In probate it's generally a windfall for the heirs, so they're not looking too closely. They start thinking of the *net* figure, the way they do on their paychecks. They don't think of it as some lawyer taking money out of their pockets. At least, not yet."

Much of the slowness and ponderousness of the probate process stemmed from the inclusion of checks and double-checks to avoid fraud. "But are we preventing fraud with this complex machinery? We're not: lawyers still run away with the money or just spend it."

Once during luncheon we got onto the topic of lawyers' earnings. "Now that's an area in which some original thinking and research is called for," Pierce said. "How much do lawyers *really* earn? The published figures are meaningless for a lot of lawyers. Most of them have other angles, other businesses on the side that provide them with income sources you don't hear about. You're talking to a lawyer and discover he has a nice piece of property. How did he get that? Oh, he shrugs, just something I picked up.

He's not going to tell you he acquired it through a dummy, that it passed through probate with a book value far below what it was really worth.*

"Lawyers aren't too dead set against delay in probate. For one thing the longer something takes the more it might seem to justify their percentage fees. But long administrations of estates often provide dangerous temptations for what the bar sometimes calls 'the weak lawyer.' There's a piece of land or a nice business whose value the heirs aren't aware of. What's to prevent a 'weak lawyer' from having it bought for a low price through a dummy and profiting on this even more than on the probate fee? A few deals like that and a 'weak lawyer' can get awful strong. Unethical? Of course it is, but if the dummy keeps his mouth shut and the lawyer is reasonably discreet, who on earth is going to find out?"

Working with Bill Pierce on the National Conference Probate Code revision has been Allison Dunham, a handsome Columbia Law alumnus who teaches law at the University of Chicago. Dunham is executive director of the Conference. Like Bill Pierce, he has a remarkable appreciation of things-as-they-are in law and an ear for the appropriate anecdote.

We met at the ABA convention in Honolulu in 1967, and he talked about probate and minimum fee schedules. He laughed at one point and said:

"You know who *I* get complaints from on the fee schedules? My law students at Chicago. Most of them are in their mid-twenties and their parents are of an age where death is not uncommon. So the family turns to the law student and says: how can we cut the lawyer's fee? The law student takes a look at the schedule and figures out that the lawyer who handles it is going to make $1,000 or $2,000 on the estate. And by now the law student is generally

*One way of pulling this stunt with legal sanction was disclosed during a 1953 investigation of the Chicago Probate Court by the Chicago *Times*. "The court itself has become a center of a gigantic, speculative real estate market. In this market, property sold out of estates with court approval is resold— sometimes again and again—at substantial profits by court-approved buyers. The profits . . . are made at the expense of the widows and children of the deceased and the financial security of the sick and insane."

sophisticated enough to know how really little work is involved in most estates, so he starts thinking: how can the family get around the minimum fee schedule? So they come to me. What do I tell them? I tell them if they're from Chicago or some other large city there *might* be a way out. Find out what the lawyer's hourly rate is: $20, $25, even $30 an hour. Tell him you'll pay him his top hourly rate to handle the probate. In large cities you'll still find lawyers who will take the estate on that basis."

How much would be saved that way? Al Dunham had a case in point. He mentioned a friend of his who had once taught probate law and had achieved a national reputation in the field. Then he moved out to practice law in Denver.

Shortly afterward I spoke to this eminent Colorado attorney of his experiment in probate. The only request he made was that I not use his name. "It could still have uncomfortable repercussions," he said. "Lawyers here are very sensitive about minimum fees."

Colorado has one of the highest minimum fee schedules for probate. It looks like this:

6% on the first $5,000 of estate
5% on the next $20,000 of estate
4% on the next $175,000 of estate
3% of the next $300,000 of estate

So that on a $50,000 estate, for example, the legal fee would be $2,300; and $4,300 on a $100,000 estate. But there are also items that normally don't go into the estate. For example, the widow is the beneficiary of her dead husband's insurance policy. For collecting that—at the expense of a single letter and a copy of the death certificate—the lawyers in Colorado also ask 1 percent of the policy. On a $50,000 policy, for example, a lawyer would collect $500 for the chore which he would, of course, have his secretary take care of.

"What happened," said the Denver lawyer, "is that the father of a good friend died. My friend asked me if I would probate the estate, which consisted of a house worth $20,000 and $5,000 in cash. He knew about legal fees, so he asked me if I would do it on an hourly basis. I was new here and I thought maybe it would be an interesting experiment to find out. I told my friend yes, but I laid down certain ground rules. I was going to charge $25 an hour, and I was going to charge him for every *minute*, for travel time, for breakage. If my work ran a few minutes over an hour, I'd charge for the full hour. He agreed. Now I pride myself on being a legal craftsman so I really gave this expert attention, and I surely spent much more time on it than the average lawyer would have. Still, with the great attention and the time rule I had imposed it came to only 25 hours, or $625 for the whole job, embellishments and all. On a $25,000 estate here the going percentage rate would have called for a $1,300 fee.

"Now I got a little nervous. An 'interesting experiment' was all well and good, but I was a comparatively new lawyer in town and the bar might think I was stepping out of line. So I wrote the Chairman of the Bar's Ethical Committee. And he said it may be unethical to charge less but he wasn't very firm on it because this was just before the October, 1961, Opinion 302 of the ABA Ethics Committee—that the 'habitual charging of fees less than those established by minumum fee schedules may be evidence of unethical conduct.' But still I got the distinct impression: all right, fella, just don't pull another 'interesting experiment.' In fact, I'd say, if I did it again today there'd be serious repercussions.

"Obviously I had introduced a dangerous yardstick into the legal services market. I had shown that a careful, even meticulous probate of a simple estate could be done for less than half of the going percentage rate by a lawyer working on a strict hourly fee basis. Now I *know* probate: I've spent years studying and writing on the subject and if *I'm* worth $25 an hour in it, you can bet a lot of lawyers around here aren't worth that much. I'd say, offhand, that there are a lot of perfectly good lawyers in Denver who could have done the same job in fewer hours and at a smaller hourly rate. And they'd have made money on the job, too."

Later when I mentioned this case to another Denver lawyer, he quoted, with only slightly disguised bitterness, a line from William James: "The natural enemy of any subject is the professor thereof."

In February, 1967, Milwaukee's Probate Judge, Michael T. Sullivan, made the revolutionary suggestion that attorneys charge for probate work on an hourly or day-by-day basis instead of the present lushly lucrative percentage arrangement. "The reaction of attorneys," he told me, "is mixed."

Allison Dunham had also mentioned a clever probate gimmick many law professors admire. The lawyer involved was an Easterner teaching at the University of Chicago Law School with Dunham. His father lived in Connecticut, and when he died he left his entire estate to his son. It was sizable: $200,000 and all in common stocks. The law professor wasn't admitted to the Connecticut Bar so he couldn't take his father's estate through the normal processes in that state without hiring a fellow lawyer. And according to the Connecticut minimum fee schedule the fee would have been $5,450.

The law professor found a simple way to avoid paying any Connecticut lawyer such a sizable fee. What made it possible was that he carried the same name as his father did—he was Junior, of course, but he never used it in his signature. So all he did was mail out change of address cards to all the corporations in which his father held stock. Now not only did he have $200,000 worth of stock certificates, but he was sure that the dividends would be mailed to him. The father's will was never offered for probate, and the son dutifully paid all his father's debts and taxes, thus fulfilling one of the important reasons for probate: the payment of the dead man's just debts.

Not all law professors have such neat ways of saving themselves money on probate. Professor David T. Smith, of Western Reserve University Law School in Cleveland, inherited a car worth about $1,000 after his father's death in Rhode Island. "That little car," he told me recently, "is going to cost me about $200 in court costs and attorney fees before I'm finished with the probate."

Professor Smith had been part of the Western Reserve team of sociologists and lawyers working on a three-year study of "Property Disposition and the Family" financed by a $95,000 grant from the Russell Sage Foundation. A book on the study is due in 1968.

Judith N. Cates, an attractive young sociologist, described the work she and the project head, Dr. Marvin B. Sussman, had been doing.

"We took every twentieth estate closed in Cuyahoga County (Cleveland) during the nine-month period from November, 1964, to August, 1965. There were some 658 estates in all. Most of them, of course, left little. Some 60 percent of the estates had $10,000 or less in them, and most of them consisted of the value of a jointly owned home. Another 30 percent left $15,000–$50,000 and a final 10 percent over $50,000.

"In every case we interviewed the heirs. We even got to out-of-state heirs in New York and Florida and sent the rest questionnaires. We also interviewed 78 of the lawyers who were involved in these estates. Oh, they liked probate work all right. They said it's pretty simple, almost always just a matter of filling in forms at the proper time, and a lot of it was so routine their secretaries did the actual form-filling. Most of them admitted they were handsomely paid for probate work.

"But a lot of the heirs weren't as happy with probate. Most of them felt that the attorney fees had been 'way too high,' but there was only one case we found where a family objected to a lawyer's fee and went to court to get it reduced. It wasn't reduced."

Between 5 and 10 percent of the families involved tried to fill out the probate forms themselves so as to dispense with a lawyer's fee, but the local probate court clerk wouldn't let them have the forms. Several heirs told Professor Cates that if the "government trusts us to fill out income taxes, why can't the government let us fill out these forms ourselves and save some money?"

The Western Reserve investigators uncovered some gamy legal tricks employed to raise fees. Judith Cates recalled one in particular:

"This man had left a $14,000 estate to his brother, who lived in

Florida. He also appointed him executor. The brother came up to Cleveland to settle the estate. He was around three months, and then the attorney handling the estate told him everything was set and he could return to Florida. The day after the sole heir left, the attorney went into probate court and got another lawyer appointed executor of the estate—because the listed executor wasn't present. The new executor's fee for doing exactly nothing was $300. The original lawyer's fee was $350."

A century ago it was illegal for any lawyer to get two fees from the same estate. A lawyer could handle the probate *or* he could be the executor of the estate, which means that he was in charge of managing the assets and distributing them to the heirs, paying debts and taxes. But lawyers and legislator-lawyers gradually whittled that expensive restriction away, and today there are only thirteen states in which a lawyer can't fulfill both functions—and collect two fees. And even in those states the rule isn't too rigid: if one lawyer is going to handle the probate, his law partner can be executor. Only in Washington, D.C., California and Idaho is this kind of double collection by law partners prohibited. And even there it is permitted if the will specifically says that Attorney so-and-so will be attorney and executor for the estate.

Understandably this is the big casino a lawyer has in mind when he is called in to draw up a will: if he can have himself appointed to both positions he is providing himself with a fine annuity some years hence. But it isn't easy. Too many husbands appoint their wives executors and stipulate that she need not provide a bond.

Most executors' fees are specified by state statute, since it is a job that is most often done by nonlawyers. The fees can be handsome. In Colorado, for example, it is $1,500 on a $25,000 estate and $4,500 on a $100,000 one. The range is from $5,150 on a $100,000 estate in New Mexico down to $1,840 in Minnesota, a fantastic spread. (Still, you're unlikely ever to see state-sponsored ads: It's Cheaper to Die in Minnesota.)

When Anna M. Nelson died in Greeley, Colorado, in 1965, her will provided many bequests for her scattered nieces and nephews, and asked that her remains be cremated and "ashes scattered to the Four Winds of Heaven." She also appointed attorney Raymond R. Pope of Greeley to be the executor of the will. After state and federal estate taxes were paid, her estate amounted to some $204,000, nearly all of it in savings accounts. For his fees as executor and attorney, lawyer Pope got a total of $22,500, or just about 11 percent of the net estate, which was approved by the probate judge. Since none of the chief heirs got more than $5,600 each—or a fourth of what the lawyer received— they were understandably upset.

Some of the heirs who lived in Oregon did some computing and found that if their aunt had died in Oregon the combined legal and executor fees would have only been $9,400, or much less than half of the Colorado amount. They pointed this out in a letter to the Colorado State Bar Association but, of course, they got no satisfaction: lawyer Pope's fees were perfectly legal and in accordance with both the minimum fee basis of the Weld County Bar Association and the state's set fees for executors. You couldn't blame the State Bar for the fact that Anna Nelson died in a particularly high-fee state. Or could you? The Weld County Bar had fixed a rather high percentage fee for legal work on probating estates, and unquestionably lawyer-legislators had had a hand in getting the state to fix healthy executor's fees. You certainly couldn't blame lawyer Pope for talking his full and just due, even if it, in effect, made him the estate's biggest single beneficiary.

You might look at lawyer Leonard S. Blondes a little more critically, though. Blondes, a Silver Springs, Maryland, attorney who is a member of the state legislature, put in for a $1,260 fee, exactly 10 percent, in the $12,590 estate of John MacFarlane. MacFarlane's widow and principal beneficiary began thinking that maybe 10 percent of a simple estate was rather too high, and she wrote of her mounting doubts to the chief local probate judge, Louise A. Terzian: "Since I have no experience and have no way of knowing if the fee is appropriate, would you please review it carefully. . . ."

Judge Terzian did and decided that the fee was exactly double what it should be, and she cut it to $630. Attorney Blondes was willing to humor the two women—the judge and his client—slightly: he would change the final accounting papers in the estate to show a $630 fee—even if he really got a total of $1,260.

Blondes later told reporter Leonard Downie, Jr., of the *Washington Post* that since he and Mrs. MacFarlane had "already agreed on the $1,260 fee he felt he could collect the approved $630 from the estate and the rest from Mrs. MacFarlane under their agreement." In short, he intended to keep the $1,260 he had collected, regardless of Judge Terzian's womanly frowns.

When Mrs. MacFarlane took it to the county bar association, she was told she could go out and hire another lawyer and file a civil suit against lawyer Blondes. At least one high bar association official, however, said she would not have much of a case. At this point Judge Terzian had to point out rather sadly to Mrs. Mac-Farlane that even though she was chief judge of the probate court —called orphans court in Maryland—she couldn't do any more because the court simply "had no control over what an attorney got outside the final accounting of the estate." One county bar official later told reporter Downie that Judge Terzian "just had some crazy ideas" about probate fees.

A cynical eighteenth-century Frenchman, Nicholas Chamfort, may have been listening in from beyond the grave. "It is easier to make certain things legal," he once wrote, "than to make them legitimate."

•   •

On February 20, 1968, the American Bar association took a timid, tentative step into the shrewd shopper's world of discount stores, charter flights, group insurance and Blue Cross. Meeting in Chicago the ABA approved a pilot project to find out if prepaid legal insurance would be attractive to the public. Before the end of the year the association hopes to offer a group legal insurance plan to a labor union somewhere in the United States.

The plan had been proposed by F. William McAlpin of St. Louis, Chairman of the ABA Committee on the Availability of

Legal Services. For several years the committee had been studying ways of making lawyers' services more easily available—and affordable—to the middle class. (Professional revolutionaries in the United States are always discouraged at the number of union members who consider themselves middle rather than working class.)

Under McAlpin's proposal, members of the participating union would pay an annual premium to be insured for the costs of attorney fees involved in a limited number of categories. These would include adoptions, bankruptcies, will drafting, and traffic cases. They would probably not include divorces, accident cases or estate probates.

Once some local union agrees, the trial plan would run for three or four years before the ABA decided whether to push for the plan on a nationwide basis.

In effect, then, with the proposal the ABA hoped it had bought a few years during which it could hold back far more radical adoptions of group legal services for the rest of us in the middle class who are not union members. Whether the ABA can prevent bolder and *immediate* plans from coming into existence is a matter that thousands of attorneys are now worrying about.

The Chicago decision of the ABA came two and a half months after the U. S. Supreme Court ruled that the Constitution protects the rights of unions to set up group legal services providing members free or low-cost legal aid. More specifically, the court ruled that the Supreme Court of Illinois was wrong in trying to prevent the United Mine Workers from saving its members money by providing them with free legal aid in workmen's compensation cases.

In a recent two-year period the Mine Workers' lawyers—working on $12,000 salaries plus expenses—had handled some 1,900 workmen's compensation cases for injured mine workers in Illinois. Under Illinois' Industrial Commission Laws, lawyers handling these "comp" cases are limited to fees of 20 percent of what they collect for the injured men. Since the UMW-paid lawyers had collected $2,600,000 in these 1,900 cases—averaging about

$1,370 per case—they had saved the injured members about $520,000 in legal fees. This is the money they would have had to pay individual lawyers on the 20 percent fee basis—if the Mine Workers hadn't provided this special service for its members.

A lot of other Illinois lawyers handling these comp cases said that the salaried UMW lawyers were just grinding out the cases; that independent lawyers would have gotten the injured miners much more. But ABA committee chairman, Bill McAlpin, who is licensed to practice in Missouri and Illinois, disagrees. "On the basis of my experience," he says, "the average recovery by the UMW lawyers was good."

What was basically involved in the Supreme Court case was Canon 35 of the ABA's Code of Ethics, which has full legal standing in most state courts. Under this canon a lawyer may not accept pay from an organization for "the rendering of legal services to the members of such an organization in respect of their individual affairs."

In effect, this restriction accounts for the fact that when the Authors Guild, for example, invites me to join and tells me all the services it is ready to provide, it specifically excludes any legal services that I might need on a publisher's contract or on a copyright problem.

And because of Canon 35, presumably, the Automobile Club to which I belong cannot assure me that if I sue anyone as a result of an auto accident case it will provide a competent attorney who would gladly handle the case on a contingent fee of only 15 or 20 percent instead of the traditional one third—or half. Because of Canon 35 the homeowners' association I belong to cannot provide me with a lawyer's services for the legal services connected with the buying or selling of my home—services the association's lawyer would provide on a nominal-charge basis rather than the present 1 percent of the home's value when bought or sold.

A relative who died recently belonged to a fraternal order that offered him low-cost life insurance, inexpensive charter flights to Europe and death benefits for his survivors. What it couldn't offer legally, because of Canon 35, was a sensible group legal service for his widow on probate. She paid a lawyer $2,300 for these services, based on a fixed percentage of the estate—services that could have been handled profitably by a group service's lawyer for $300.

Bill McAlpin agrees that the Supreme Court ruling "wiped Canon 35 off the books." Yet, the canon is still around as far as middle-class groups are concerned. There has been no rush of fraternal orders, for example, to set up group legal services for its members.

Obviously, lawyers are waiting for guidance from their bar associations. Whether any enterprising service-minded attorneys are going to be willing to conduct their own group legal service experiments before the ABA makes a careful decision on its limited union experiment four or five years hence, remains to be seen.

Most U.S. lawyers, I'm sure, are opposed to the idea. If the ABA waits to get a consensus from its members before it suggests something more relevant than a long-range, limited experiment in legal insurance, there is going to be a terribly long wait.

In August, 1967, at the ABA convention in Honolulu, I sat in on a debate on group legal services. There were, perhaps, seventy-five lawyers present and if the applause was any indicator of their choice, group legal services doesn't have a chance. After the debate a Florida lawyer spoke out bitterly:

> I practice in a typical retirement town. I can see the day when retirees come down to my town and are told when they have any legal problems they should go to such and such a firm because the corporation they had worked for has a deal with the firm for it to represent employes and retirees. . . . That camel we're letting into the tent will trample us to death.

As I walked out, a small-town Wisconsin lawyer shook his head and said to me: "They don't learn a damn thing. They're always worried about making as much as the doctors, but they don't realize they're heading into the same kind of mess the doctors got into by not feeling the public's pulse. They'll stall for ages on group legal services—and commiserate with each other on why people don't respect lawyers anymore."

As of July, 1968, there were still no modern, sensibly priced expert legal services available for the American middle class. What there was, was of uncertain quality, priced generally so that the lawyer becomes a silent partner and is available only on the lawyer's terms. In short, there are no guarantees of satisfaction, quality of services, or assurance of fairness.

Nothing's changed.

10 PRO SE: *BAKER'S BATTLE*

Mr. Cleave, when tried before Lord Lyndhurst in the Court of the Exchequer, acted as his own counsel, and began his speech by remarking that before he sat down he feared he should give an awkward illustration of the truth of the old adage, namely that he who acts as his own counsel has a fool for his client. The judge at once remarked, "Oh, Mr. Cleave, don't you mind that adage: it was framed by the *lawyers.*"
—Curiosities of Law and Lawyers

In the spring of 1966 I flew to Janesville, Wisconsin, to spend a few hours with John Gordon Baker, "a dangerous crank." A bar association official called him that.

To lawyers, cranks come in all shapes and ferocities. They send long letters—carbon copies mostly—from mental hospitals; they come in with "proof" they are the real heirs to all Manhattan below 23rd Street; and they circulate petitions calling for the impeachment of Chief Justice Earl Warren. But the most dangerous, most vexing and in some ways the costliest cranks are what one lawyer calls "the *pro se* nuts." *Pro se,* in Latin, is simply "for himself." If you represent yourself in court in a civil or criminal action you are *pro se.*

There are professional *pro se* litigants who make penurious but proud careers of their perennial suits. In New York there is one man who has spent much of the last fifteen years suing drug companies, broadcasters and advertising agencies for several hundred million dollars. He claims he invented certain advertising gimmicks and wants adequate royalties for every single use. (As a legal pauper he doesn't have to pay court filing fees of any kind.) He has yet to collect his first dollar. In Nassau County, Long Island, a fifty-four-year-old ex-telegrapher and house painter has more than a billion dollars worth of lawsuits in motion against the State of New York, the City of Long Beach, various Long Beach policemen, a doctor, a nurse, and his neighbor. It all started when one of his teen-age sons was struck by a neighbor; he took his son to Long Beach Memorial Hospital and there he was given medicines which, he says, caused him to have a heart attack.

In Chicago, Sherman H. Skolnick, a thirty-eight-year-old paraplegic, has been suing the Chicago Bar Association for $400,000, Chief Judge William J. Campbell of the Federal District Court for $2 million, and the city of Chicago and the State electoral board for lesser sums. Two brothers, Ralph and Percy Cothran of San José, California, spent years in their *pro se* suits against a local water company.

Lawyers have learned to be wary of the *pro se* litigants. Not long ago the *Practicing Attorney's Letter* told its readers why:

> It's paradoxical and clients may be incredulous but lawyers know it to be true: one of the most difficult of trial adversaries can be the litigant who goes to court without a lawyer. He has the right to do so, if he wishes.
>
> The very defects which would be catastrophic to an attorney—lack of legal knowledge and experience—tend to help the self-representer. They gain him sympathy . . . many a judge will relax the procedural rules for him. More than that, the judge may assist the layman in setting forth a *prima facie* case or defense, and help him ask questions to be asked parties and witnesses. Some judges even unconsciously become the layman's "advocate."
>
> To make matters worse, if the case is tried before a jury, jurymen will identify with a fellow-layman. To them he looks like a guileless underdog engaged in an unequal battle with a shrewd, overly technical lawyer. What a humiliation it is for an attorney in such a case to suffer a defeat.

When John Gordon Baker went into court representing himself he didn't get any judicial sympathy or help. In fact, the State Board of County Judges said Mr. Baker had no right to come into their courts *pro se*. Backing them up were the lawyers of Wisconsin through their State Bar, and even the 130,000 lawyers who belong to the American Bar Association. John Gordon Baker aroused their passionate antagonism because he was, potentially, the most dangerous threat to the billion dollars in annual legal fees that U.S. lawyers earn through probating wills and taking estates of the dead through the courts.

Toward the end of Baker's litigation I talked to an interested bar official, asking him to compare Baker and Norman Dacey, whose book, *How to Avoid Probate,* had just come out.* "Dacey is just a nuisance," he said. "He's got a skirmish going out on the flanks. Even if he wins there he's got to lose the main battle. Baker's in a frontal assault. He wins and we're in real trouble."

Curiously, Dacey the skirmisher got all the publicity which, of course, helped sell 750,000 copies of his $4.95 book. Baker the front-line combatant got no more than a single cryptic paragraph in a Wisconsin daily during the entire course of his campaign.

In many other ways, too, John Gordon Baker is a most atypical crank. He is well educated (University of Wisconsin), prosperous, a hardheaded manufacturer who employs 230 people, and a life-long Republicans. In short, he is all the things litigious *pro se* characters usually aren't.

Until he took on the entire organized legal profession of the country, Baker had been a consistent and, on the whole, happy user of well-paid legal talent. He is president of a family firm, the Baker Manufacturing Company, of Evansville, Wisconsin. The firm, one of the state's oldest foundries, does about $9 million a year in water system equipment, well supplies and iron castings. There is a generous profit-sharing system with its employes, and many of them, or their heirs, are among the 300 stockholders of Baker Manufacturing.

John Baker is conservative and a traditionalist. He is proud that he still lives in the Evansville house he was born in sixty-one years ago. The Bakers have two grown daughters, one who recently got her Ph.D. at Harvard and another at the University of Wisconsin where Baker got an engineering degree.

Baker Manufacturing generates a normal amount of routine

*See Chapter 11.

legal work and some patent litigation. But there was never enough to hire its own full-time staff lawyer, so for many years Baker used a Madison, Wisconsin, law firm, Ross, Stevens, Pick and Spohn.

In a nearly deserted Janesville hotel dining room, John Baker, tall and white-haired, explained:

"They had been doing our legal work on an hourly basis. For a long time it was $15 an hour and then they raised it to $20. It wasn't all routine. Sure, there was corporate work, bylaws and minor litigation, but there was also a lot of head-scratching work. Our annual legal bill ran to $2,000–$3,000 and we always felt we were getting good value. No complaints."

The trouble started after Baker's mother, Eliza S. Baker, died at eighty-seven on October 24, 1961. She left an estate of some $172,000, and under her will it was to be shared by her son, John Baker; a daughter, Elsie Baker of Los Angeles, and two grandchildren, Margaret Kearns and John Baker.

Soon afterward John Gordon Baker of Evansville, who had been appointed executor under his mother's will, asked attorney Myron Stevens of Madison to start probating the will. In addition, following his lawyer's advice, Baker hired an accounting firm to prepare the estate's federal and state tax returns.

"When I asked Stevens to go ahead," Baker recalls, "I assumed it would be on the same hourly basis we had employed for years. I knew it was a simple estate without complications or conflict or tricky provisions and I guessed there might be, say, twenty hours of legal work. Just to make sure, I asked Stevens. He told me that on probate the State Bar's minimum fee schedule worked strictly on a percentage basis, and he figured that the fee for handling the estate would be about $4,800. I was flabbergasted. It was ten times more than I expected. He said it was what any lawyer in the state would charge. The minimum fee schedule was designed to prevent unethical lawyers from undercutting and doing sloppy work. I said did he consider it unethical to charge the firm $20 an hour for legal work when there were firms in Milwaukee charging $40 an hour. No, he said, that's different. Probate was 'set work' with fixed percentage fees only. Well, I reacted pretty strongly. It was the time of the General Electric and Westinghouse price-fixing scandals, and I said I didn't like the idea of lawyers getting together and fixing obligatory fees without asking the public!"

Lawyer Stevens offered to drop probate at this point—early 1962—and Baker accepted. Stevens estimated that he had completed 40 percent of the necessary work so that his fee would be $1,920, which Baker paid out of the estate funds.

Now Baker began shopping but he soon found that in law there are no discounters and that "special arrangements" in probate fees were available only to the widows and orphans of a brother lawyer. And he got the dangerous idea: why couldn't he prepare the forms himself and complete the entire probate?

"It took me about twenty hours in all, but then I wasn't familiar with them. I'm sure a legal stenographer in a busy office would run through them in three hours at most."

The papers he prepared included:

Final Account and Petition
Notice of Hearing on Final Account and Determination of Inheritance
    Tax and Information Required by the Department of Taxation
Proposed Order Determining Inheritance Tax
Waiver and Consent for Final Settlement

"It sounded very impressive," Baker said, "but they were just routinely worded papers that had been done thousands of times before. Different names, amounts and dates and that was it. It didn't call for three years at law school. Anyone with average intelligence could have done it. And this was the work that was so special that the Bar Association decided it couldn't be done just for mere hourly rates but only on a percentage, or partnership, basis."

Baker turned all the completed forms in to the Rock County Probate Court headed by Judge Sverre Roang, a heavy-faced man with short, bristling hair. As it happened Judge Roang was chairman of a national committee of probate lawyers and judges working to create a special model probate code. The committee's main aims were to simplify probate procedures even further by removing various formalities. But nothing in the proposed code would allow a layman such as Baker to prepare the necessary probate papers himself. And there was nothing in the code about reducing attorneys' fees in probate. In effect, the proposed code, by reducing the amount of paperwork even further, would simply make probate even more profitable for lawyers.

Judge Roang refused to consider Baker's papers—until he hired a lawyer. And if he didn't, the court would appoint another executor who *would* hire a lawyer. At this point Baker had his first doubts, and as a normally prudent businessman asked for a legal opinion. He went to attorney John C. Wickhem, who checked the law and told his client that he was perfectly within his rights to go ahead without an attorney if he wanted to. He quoted the Wisconsin State Constitution:

> Any suitor, in any court of this state, shall have the right to prosecute or defend his suit either in his own proper person, or by an attorney or agent of his choice.

And obviously in this case John Gordon Baker was the agent of his choice. This legal opinion cost Baker $500, but now he felt that he had solid underpinning to appear without a lawyer in probate court.

Baker sent the judge lawyer Wickhem's opinion, plus another from a Los Angeles attorney who represented Baker's sister, Elsie, one of the other heirs. The Californian, Alvin O. Wiese, Jr., wrote that he was surprised the issue had been raised at all:

> I cannot understand this problem since Executors and Administrators frequently and without difficulty, represent themselves before the Probate Courts in California. . . . I wholeheartedly concur . . . that laymen are entitled to represent themselves in legal procedures if such is their choice.

But Judge Roang was not to be persuaded. He went further. If Baker wanted to appear before the Judge to argue his right to probate the estate without a lawyer, why Baker would first have to get a lawyer to make the argument. Shortly afterward, Judge Roang ordered all of the Baker estate papers to be returned, so that the estate remained unsettled. He also told Baker that if he persisted in his conduct he could be fined for practicing law without a license.

For a time Baker looked around for a lawyer to handle the argument before Judge Roang, but he found that lawyers were quoting fees that would have been considerably higher than what he would have paid for probating the estate. His hunch that the fees mentioned were deliberately inflated was reinforced when some franker lawyers told him that they wouldn't handle the case for anything—they didn't want to "endanger their probate practices."

With an engineer's logic Baker decided that if plan A doesn't work, why not try plan B? Finding B meant going through law books.

"I found that I could quickly appeal to the State Supreme Court on a writ of *mandamus.* This is something done when everything else fails, if a government body refuses to act when it should."

(*Mandamus,* Latin for "we command," is a writ issued by a superior court to a lower court or governmental agency directing it to restore to the complainant rights or privileges of which he has been illegally deprived.)

On May 24, 1965, the writ of *mandamus* which Baker had carefully drawn was presented to the Supreme Court of the state. The court issued a writ, and now Judge Roang had to tell the Supreme Court why he had not allowed Baker to act as his own attorney.

On October 7, 1965—four years after his mother's death—Baker appeared in the Supreme Court to argue his case. It had cost him $125 to have his 113-page "Petitioner's Brief and Appendix" printed.

I asked Baker how his wife regarded the whole business. He nodded. "At first she was very sensible and realistic: she felt it was a big mistake for me to get so involved. After all, the few thousand dollars weren't going to impoverish my family or my sister's. 'Is it all worthwhile?' she asked me. But before I went to Madison to argue the case she had come all the way around: she felt I was right. There was an important principle involved, and in life you mustn't always be *that* sensible."

In the State Supreme Court in Madison, Baker realized that a hassle in an obscure county court suddenly had nationwide implications. The State Bar Association had filed a brief against him; so had the State Board of County Judges and even the American Bar Association, whose vigilant Unauthorized Practices Committee had spotted the Baker matter as a potential time bomb. Now Judge Roang, a minor member of the U.S. judiciary, had a lot of big brothers in his corner.

"At first I was a little surprised," Baker recalls. "But as soon as you thought about it a minute, you could see the implications. If I could probate the estate without any attorney, so could any executor. By this time I knew that probate work was the most lucrative the lawyers had. Here they get comparatively high fixed percentages for a form of clerical work, most of which their stenos did anyway. If *I* could do it, why in a few months some law-form publisher would have a kit out enabling anyone to do it easily just by filling in blanks and stuff. If only a third of the executors chose to do it themselves, the lawyers would be losing hundreds of millions every year. I was touching a live nerve. A widow is left $50,000 by her husband: if she fills out the forms herself and makes a visit to the probate court she could save herself nearly $2,000 in this state. That's real money: if she got a job as a clerk in an office at $75 a week she'd have to work nearly six months to earn that kind of money. And here on her husband's estate she could earn that just by filling out some routine forms that might take three or four hours. Which would *you* choose? You can't find a buy like *that* every day."

In his formal arguments Baker held to three main and reasonable points:

First, he cited the State Constitution which permitted any individual to represent himself or be represented by an attorney or *agent* before any court. He insisted, with considerable logic, that attorneys and agents weren't the same thing, and therefore an agent did not have to be an attorney. An agent could be plain John Baker, citizen: "If the framers of the [State] Constitution had intended the word 'agent' to mean 'attorney' they would have used one word, not two." Further, his constitutional right "to obtain justice freely, and without being obliged to purchase it," had been abridged. Not only was he being required to purchase it, but he was being asked to pay a high price because "the county court will arbitrarily allow a fee which is substantially in excess of the reasonable value of services."

Baker pointed out that in California and Minnesota, to mention just two states, he would have been able to appear in probate court without an attorney. Apparently this had *not* resulted in chaos or confusion or undue administrative burden for the courts there.

In his concluding oral remarks before the State Supreme Court —"I wasn't too nervous," Baker recalls—he said he had shown evidence of

(a) organization by the State Bar of Wisconsin for monopolistic control of legal fees on a statewide basis contrary to the public interest, and
(b) County Court's condoning and making possible such control.

On November 30, 1965, the seven-man State Supreme Court turned in a unanimous decision, written by Justice Thomas E. Fairchild (he has since been promoted to the Federal Circuit Court of Appeals in Chicago). Justice Fairchild knocked down Baker's arguments this way:

An "agent" could *only* mean an attorney, regardless of how previous State Attorney Generals had interpreted this. As to the fee being excessive, why, said the court, Mr. Baker will have the right to appeal to this court if he thinks the county court permits the lawyer too high a fee. After all, the State Bar minimum fee schedule "rests for its validity upon the collective judgment of the committee or groups that passed upon it as a scale of fees generally fair for the type of services listed." In short, if a bunch of lawyers say it's fair, it must be.

But most importantly, the Supreme Court said that Baker had no right to appear without a lawyer in the matter because as an executor in an estate in which several others were also beneficiaries, "they would not have the benefit of legal analysis of their rights if the executor proceeded without an attorney."

The court admitted that it wasn't a question of always needing expert legal judgment in a routine probate. It may happen

that in a proceeding there may be no difficult legal problems that a lay executor could not successfully handle. . . . Nevertheless the need for protection of beneficiaries in general from practice by unlicensed persons justifies the general rule and its application to this instance.

Just to nail things down properly the court went further: *even if Baker had been the sole heir to his mother's estate, he would be required to hire an attorney.* There was no way out for petitioner John Baker: some Wisconsin attorney had to be hired for $4,800 on this estate.

I talked to John Baker a few months after the Supreme Court verdict. "Oh, I had thought vaguely maybe I ought to take this to the U. S. Supreme Court, but I just felt the cards were stacked against me. Anyway, I had a business to run. I hired another set of lawyers to settle the estate and that cost $2,400, making the total legal bill on an estate in which I had prepared all the forms, a total of $5,300, or $700 more than the original minimum fee schedule.

"I talked to a relative of mine, a lawyer. He said I didn't have a chance from the start. The legal profession, a kind of secret society, had to look out for itself. There was too much at stake here. I didn't really think I was going to win, but once you get started on this kind of thing you have to see it through. It was too naked, too brazen to let it go by without a protest. Well, I made my protest and nothing's really changed, but I think the lawyers were shook up a bit. That's something."

       •   •   •

I was puzzled at how little publicity the case had gotten in the Wisconsin press. There wasn't anything, anywhere, except a single, rather cryptic one-paragraph item in a Madison, Wisconsin, daily after the State court ruled against Baker.

I asked Baker if he hadn't thought of calling in any of the Madison or Milwaukee papers to alert them to the significance of the case. "Never occurred to me," he admitted. "Maybe I should have."

After my long talk with him I went to Chicago to see some of the lawyers on the ABA's Unauthorized Practice of Law Committee, which had also filed a brief against Baker. I asked them about the strange lack of publicity the case had outside of law reviews. "Were we lucky!" one of the UPL lawyers exclaimed. "The whole profession would have gotten a helluva black eye if Baker had called in the papers. Thank God he's a gentleman. Misguided, of course!"

I described the Baker case briefly in October, 1966, in a *Reader's Digest* article, "The Mess in Our Probate Courts," but I was a little bothered that John Gordon Baker was still my exclusive news property. I suppose I felt a little like the foreign correspondent who gets what he thinks is a great beat and cables New York a long story which gets played prominently on page one. The managing editor sends him a congratulatory cable. Two days later he gets another cable: GREAT BEAT. WHY IS IT STILL EXCLUSIVE?

So I set out to make John Baker's story less exclusive. He had fought well with the enemy's weapons, on the enemy's grounds, had written a splendidly lucid and impressively persuasive brief; and now he was out money and a lot of time. The least I could do was help alert the Wisconsin press, which had completely overlooked him and the issue he raised. In late February, 1967, I was in Wisconsin again and sought out Ed Kerstein, the knowledgeable legal and court expert of the *Milwaukee Journal*. He hadn't heard of the case from the paper's Madison bureau but quickly agreed it deserved a feature even eighteen months after the court ruling. He did a long perceptive story about this "landmark decision" on March 1 which pointed out the full dollar significance an adverse decision would have had on Wisconsin lawyers.

Then, feeling a little like an advance man for a departed road show, I went on to Madison. There, I knew, the *Capital-Times* kept a sharp eye out for State Bar activities. In fact Philip S. Habermann, executive director of the Wisconsin State Bar for the past twenty years, once wrote sourly of this daily that it "delights in belaboring the bar, bench and individual lawyers on any occasion."* How could they have missed the Baker story which had its final denouement only a few hundred yards from the *Capital-Times* building in Madison?

Both Miles McMillin, who practiced law until 1945 when he became editorial page director of the paper, and Dave Zweifel, the paper's court and legislative expert, couldn't understand how they missed the Baker case. "Of course, it's not the kind of case the State Bar would send out a PR release on," McMillin said, "but we should have had it." On March 7, 1967, Dave Zweifel made up for the omission with a splendidly biting account, "He Tried to Buck the Probate System."

So, some eighteen months after the Supreme Court decision, John Gordon Baker got the local recognition—and pointed local discussions of the issues involved. As far as I was concerned it wasn't all one-sided. After talking to Ed Kerstein and Dave Zweifel about how the significance of the Baker case had been missed by two of the state's leading dailies, I got an interesting idea which is discussed further in Chapter 16.

---

*Mr. Habermann had a backhanded compliment for me, too. He wrote, late in October, 1966, that my article, "The Mess in Our Probate Courts," was an "even worse attack" on the probate courts than was found in the Norman Dacey book, *How to Avoid Probate.*

11 OUR UNKNOWN HEIRS

More lawyers live on politics than flies on a dead camel.
—Old Tammany Hall saying

Senator Robert F. Kennedy caused a stir in the recent primary campaign when he said during a tour in support of Justice Silverman that there were "documented" cases in which court-appointed guardians had received high fees.

It turned out that most of these stemmed from an article a few years earlier in *Harper's* magazine. Members of the Senator's staff had checked with the author and editors and satisfied themselves that the facts were accurate.
—*The New York Times,* July 5, 1966

The *Harper's* article was mine. I had written "Your Unknown Heirs" in 1961 because a friend's widow said something I didn't really believe, because the whole thing seemed preposterous.

In a way the article became an apology to her for my original skepticism. I am not a *polite* skeptic so I had to undo much more. I spent four months digging all over the country and found situations so acceptedly and slyly corrupt, so scrofulous, that I lost what lingering innocence I may still have had about the basic probity of some lawyers and judges.

Like any article writer, you start by checking what others had written on the subject. There was *nothing* on the subject, in the popular magazines or even law reviews going back to 1900.

There were three possibilities: (1) the whole business was so local it simply never rated national attention; (2) it was cloaked with such silence that no competent writer had ever gotten a whisper; or (3) maybe it just wasn't so.

After my investigation I knew it was not local. In one form or another, variations of the legalized extortion existed all over the United States. Nor was it that secret. The details were generally available to any competent reporter willing to dig into the local probate or surrogate court records. Yet, with a few honorable exceptions, even the local aspects of this permissive pilferage were seldom publicized.

My *Harper's* article, the first *national* survey of the way politically connected lawyers and judges were milking estates quietly, became a much quoted first. I was praised by reform Democratic Clubs in New York, denounced by assorted probate and surrogate judges around the country, and had the mixed pleasure of seeing sizable chunks of the article borrowed, without permission, for an enduring best-seller, *How to Avoid Probate.**

While working on this book I naturally checked to see how things had changed since 1961 in regard to the special guardian and appraiser fees legally taken out of estates. Very little has changed: some minor reforms in New York and Washington State, and nothing more.

In 1965 some 100,000 Americans died leaving behind estates worth at least $60,000 each. The total worth of their estates was nearly $22 billion. Funeral costs for them were $150 million. But the administrative and legal expenses of getting their estates through probate was nearly $800 million, which makes the touted high cost of funerals seem almost reasonable compared to the over five-times-higher cost of preparing the paper and legal work designed for interment in probate court files. Interred alongside, like royal appanages, are the documents that attest to the fact that sanctioned theft had taken place with the approval of the law and the benison of the judge.

·   ·   ·

It started with the death of a friend, Harry. We had moved our families to this suburb about the same time. In the late thirties

---

*Belatedly and somewhat cryptically, author Norman Dacey did acknowledge use of my material in subsequent editions of his book.

and early forties he had been one of a handful of New York labor leaders who had warned of and fought off the attempts of Communists to grab control of some key unions. He helped build his union vigorously, but after his first heart attack he stepped down. Even in partial retirement he was a vigorous organizer of local political movements, a stirring, effective leader. His death was felt measurably by all of us who had worked with him.

Several weeks after the funeral Julia, his widow, was having dinner with us when she said: "Have I got a story for you! . . . What a racket!"

Harry left a modest estate to Julia and their two young sons. A family friend and lawyer who was handling the estate warned her she would be up against a peculiar and slightly expensive problem: a special guardian.

As she explained it to me, the surrogate court had to appoint a special guardian "to make sure the rights of our sons weren't being compromised. Me, they won't trust. They have to bring in some outside lawyer. Then I started hearing stories of how much these courthouse characters can ask for. And you've got to pay them or the estate never gets settled."

Her indignation and vehemence must have brought crinkled skepticism to my face. "Wild, isn't it?" she said. "I didn't believe it, either, first time."

Now her brother-in-law, who knew his way around politics in the county, entered the picture. He said he could save Julia some money here. As he explained it to her, every surrogate kept a patronage list of lawyers he appointed as special guardians. The more influential ones, the men he owed bigger favors, of course got the larger estates and correspondingly larger fees. But to some extent, on these smaller estates the patronage list was controlled by a certain court clerk. Now her brother-in-law had a lawyer friend who was on this list, and although the normal fees for an estate the size of Harry's would be about $500, the lawyer friend, as a favor, would do it for a token $100. But the court clerk had to be paid, too. For $150—cash, please—he would see to it that the lawyer friend would get the special guardianship in the estate. Such Byzantine intrigue for a placid suburban county; such Machiavellian maneuvering to outwit costlier villains!

The clerk was paid and the friendly special guardian came to Julia's home one Saturday afternoon. He called Harry's sons in and said:

"Boys, I know you want to be playing outside, so I won't waste your time. Tell me: when your father made out his will in December, 1965, was he sane?"

"Of course he was," the older boy burst out. "What's the matter with you?"

The special guardian said: "Don't get excited boys. That's all I have to know."

He later phoned two witnesses to the will and filed a brief report in which he concluded that the will was valid. Perhaps two hours of work in all for the $100. But then it had been a big favor. With the $150 to the court clerk, Julia and her sons had paid out, in effect, $125 an hour for "work" that any fairly intelligent legal stenographer could have done—at $3 an hour.

Although my skepticism was apparent, I couldn't believe that Julia had made it all up; she was too sensible. It was *too* wild. The fact that I had never heard of special guardians—and considered myself pretty well informed as to most current rackets and swindles—didn't mean they didn't exist. Inwardly, I assumed that there was *something* but that, in her indignation, Julia was exaggerating. There were probably perfectly valid reasons for the special guardians, and probably there was a lot more work involved for the lawyer who got the appointment than I knew about.

I asked a few lawyer acquaintances. Every one had had some experience with the institution as a result of probating estates for clients. Several gave me specific cases and where to find the court records. Another said, with a bit of legal mockery: "Not only is it a fat racket, it's even a violation of the Canons of Ethics. Look at Canon 12."

I did. The American Bar Association has a long list of thou-shalt-nots for lawyers and for judges, too. Canon 12 of the Judicial Ethics says that when a judge appoints persons to aid him in the administration of justice, "he should not permit his appointments to be controlled by others than himself. He should also avoid nepotism and undue favoritism in his appointments."

The best measure of what I finally uncovered was the two opening paragraphs of the article which appeared in the August, 1961, issue of *Harper's*. (A few months later an authorized condensed version appeared in *Reader's Digest*.)

> In most states of this Union, a man or woman who dies leaving an estate where children inherit may rest uneasy for one reason at least: a big piece of it may go—not to heirs—but to officers appointed by the probate and surrogate courts. Even if the children are involved only indirectly, the estate may have to pay this cut.
>
> This legal system provides political patronage for thousands of the courts' "special guardians" or "appraisers." Unobserved by the public, they are the last earthly mediators between the solvent dead and their heirs. Every year over-tolerant judges, archaic laws, and needy political machines combine to take millions silently out of small and large estates. These persistent pluckings are some of the most widespread, most profitable, and least known evils in our courts.

One of the cases I looked into was that of the Woodward estate. When Long Island millionaire sportsman William Woodward, Jr., was killed accidentally in 1955 he left about $10 million equally divided between his wife and two sons. The exactions from the estate proceeded in this order:

First, New York Surrogate* William T. Collins appointed Harold H. Corbin, a New York criminal lawyer with good connections, to "prove" the will. He did essentially what the special guardian had done with the will of my friend, Harry. For this very minor work Mr. Corbin asked for and got a fee of $2,500— from the estate. It was the lightest of touches.

Then in 1957 the surrogate again appointed Corbin special guardian for the well-protected Woodward boys. And now an-

---

*The name of the court may vary, but the game is the same. It could be probate, county, orphans or even superior court (as in California).

other lawyer was called on. This was Edward V. Loughlin, a former leader of Tammany Hall, who was appointed special guardian for the young distant Woodward cousins who *might* inherit under fairly remote circumstances. Corbin and Loughlin asked the surrogate for fees of $47,500 each. He cut them slightly, to $45,000 each. So the first time around the Woodward estate was out $92,500.

In 1961 when the estate was settled, there naturally had to be a final accounting, calling for the appointment of more special guardians to see that the various children involved had been done right by. Irving Saltzman, special guardian for the young cousins, asked for and got $20,000 for protecting the interests of the remotely potential heirs who actually got nothing from the estate. Edward V. Loughlin, who had quit as Tammany Hall leader in 1947, was still influential enough to rate still another plum of $25,000 for his special guardianship in the accounting proceedings.* He was, presumably, still protecting the interests of the two sons of the dead man. In all, then, some $137,500 had been paid out to lawyers who had not been called upon in the will to probate it or act as executors or even as personal guardians of the children involved. There couldn't have been a remoter, more impersonal—nor a more profitable—relationship.

The two $45,000 special guardian fees in this case deserve particular attention. Each Manhattan surrogate, who is elected for a fourteen-year term, earns $37,500 a year. In these two cases the judges awarded fees considerably larger than their annual salaries and for work that without question did not take a full working year. A full week's work would have been a lot. There is, of course, an art to making it appear as if the special guardian has done a lot of work—on paper, anyway. But since the larger estates are usually handled by banks and trust companies, which are checked constantly by federal and state agencies—and by their own internal

---

*And even fatter fees. In 1960 this great favorite of Manhattan's two surrogate judges was appointed special guardian in three large estates valued at $21,000,000. Loughlin is widely believed by *cognoscenti* to have made $100,-000–$150,000 a year out of special guardian and referee fees.

controls—the idea that a special guardian is also needed to make sure the estate's securities are *really* there seems superfluous. One special guardian who knew this once came into a New York trust company on a Friday at noon. He said to the trust officer, "Let's see these four securities the estate has. If you have these I assume you have all the rest, and besides I want to make the first race at Jamaica." He was in the bank twenty minutes and he asked for and got a special guardian fee of $6,000.

Still, it is hard to get exercised about a dead rich man and the manner in which part of his estate is distributed to political favorites of a judge. Your reaction is probably like mine: I wish I had got part of that $10 million. I wouldn't have said one cross word to any of those special guardians.

But it is not really a private arrangement of no interest to the public. A New York attorney, Joseph S. Iseman, after reading my *Harper's* article, wrote and explained a point I had missed. He felt this spoils system was still tolerated because

such fees are almost always deductible in determining federal and state estate taxes. . . . The fact that these levies are borne in large part by the taxpaying public explains both the lack of complaint from heirs and the bar's apathetic attitude toward this problem.

Under our progressive tax structure, the larger the estate (and, hence, the juicier the fees) the less the patronage burden is borne by the heirs and the more it is borne by the rest of us. A very large estate has virtually no incentive to buck the system. . . .

Admittedly, then, these patronage fees result in Internal Revenue getting less from these estates but, really, who of us can get exercised about *that?* In our society, legal tax avoidance is an art for which practitioners are paid well. Besides, most of the lawyers who are beneficiaries of the surrogate and probate court largesse probably are wise enough to declare their full income, so that in one form or another Internal Revenue—and the country—does get a good part of the patronage fee ultimately. No, the *tax* aspect of the problem wouldn't rouse many of us.

What was far more pertinent—and frightening—to me was the

closed, tight, corrupt system which elected judges and favored attorneys had erected and perpetuated. An enormous, barely visible system of legalized extortionate handouts to one another, or to their sons, relations and henchmen. A system that could only encourage a very cynical attitude about other people's money on the part of judges, lawyers, court personnel, and sometimes even reporters covering the courts. In the Midwest where the appraiser system on estates is widely employed, several newspapermen were the recipients of these patronage appointments. And, of course, presidents of the local bar associations.

When *Newsday,* the vigorous Long Island daily, made a thorough study of the larger special guardian fees awarded in 1965–66 in Nassau and Suffolk Counties, it found that Francis B. Froehlich, president of the Nassau Bar Association, had received $22,-500 in such fees; Charles R. Carroll, his predecessor, had gotten $12,000; and H. Alan Zwissler, president of the Suffolk Bar Association, received $2,000.

The remarkably pervasive influence of the system is pretty well illustrated in the case of a respected New York attorney, O. John Rogge. In 1948 Rogge, then a vigorous forty-five-year-old firebrand who had represented many small unions, became the American Labor Party candidate for surrogate in Manhattan. The ALP was a left-leaning third party nurtured by nascent memories of the Popular Front days of the thirties. No one gave Rogge a chance, but he campaigned hard. He called the surrogate's court a "political pork barrel" and promised, if elected, to appoint special guardians only from a nonpolitical panel of lawyers. He told how the surrogate's court of Manhattan, handling more than $700 million dollars' worth of estates every year, had become the richest single source of patronage in the city. (In 1965 it was $941 million.) He repeated the *bon mot* of Mayor La Guardia, who earlier had called the court "the world's most expensive undertaking establishment." So expensive, in fact, that although La Guardia, New York's splenetic reform mayor, starved Tammany of all political patronage, the Democratic organization and its clubhouse lawyers were able to survive very well just on the surrogate patronage.

Rogge did more. He had aides check on the 749 special guardians the surrogates had appointed in 1947. "Some 258 of these," he told audiences around the city, "went to 19 men and women, most of whom are identified with either the Democratic or Republican machines." He issued lists of the appointees. He told how they had to kick back part of their fees to their party district leaders and to Tammany itself.

Like that other third-party candidate running in 1948, Henry A. Wallace, John Rogge didn't make it, either. But he was never more effective than in defeat: his party took enough votes out of the Democratic column to elect for the first time a Republican surrogate, George Frankenthaler, who squeaked in by 1,200 votes.

When I was researching my 1961 magazine article, I thought it might be useful to call Rogge, who seemed to have gathered quite a bit of material in his vigorous 1948 campaign for surrogate. I discovered a new John Rogge.

"Hell, man, what's wrong with special guardianships? I got a few myself from Frankenthaler, you know. Including a real fat one. Maybe he was grateful my running helped elect him. The way I look on these specials now is: here's a lot of money up for grabs. A lot of people who don't deserve it—the heirs—are going to get it. So I have no hesitation in asking a high special guardianship fee. Sure, it's a political reward. What's wrong with that?"

Since he had been so extraordinarily frank I called on Rogge again, in 1967. He was now sixty-four and a partner in the very potent law firm of Congressman Emanuel Celler, chairman of the House Judiciary Committee. This post makes Celler far and away one of the most powerful lawyers in the country.

I told Rogge what I was doing and asked if he had any different views on the surrogate court patronage system. He laughed. "Well, I've become older and mellower. Maybe I wasn't too critical of the special guardianships the last time we spoke. But that Silverman-Klein campaign for surrogate in 1966 made me do some thinking. You were right in 1961 and I was right in 1948. The present system stinks. We got to take the patronage out of it. Maybe that Canadian system you mentioned is the right idea. I'd like to see us try it."

In my *Harper's–Reader's Digest* articles I had advocated a trial run of the system used in Canada to avoid the probate court patronage. There, in each province a full-time appointed public official acts as official guardian in behalf of minors mentioned in wills. He gets fixed and very nominal fees for his work.

My suggestion was picked up by Senator Kennedy during the 1966 race for the New York surrogate. After his choice, Justice Samuel J. Silverman, had been elected, Senator Kennedy testified before the New York State Legislature's Committee on Court Reorganization on November 29, 1966. He called for the abolition of the special guardian system and its replacement by a corps of salaried public guardians, estimating that 60 of them could handle all the cases in the state at a cost of about $1 million, far less than the fees now paid to the court-appointed special guardians. In 1965 all 63 surrogates in New York State handled 30,615 estates with a gross value of $3.7 billion. Of this the six New York City surrogates—two for Manhattan and one each for the other counties making up the city—handled nearly 13,000 estates with a gross value of almost $2 billion. The best estimate is that in New York City special guardians get fees of nearly $3 million a year. *The New York Times* account of Kennedy's testimony went, in part:

> The committee heard him in silence and asked no questions, but after the Senator left, members of the committee, and some surrogates called as witnesses, denounced him for repeating "hearsay" statements impugning the system. . . .
>
> Surrogate Samuel S. diFalco of Manhattan . . . waving his hands at the portraits of former surrogates adorning the walls . . . declared: "These surrogates must be turning in their graves at the testimony of so-called witnesses who said something is wrong with the surrogate's court. There's nothing wrong with the surrogate's court."

Senator Kennedy was also denounced by State Senator John J. Hughes of Syracuse, who was particularly sensitive. Hughes, the former Onondaga County Republican leader, was and still is a potent determinant in that county of who gets the safe Republican nominations for judgeships, including the local surrogate. In 1964, Hughes received a fine plum from Onondaga Surrogate Laurence B. Wood. Hughes was appointed special guardian for fifteen infants who might eventually take a part of the $5 million Ernest L. White estate. In July 1968 Surrogate Wood allowed Hughes a fee of $14,101.

Others denouncing the Kennedy proposal to take the patronage out of special guardianships included every bar association in the state. They presented, according to *The New York Times*, "a united front against the Kennedy proposal for the creation of a State Office of Public Guardians."

Why should the bar be against so sensible a proposal? I could understand individual lawyers being fearful of standing up against exactions on estates they were handling. I recall a Boston attorney with a large probate practice explaining what would happen: "The judge would look down his nose at me and say, 'What's wrong with the fee?' and I'd be dead. I might as well get out of law, because I'd be through here."

I asked a friend of mine, a former New York court administrator, for an explanation of the bar's solid stance against this reform. He smiled at my naïveté:

"Say you have this public guardian on estates. That means you have a third party, probably a very nosy one, in the estate. If the estate lawyer is pulling some fast dodges, a little juggling, maybe one or two *slightly* unethical gimmicks, why, there's now a public official who can blow the whistle. Lawyers look ahead. Here's a public official, a lawyer, and what can he be thinking about? The same thing most lawyers dream of: becoming a judge. Now how can he get a judgeship? Just by showing what a diligent, upright official he is in checking out these estates. A man like that could be real dangerous."

I got another insight into the relationship of the bar and the present special guardian system from former Manhattan Surrogate George Frankenthaler who served from 1948 to 1956. (He died in May, 1968).

"There's a piece in the system even for the lawyer who isn't a favorite of the surrogate. A lawyer handling an estate or one who knows an estate is due in the surrogate's court goes to the judge and says: 'Here's your chance to appoint Bill Smith. It's a nice sized estate and he's on your list.' Then the lawyer goes to Bill Smith and says: 'Hey, Bill, I just got you appointed. How about a piece?'

"Another dodge is lawyers playing one surrogate against another. A lawyer would come to me: 'Judge, I've got a good case for you.' He means, of course, that there'd be a nice fee for one of the men on my list. But you've got to listen with a special ear for these casual talks. What he's saying on the ultra-high frequency you get used to in the surrogate's court, is that he could just as easily take this estate and bring it into the court so that the *other* surrogate gets it next month. Having gotten over that unvoiced message he then asks: 'How about appointing so-and-so next month when I bring this estate in?' Well, I know a lot of surrogates went along with those cute tricks. I didn't.

"The two surrogates in Manhattan take turns each month on certain incoming matters. A lot of lawyers would deliberately avoid serving a citation the month I'd be sitting 'in chambers.' They knew I was tight on special fees and they weren't interested in keeping costs down. They had a deal with someone on the other surrogate's patronage list—a form of fee-splitting, really— and the more the surrogate was going to permit the special guardian to get, the more this lawyer handling the estate would get. Come to think of it, it was pretty crooked.

"Everyone knew the surrogates had patronage lists. But how did you get on them? At Christmas lots of expensive gifts came in. I mean *expensive*. I'd return all of them more than five dollars in value. Some of the court clerks probably thought I was crazy, because Christmas week at surrogate's court was spectacular. Most of the larger firms handling estates would give each clerk and employe here fifty dollars so that most of the employes doubled their salaries. Others could have opened liquor stores with the cases they got. We finally stopped this but it wasn't easy.

"There were other things you saw but couldn't do much about.

A special guardian wants a particularly fat fee out of an estate. He goes to the executor or attorney for the estate and holds him up. How? He just says, look, I want so much. If I don't get it I'm going to tie up this estate in objections for the next five years. And he could. Any lawyer could find *some* reason why there should be a delay in the interests of the children he's supposed to be 'protecting.' Some of the surrogates went along with this blackmail, I'm sorry to say. When the held-up lawyers would come to me with such complaints—always in a whisper—I'd say, 'All right, will you back it up if I talk to the Appellate Division?' and the man would shrink back and say, 'For God's sake don't get me involved. I got a lot of estates coming into surrogate's court.' What could you do? There's no avoiding it: a warped surrogate could always find justifications for outsize special guardian fees."

I asked former Surrogate Frankenthaler a question that surely must have bothered many reporters and editorial writers during the great 1966 surrogate battle in New York when Senator Kennedy interceded and helped win the election for Judge Silverman. Yet it was never asked publicly:

In New York State the surrogate judges are able to hand out patronage running to several millions of dollars every year. Is it reasonable to suppose that *none* of it ever comes back to them, personally; that sooner or later some of them don't wonder why they, too, shouldn't be beneficiaries of the unintended largesse of some dead man?

Frankenthaler nodded. "Oh there *are* stories you hear of surrogates getting jewelry, trips to Europe and that kind of thing as a kickback."

More recently I put the same question to a man who has spent many years in the New York State courts as an administrative official. His answer was judiciously roundabout but clear: "I don't think it unlikely that a surrogate who has power to hand out millions in patronage won't get some of it back one way or another."

All this is only hearsay, as the lawyers put it, hardly evidence. *But it is what those intimately connected with the operation of our probate courts believe to be true.* "Intelligence," said Santayana, "is the power of seeing things as they are."

In the fall of 1967 I had lunch with a veteran aide of the surrogate's court about what reforms Surrogate Silverman had been able to introduce. I already knew that the state legislature, as a result of the many exposés during the 1966 surrogate campaign, had modified the law somewhat so that special guardians were no longer called for in some cases. But since these involved mostly minor $50 and $75 fee cases, no one was too sorry to see them eliminated.

"Well, he's sticking to his campaign promise to publish the names of his special guardian appointees every week in the *New York Law Journal.* DiFalco still doesn't, of course," the court aide said. "And Silverman is keeping the special fees down, way down. Which means that the banks and trust companies love him and try to funnel their estate cases his way. The lawyers with estates who want a cooperative 'friend' designated as special guardian take their cases to Surrogate diFalco, who's still operating on the old gold standard. He just gave another big special guardianship in a $14 million estate to his former law partner, Arthur Field, who has the judge's son, Anthony, in his office, too. Young Anthony is doing real well for a lawyer recently admitted to practice who didn't go to any of the Ivy League law schools."

My luncheon companion, a nonlawyer, went on: "This is a lawyer's town, and if you're well connected you're going to live high even if you weren't on law review. But nine tenths of the work here in surrogate's isn't *law* work; it's routine paperwork and bookkeeping. Actually, the chief clerk here can handle most of what the surrogates are supposed to sign. Maybe that's why there has to be so much gravy around this court: if there wasn't, nobody in his right mind would come near it. Nearly all of it is a big goddam bore and sometimes I look at Surrogate Silverman on the bench and he's probably thinking: why did I ever let Bobby talk me into running for *this?* I bet he'd love to get back to Supreme Court. Except for being able to hand out juicy plums the surrogate's job is just a glorified bookkeeper's job."

•   •   •

Public scandals about New York surrogates are rare. In 1899 an investigating commission found that Surrogate Cohalan appointed a lot of his relatives to guardianships. The whole family was in a great position for mutually supporting nepotism. Of seven brothers, two were State Supreme Court justices and one a surrogate. Several of the others were lawyers.

In recent years only one New York State surrogate has been officially criticized publicly by the Appellate Division, which supervises the conduct of surrogates as well as State Supreme Court judges. In 1964 Surrogate Lott H. Wells of St. Lawrence County in upstate New York was criticized officially for displaying "officious conduct" and "singular unawareness of the judicial function" and "the rights of parties in our system of litigations." The case didn't involve special guardian fees but an estate in which his wife had an interest.

In other states, too, there is a remarkable dearth of instances of criminal conduct by a probate judge. One of the very few known took place in Houston, Texas, where forty-five-year-old Judge Clem McClelland was the first full-time probate judge of Harris County.

McClelland's downfall in 1962 came primarily because he was too businesslike. Other probate judges might be deliberately casual in their patronage fees to members of their family or relatives or friendly lawyers trusting that in time bread cast on the waters would come back at least enriched, if not wondrously converted to cake.

McClelland preferred not to trust to goodwill, faith in one's fellowman and human gratitude. Still, certain amenities had to be followed, so he used the Tierra Grande Corporation. The hundreds of friends and others who got appraiser appointments in McClelland's court were told exactly how much stock to buy in Tierra Grande. As his front, McClelland had a friendly lawyer, J. Bryson Martin, holding the presidency of Tierra Grande, an "investment corporation."

Not only appraiser fees but even outsize fees awarded to lawyers acting as administrators of estates that came before McClelland's court had to be invested in Tierra Grande. For example, lawyer Richard H. Putney, who was given a $10,000 legal fee in the $160,000 Clara L. Currie estate, was told by the judge to "put my half in Tierra Grande." And money in Tierra Grande, a prosecutor put it later, "was the same as putting money in McClelland's pocket." In the same Currie estate, McClelland ordered attorney Putney to "lend" another "friendly" corporation $40,000 without interest or security.

To get cash for these strange loans and legal fees, McClelland ordered the Currie estate to sell 1,900 shares of Texaco stock on the ground that the blue chip was "speculative."

McClelland got so bold at one point that he ordered attorney fees in various estate matters paid to Jerry S. O'Brien. The only trouble was that O'Brien wasn't a lawyer but simply an accommodating insurance friend. Since he wasn't a lawyer McClelland saw no reason why O'Brien should get a 50–50 split. On one $3,200 "legal" fee to O'Brien, he demanded and got $2,800 back the very next day.

After much backing and filling in the Texas courts, McClelland was convicted of stealing $2,500 from another estate in his court. He was given a ten-year sentence which he began serving in 1965. His fellow accomplice, lawyer Martin, got a four-year term —for bribing McClelland. But under Texas' curiously lax disbarment procedures McClelland wasn't disbarred until after he was in prison for nearly two years.

On the surface it would seem that if there has been only one major and criminal involvement of a probate court judge in recent years—out of the 3,000 or so probate judges in the country— why, they're probably as clean-living a bunch as you'd find in the U.S. judiciary. Not necessarily. The opportunities to do well on the probate bench by enriching relatives and political friends are so extensive that there isn't too much temptation to be *needlessly* and blatantly crooked.

There are lots of questionable appointments of special guardians that have, thus far, not engendered any judicial wrist-slapping. For example:

Anthony diFalco, the young lawyer-son of the Manhattan surrogate, is a particular favorite of the city's surrogates. He has received lucrative appointments as special guardian from former Surrogate Cox in a $5 million estate. That is, Cox vehemently insisted *he* had appointed his colleague's son. Actually, Surrogate diFalco did handle some aspects of the estate in court.* DiFalco has also received specials from Bronx Surrogate McGrath of the Bronx. Reciprocity is only fair, and Surrogate McGrath's son, Kevin, gets special guardian appointments from Surrogate diFalco. In Brooklyn, lawyer Myron Beldock is frequently favored with special guardianships by Surrogate Edward S. Silver, as well as by similar fees in Manhattan. Lawyer Beldock is the son of George J. Beldock, presiding justice of the Appellate Division, which supervises the operation of the Brooklyn Surrogate Court.

In 1966, the *New York Post,* in a splendid piece of investigative reporting, uncovered the fact that at least eight lawyer-sons of sitting State Supreme Court Justices have received sizable special guardianship fees. In the first eight months of 1967 not only were the lawyer-sons of Supreme Court Justices favored, but so was the wife of one justice, a brother-in-law of another and two brothers of a third.† There was a greater measure of discretion in nearby Nassau County. There Surrogate John D. Bennett gave $12,500 in special guardian fees to Robert Scholly, an attorney with whom Bennett's son works as an associate.

"Things aren't good but they used to be a whole lot worse,"

---

*Another probate judge-father was more direct and even more generous to his lawyer-son. On December 14, 1960, Boston Probate Judge John V. Mahoney appointed his son, George, to a $10,000-a-year trusteeship of a multi-million-dollar estate in the Judge's court. In effect, a generous annuity for his son that would last a lifetime. But the stink was too great, and George had to resign his "trusteeship."

† It took a Massachusetts probate judge, John V. Phelan, to be kind to his *daughter-in-law-to-be*. While she was still attorney Shirley Lipinski and three months before marriage to his son, Robert, the judge appointed Shirley administrator of a $300,000 estate. She got a nice $6,000 wedding present for her work—from the estate, in 1962.

says one active sixty-five-year-old New York attorney who's practiced forty-three years. "We used to have a lady lawyer around who got a lot of these specials because her daddy was ranking judge. Only trouble is she was drunk all the time, and she could never get around to do what little paperwork there was. So if you got her you had to figure on two fees: the special fee and the private hospital fee for drying her out. And those are damned expensive little places."

Besides such good favors to judges' children and lawyers' relatives there are also fat fees to the former law partners of judges. When Surrogate diFalco chose a special guardian to "protect" the interests of two children of John J. Schubert, of the theatrical family, he turned to his former law partner, Arthur N. Field, who is now in a law firm with which the surrogate's son, Anthony, is associated. Lawyer Field asked for and got a fee of $15,000 even though the two children received only $12,000 each. In Suffolk County, New York, Surrogate Pierson Hildreth gave his former law partner, LeRoy Van Nostrand, Jr., a neat $8,000 special guardian fee.

When I did my original investigation in 1960, Surrogate Joseph A. Cox of Manhattan was aggrieved at my imputation that he and his fellow Surrogate diFalco were allowing outsize fees in special guardianship cases. "You think we're high here? Why, we're *reasonable*. You want to see high fees, go to Brooklyn. They're five times higher."

From 1955 to 1964, Maximillian Moss was Brooklyn's surrogate, and his reign is still regarded by its beneficiary lawyers with the awed benevolence museum curators reserve for the Medicis. "Tzimmes every week," is the way one Brooklyn special guardian recalls the elysian past. (*Tzimmes* is a rich Jewish dessert of carrots, raisins, fruit and other splendidly caloric ingredients.)

Moss, a gregarious Brooklyn lawyer, was raised in Tennessee. He went to night law school and became managing clerk of a prestigious Brooklyn law firm, Cullen & Dykman. It handled the large estates of the wealthy families who lived in the brownstones of Brooklyn Heights overlooking New York's lower bay. In his way, Moss became a beloved Mr. Brooklyn, helping raise funds for every charity in the borough from the Boy Scouts to the Salvation Army, and in time he became founder and president of the Jewish Community Council, which united the many Jewish charitable and community groups of the borough. It also served to reinforce Moss' already great political power as surrogate. He had, in effect, created a social-legal counterpart of that mathematical curiosity, the Klein bottle, whose spout curves back into its mouth, so that it became a one-sided surface which is closed and has no boundary.

Moss, as community and fund-raising leader, had a large force of willing lawyer-aides who would be paid for their charitable efforts by being awarded generous special guardianships. These, in turn, would be extracted quite legally from the estates of the well-to-do families of the borough. (Brooklyn, with 750,000 Jews, has the largest Jewish population of any U.S. county.) These same wealthy families would be solicited for the charities Max Moss helped raise money for. So even if the rich dead man provided in his will for these charities he was, unknowingly, also making a provision for the favored lawyers helping Surrogate Moss. Of course, the largest special guardian fees went to those lawyers whose political instincts were even stronger than their charitable ones. For a politician, charity begins at home base—the clubhouse.

Moss was succeeded as president of the Jewish Community Council by Abe (Bunny) Lindenbaum, an old friend of his who was a wealthy real estate attorney. Lindenbaum, a short, friendly 240-pounder, was clearly Moss' favorite special guardian, and one lawyer who knew both men recalls the gossip of the period:

"Every morning Abe would go to the courthouse to get his specials for the day. He couldn't have made less than $100,000 a year in specials alone. In Manhattan Eddie Loughlin was it, and here we had Bunny Lindenbaum. Every Brooklyn lawyer who was on the 'clubhouse' list [Democratic Clubs, of course] used to dream that maybe Abe would drop dead and he'd become Moss' favorite. I used to get lousy $100 special guardianships twice a year, and once when I raised a kick they threw a 'big' $750 one my way. Abe wouldn't even touch any that low.

"The way it worked in Brooklyn was after you got the appointment you talked to the clerk of the court. Often he would tell you how much to ask for. And he'd know to within a buck. Because the attorney fees in the estate wouldn't be approved until the special guardian's fee was."

I asked this Brooklyn lawyer, who had been active in clubhouse politics for more than thirty years, the question I had asked others. He was firm: "No surrogate is going to allow special guardians to make all that money and not get *some* of it. Be *reasonable*."

Lindenbaum had a little trouble in 1961. He ran a fund-raising luncheon for Mayor Wagner and got $25,000 from a group of builders and real estate men. The only problem was that Lindenbaum was then a member of the City Planning Commission, which had to approve zoning changes. (Properly rezoned, a piece of property worth, say, $30,000 could easily become worth $150,-000.) There was an investigation by the City's Board of Ethics which said that while Lindenbaum's activities were not illegal, they should be made illegal by legislation. After that Lindenbaum's plums from Moss fell off somewhat. So that in 1962–63, for example, his fees from special guardianships and referee appointments amounted to only $65,000. He is still getting these patronage appointments from Brooklyn Surrogate Silver, the borough's former district attorney.

A younger Brooklyn attorney who is currently in power in the Democratic County Committee—he does much of its legal work in primary elections—talked freely recently about special guardianships and other connected matters:

"I've been working hard for a long time for Stanley Steingut [Brooklyn's hereditary Democratic leader], so it's only right I get some specials. They used to be little stinkers, $75 or $100, but now I'm getting some dillies. I just got one on a $140,000 trust where I'm doing the guardianship on the accounting and my fee is going to be $5,000. If I keep my mouth shut and keep on having a strong back and stay useful I might become county leader someday. Well, who's gonna pay for my time in politics? What's wrong with my getting specials?"

The trust work he referred to is a source of special guardianship patronage that doesn't come out of surrogate's but from the State Supreme Court. The Supreme Court has jurisdiction over the so-called inter-vivos, or "living trusts"—the kind Norman Dacey advocated in *How to Avoid Probate*. In a living trust the donor can effectively give away his property during his lifetime although he retains control over it. Here, too, if there are minor or incompetent heirs involved, the Supreme Court will appoint special guardians to protect their interests by checking out the periodic accountings of the trust's paid holders, usually banks or trust companies. There are about 100,000 of these trusts in New York State alone, and their value runs well into the billions. Since they need occasional accountings—and guardians—they are a perennial source of patronage. Every now and then lawyers and their legislative friends try to get the law changed so that these trusts have to have more frequent accountings and naturally more frequent special guardians. So far the banks and trust companies have managed to defeat these efforts but as one trust company vice-president explained:

"It's getting harder. The lawyers talk darkly about 'we ought to know what's going on in these big trusts'; and privately, of course, they figure that by requiring an accounting, say, every eight years, there would be special guardianships in that estate, say, at least seven or eight times during the life of a living trust, which can go on only for a limited span: the lifetimes of the trust's beneficiaries plus twenty-one years." (Only trusts for colleges and hospitals can run forever.)

"The guardian's job is what he wants to make it. On a $100,000 estate or even a trust, he just doesn't have a day's work even if he counts the securities in the vault five times over."

One Manhattan lawyer who got some notoriety as a result of his special guardian appointment in the accounting of a trust was former Mayor Robert F. Wagner. On January 14, 1966—two weeks after he became New York's ex-mayor—he was named special guardian of two trust funds valued at $5,500,000. The funds had been set up in 1926 by two sisters, and the current beneficiaries are their sons and the children of the sons. Neither of the families are in New York, but since the trust is managed by the Manufacturers Hanover Bank in New York, it fell to New York State Supreme Court Judge Abraham Geller to appoint the outgoing mayor for "a nice going-away present," as one slightly envious New York lawyer put it.

Such departure gifts—so much more practical than luggage or gold watches or desk sets—are almost a tradition in the East for outgoing mayors and governors who are also lawyers. Not long ago the outgoing mayor of Buffalo got a $25,000 fee for his "work" as special guardian in a large estate. When he was about to leave office at the end of 1960, Governor Foster Furcolo of Massachusetts was given a fine departure present as an appraiser in a $600,000 estate. In fact, he was given his patronage present six days before he left the job—while he was still governor.

Ordinarily appointments in trust cases almost never make the newspapers, but in Mayor Wagner's case some envious enemy tipped off a reporter for the *New York Post* and the next day, May 7, 1966, *The New York Times* had it, too: WAGNER IS NAMED GUARDIAN OF 11. Wagner had the misfortune to come up against the opposition of three of the mothers of the children involved— the wives of the sons of one of the founders of the trust, Mrs. Blanche S. Benjamin. Through their lawyers, the wives protested the mayor's appointment on the ground they could do the job themselves and thus save the trust a lot of money.

This called for a judicial decision in the New York State Supreme Court, and it fell to the lot of Justice William C. Hecht, Jr., who is also charged with the task of checking on fees to lawyers who act as referees in incompetency cases.* Justice Hecht said that he was confronted here with the question, "Whether the estates should be saved the expense of a guardian who is a stranger to the infants, or whether there is an adversity of interests be-

*See Chapter 13.

tween the respective mothers and their children which would make it desirable to retain the guardian." Justice Hecht ruled that the trusts must be scrutinized by an outsider—the former mayor.

The three mothers accepted defeat but not Jonathan S. Benjamin, a thirty-six-year-old sheep rancher in Cheshire, Oregon, who is the father of three of the eleven infants Wagner was appointed to "protect." He and his wife, Joyce, are the parents of George, twelve, Emelia, nine, and Elizabeth, two and a half. (Emelia is named after her aunt, one of the founders of the trust. Jonathan's mother, Mrs. Blanche S. Benjamin, was her sister.) Jonathan Benjamin's two brothers, Edward and William, are New Orleans lawyers. Jonathan wanted to make a test case out of it—"let's carry it to the U. S. Supreme Court"—but his brothers wouldn't go along.

Jonathan Benjamin, who raises sheep for a living and pursues lost causes as a hobby, wrote me:

"It's a ridiculous outrage. Mayor Wagner hasn't even seen fit to write his three wards in my house. Some guardian. My son, George, is now determined to become a lawyer—and heaven help Wagner, for the boy is feeling vindictive and rightly considers his rights under the Constitution denied. Vengeance is a lousy motive and I am seeking to bring about his understanding. Very difficult."

The publicity on the matter was embarrassing to Wagner, and there is reason to believe that a compromise fee was agreed on to avoid any further litigation. Wagner asked for and got a fee of $15,500. Ordinarily he could have gotten $25,000 on a trust this size, so perhaps it does pay to raise a fuss. One year later, on May 21, 1967, the former mayor appeared before the state's Constitutional Convention and urged it to write a strict code of ethics for legislators and state officials. This, he said, "would increase the confidence of the people in our government" and "act as a beacon light for public officers in their most needful moments." But he didn't say anything about the "needful moments" of ex-mayors sent out into the world without office and only a $15,500 farewell present extracted by wholly legal means from eleven children he didn't know and would never meet—unless George Benjamin is still vengeful when he becomes a lawyer, possibly twelve years hence.

New York State doesn't have a monopoly on special guardian rackets. They can be found in many other states, including Massachusetts, New Jersey, Florida, Rhode Island, Illinois, Wisconsin and Connecticut. In some states, such as New Jersey, Massachusetts and Florida, the special guardian bite comes on top of another gouger of estates known as an appraiser. But in some forty-two states the appraiser is frequently the preferred method of handing out patronage on estates.

California's experience is instructive on how hardy and durable the appraiser is even after repeated exposés. Houston I. Flournoy, a thirty-seven-year-old former Republican state assemblyman and college professor, ran for state controller of California on a platform that stressed reform of the state's inheritance tax appraiser racket. The state has 154 appraisers, appointed by the controller. These appointments enable the controller to build an impressive political machine, since the appraisers, who receive up to one percent of the estate's value, can gross up to $75,000 a year out of part-time work. In all, California appraisers make about $4 million a year. In effect, some appraisers make more by their very part-time work than the governor makes for his full-time, arduous year, for which he is paid $40,000.

Under Flournoy's proposal the state would save at least $1.6 million a year and the heirs to the appraised estates at least $2.7 million.

What does the appraiser do? A veteran California Superior Court judge who has handled many estates in his court filled me in:

In most cases it's just a matter of sitting down to check the value of the estate's stocks and bonds in the *Wall Street Journal*. Some of them don't even do that but just approve the appraisals already made by the bank or trust company handling the estate. But if they have a real problem—say, unimproved land—they're allowed to bring in a professional appraiser on a per diem basis. To make things sweeter, appraisers can also get a nice little allowance for their "clerical" help. All this, of course, comes out of the estates being "appraised." The whole appraisal business makes no sense here—except as patronage.

This was the system that Controller Flournoy pledged himself to abolish. Bills introduced into the state Legislature in 1967, soon after he took office to reform the inheritance tax appraiser system, passed the Assembly but not the Senate. In September, 1967, I asked Flournoy why. He wrote:

> I can only speculate. . . . The opposition was primarily from the Democrats on the Governmental Efficiency Committee, and these are fundamentally the senior members of the State Senate. I suspect that some of them find no fault with a political patronage system. I think the California Bar Association, which opposed me strenuously in the State Senate, also had an impact upon some of them as well.

The bar's opposition didn't surprise me. Elsewhere bar associations have come out strongly for the retention of the appraiser system, leading some unkind critics to suggest that perhaps attorneys for the estate might in some fashion *share* in the appraiser's fee on that estate. But most California lawyers I talked to were in favor of the appraiser system, simply because they would rather deal with a man who is out to make his fee as quickly and simply as possible rather than have to deal with a civil servant who might give them a hard time.

In Jacksonville, Florida, a leading attorney, who is furious at the whole appraisal racket provided some details:

"We should abolish appraisals in estates altogether. They are useless except as patronage for county judges here. They set the fees ridiculously high to reward their friends. The tax collector pays no attention to these appraisals. He makes his own appraisals. And the executor of the estate is perfectly able to find out what things are worth.

"Here's an estate my office handled recently. There was $49,500 of real estate and furniture and jewelry and a car for a total of $53,000. Ordinarily that would call for a modest fee of $100 for the appraiser. Well, no one's going to raise a fuss about *that*. But there were two other items in the estate: a bank account of $18,-000 and some 15,000 shares of IBM stock, worth then about $6 million. Now the money didn't require appraisal. And the stock is appraised for everyone, every day in the newspaper stock market tables. But the appraiser comes along and demands $6,238 for the hour's work as 'appraiser.' They say that is only one tenth of one percent of the 'value of the estate.' But actually it is 12 percent of the property actually appraised. The county judge saw nothing wrong with the fee asked by his friend."

Since the patronage appraisers are anxious to get as big a fee as possible, they are naturally tempted to view an estate through the rosiest of glasses. Elias A. Wright, a Seattle, Washington, attorney, recalls one appraiser who "insisted on appraising the property for about three times what it was worth, saying they were paid commissions regulated by the amount of the appraisal."

Next door, in Oregon, the state saw the ultimate in togetherness when District Judge Edwin L. Jenkins of Hillsboro found the easiest way to handle probate patronage was just to keep it in the family: in estates that came before him, he appointed his wife as appraiser, and even as administratrix of estates he felt required such services. But he went too far and in November, 1966, he resigned after the Oregon Supreme Court found him guilty of improper conduct as a judge. Partly as a result of the disclosures in his case, the state finally got around to abolishing the whole appraiser system for estates.

In Wisconsin, after considerable newspaper pressure, the appraiser law was changed to eliminate listed stocks and bonds from the items the appraiser included in estimating his fee.

In December, 1962, a mysterious Leslie F. Martin of Mason, Ohio, made an interesting discovery in the court news of the nearby newspaper, the Lebanon *Western Star,* and wrote about his find to the editor. His letter went, in part:

, . . in reading the Court News of the past two years I have noticed one name recurring week after week as appraiser in every single estate. That name is Scott Ray, Jr. I further find, after inquiry, that he is a brother of Probate Judge Ray, who appoints the appraisers. Now that appraisal fee must amount to quite some little amount.

Surely this is contrary to ethical practices, and I wonder why the Warren County Bar Association condones such out and out flagrant abuse of patronage.

The *Western Star* ran Mr. Martin's letter, and Judge Robert G. Ray of the county probate court reacted vigorously. He filed a suit for libel against the newspaper and also removed all the probate court legal ads from the *Western Star*.

In the summer of 1966 Fred E. Jones, attorney for the newspaper, wrote me to explain why the libel case hadn't come to trial:

Quite frankly, the Probate Judge has shown no disposition to push the matter to a conclusion, and I suspect his lack of interest is attributable to a suspicion that he will not prevail. . . . The suit has received no publicity since it was filed. The Judge's brother is still serving as an appraiser with regularity, particularly if the size of the estate is substantial. . . . The Warren County Bar Association has never taken any action in the matter. This is a small Bar, and most of the lawyers are reluctant to become involved.

They didn't have to, because the public got involved. In November, 1966, Judge Ray was defeated for reelection as probate judge. His patronage handouts to his brother were generally believed to be the main reason. Like Junius, the identity of letter-writer Leslie F. Martin has never been ascertained, but he surely wrote an interesting letter.

Fortunately, there are some probate judges opposed to the appraiser and other estate exactions. In northern Kentucky, James A. Dressman, Jr., was elected county court judge in 1961 on a platform of reforming the appraiser system there. Since he had probate court jurisdiction, too, Judge Dressman was able to do something. First, he found that the traditional one tenth of one percent appraiser fee went to each of three appointed appraisers quite illegally. The state code called only for $1.50 a day to each appraiser. As soon as Judge Dressman enforced this pay scale, the desire to appoint friends as appraisers ceased in his county. John A. Kohrman, a Covington, Kentucky, attorney, has led a long fight in his state and in the ABA itself to eliminate the appraiserships completely.

Not all probate judges intent on eliminating the needless appraiser fee system have found public support, let alone bar approval. Joseph W. Knott, an attorney of Stratford, Connecticut, was elected probate judge for a four-year term in 1958. In Connecticut the state statutes call for the probate judge to appoint two or more disinterested people to act as appraiser. The statute doesn't set forth any qualifications, nor does it establish any fees. But through practice the fee has become one tenth of one percent of the gross estate. Joseph Knott knew that a former president of the Connecticut Bar Association, Charles M. Lyman, had called the appraiser system "nothing but a legalized racket." Perhaps he could eliminate it in his court. He got an idea: "After a time it became apparent to me that it was unfair to ask a widow with a small estate to pay the $25 or $50 to these appraisers."

He started on a trial basis a system of having appraisals made, *without fee,* by the widow's insurance broker or real estate agent or even next-door neighbor. The trial was successful, and he extended it to all estates coming into his court.

This reform proved a tremendous success. The heirs appreciated the opportunity to save appraisal fees. . . . A few attorneys and trust officers resented the reform, as it removed the opportunity they had long enjoyed of doing favors for friends, but the vast majority . . . liked it. . . . The plan was not regarded with favor by probate judges in districts near Stratford because it tended to pinpoint the continued abuses prevalent in their courts and, I am sure, caused them some embarrassment explaining to heirs why court-appointed appraisers had to be employed in their courts.

After four years in office, I did not receive the endorsement of my party [Republican] for reelection, ran as an Independent and lost. My successor in office immediately discontinued the reform, restored the old plan, and in November, 1966, was reelected for a second four year term.

Understandably, Joe Knott is a little bitter. In seeking a moral for his experiment in honesty and the elimination of patronage he feels that "the public is just as much to blame as the probate judges and politicians. Their indifference to the abuses heaped on them would almost seem to justify a continuation of the same abuses."

But Joe Knott's example hasn't been in vain. At present at least two other Connecticut probate judges are doing away with paid appraisers. Judge Stephen Sweet, a Republican, does it in Middletown, and a Democrat, Judge James Kinsella, does it in Hartford.

Another vigorous battler against Connecticut's appraiser racket has been Howard T. Sackett, II, of Fairfield. Sackett, a World War II bomber navigator, went to University of Virginia Law School after the war and did so well that he was appointed law clerk for the Chief Judge of the U. S. Court of Appeals.

As a lawyer in exurban Fairfield, Sackett handled a number of estates. He quickly became aware of the abuses in the state probate system. Each of the state's 126 elected probate judges operates on a remarkable "franchise" basis. All probate fees are paid to the judge, who pays his office expense and keeps what's left over. In the more prosperous districts the "left over" part is often greater than the governor's salary. And since the probate judge can also conduct a law practice on the side, he can do splendidly. Just how much the judges clear is difficult to find out, points out Sackett:

Each year the probate judge files a sworn financial statement with the State Tax Commissioner showing his gross receipts, expenses, and "profit." Unfortunately, I think there are several probate judges who habitually falsify their statements.

The appraiser system, involving fees to friends and political supporters can also be used by probate judges to enrich their own law practices. Howard Sackett gives some examples:

In Fairfield the probate judge passes out thousands of dollars worth of appraisal appointments to particular real estate brokers, who in turn send real estate closings to his law firm.

In several nearby towns probate judges see to it that the mortgage officer of the largest mortgage lending institution in the county is frequently supplied with appraisal appointments. That mortgage officer then sees to it that a substantial number of mortgage closings are sent to those probate judges. In Fairfield, this has been a standard practice for at least twenty years, with both Republican and Democratic probate judges.

During his campaign for probate judge in 1966, Sackett revealed that the appraiser fees went to the state's higher court judges, too. For example, State Circuit Judge Rodney S. Eielson, of Trumbull, received a $3,000 fee from an estate probated in 1962—for doing virtually nothing. Sackett had his secretary do the appraising on the stocks which made up the great bulk of the $4,900,000 estate. It took his secretary forty-five minutes.

Still, there was no law against a sitting judge taking a $3,000 piece of patronage. But Sackett in his years of digging into the system found that many times the chosen appraisers were county and state officials such as selectmen, zoning commissioners, state liquor authority commissioners and sewer commissioners. Having handed out patronage to these officials the probate judge in his other role as a private lawyer naturally was in an advantageous position when he appeared before these officials on behalf of a private client. As Sackett put it in his campaign literature: "Money is taken from innocent victims and is used for improper influence in government."

Howard Sackett was defeated, partly because many of his fellow Republicans, interested in keeping the old appraiser system, worked against him.

If the voters can't always be depended upon to see where their best interests lie, perhaps it is up to the only citizens who do know how bad the situation is because they see it from the inside. Sackett touched on this in a letter that appeared a few years ago in the *Journal of the American Bar Association.* He was responding to a letter complaining about the "image" lawyers were getting in a TV show about crooked lawyers and a crooked probate judge:

I believe all lawyers know that corruption in government, especially in the courts, cannot exist without the participation of some lawyers, the approval of many lawyers, and the apathy of most lawyers. . . . We cannot complain about a poor "image" [of the lawyer] if the reality is poor; and isn't it about time for the Bar to start a job of housecleaning so that reality will conform to the "image" we want to project?

So far the would-be reformers haven't been too effective. Legislatures, composed of lawyers in the main, aren't likely to make any basic changes in a system of court patronage that often makes the difference between a lawyer-legislator living moderately and living *really* well, the difference between a Volkswagen and a Cadillac. The idea that it is only a dead man's money, and what right do the undeserving heirs have to raise a fuss, is an article of faith by now. But this rationale for the system, this balm for an occasional twinge of legal conscience, surely can't withstand forever people snickering, editors writing and heirs complaining. Still the main housecleaning will have to be done by the lawyers themselves. Every one of these thefts from estates that are given legal sanction means the bar has given its assent, implied or actual, to corruption in our courts.

12 THE STERLING WILLIAMS DRAMA: O'NEILL OUT OF HOWARD

Not very long after I had reached the Capital I strolled into the Personal Bereavement Court. . . . The next case was that of a youth hardly arrived at man's estate, who was charged with having been swindled out of a large property during his minority by his guardian. . . . The lad pleaded that he was young, inexperienced, greatly in awe of his guardians, and without independent professional advice.

"Young man," said the judge sternly, "do not talk nonsense. People have no right to be young, inexperienced, greatly in awe of their guardians and without independent professional advice. If by such indiscretions they outrage the moral sense of their friends, they must expect to suffer accordingly." He then ordered the prisoner to apologize to his guardian, and to receive twelve strokes with a cat-o'-nine tails.
—SAMUEL BUTLER, *Erewhon*, 1872

The lawyer came first; it was he and not the physician, who had to manage the consequences of mental disease insofar as they affected the interests of the community. The lawyer was then the first who had to see to it . . . that property mismanaged or abandoned by a person mentally deranged be taken care of in some normal, legitimate way.
—GREGORY ZILBOORG, *Legal Aspects of Psychiatry*, 1944

When Mrs. Mary Edith Williams died on March 6, 1955, in Minneapolis she was eighty-five, wealthy, and had spent most of her last fourteen years in a wheelchair. Since she came of an old Minneapolis family and was an active DAR member, she got a respectful obituary in the local dailies. She died almost alone: her nurse and housekeeper were with her in the large house in the once-fashionable Kenwood section, but her only child, Sterling, was in a sanitarium recovering from delirium tremens, and her legal guardian, attorney Oscar A. Nordquist, was sunning himself and his family in Fort Lauderdale, Florida. Ever since he had managed to have himself appointed her guardian, lawyer Nordquist had been enjoying a greater prosperity than he had ever known.

Often the dolorous drama of Mrs. Williams and her son and their lawyer-guardian sounds like the unlikely collaboration of Eugene O'Neill and Lillian Hellman interweaving such themes as the generational deterioration of a family and the cunning force of greed.

The family fortune was built by Sterling Williams' grandfather, who had been one of the founders and president of the Minneapolis National Bank. Sterling's father, James L. Williams, in turn, became president of the bank on his father-in-law's death. He also dealt profitably in real estate, and on his death in 1916 left a sizable estate to his wife. They had one child, Sterling, born in 1897.

The large red brick corner house where Sterling now lives with a nurse is redolent of the early twenties. The furniture is mission oak, and the books have the flavor of James Curwood and Oliver Optic. Now seventy-one, Sterling has no upper teeth, so his speech comes through accented with a regular "chomp, chomp," but what he says is otherwise clear and coherent. In his white socks and speckled blue cardigan he looked like a typical retiree enjoying his leisure rather than a man who had been through a fifty-year nightmare. Recently, during a visit he recalled for me some of the events that followed his father's death in 1916.

"My mother was a leaner and I'm the one she leaned on." When his father died his mother took him out of the University of Minnesota so that he could accompany her on a long visit to Gulfport, Mississippi, where she had some friends. "Funny thing. She kept telling friends that she was traveling for *my* sake. She'd tell them I was just a 'poor, sick boy,' even though I was a pretty good boxer and wrestler in college.

"When we started traveling she always had a nurse in attendance. She took my father's death pretty hard. So I went along and usually acted as her chauffeur. We lived for a while in Los Angeles, and I was able to get another semester in at UCLA and one at the University of Southern California. We'd come back from time to time to Minneapolis, and I got a job in the Northwestern Bank, but in a few months she'd decide we had to travel again for her health."

Sterling told me he had never heard of a play called *The Silver Cord* by Sidney Howard. He asked me to tell him what it was about. I said it was about an overpossessive mother with two sons. One managed to get away from her—with the help of his wife. The other didn't. When I finished he nodded slowly. "Yes, yes. That's the way it was. She just couldn't let go of me. But I had a half-brother who got away. He died during the flu epidemic of World War One."

Sterling became a drinker and later a steady user of codeine, which he got by taking a lot of elixir terpin hydrate. Then followed commitments to institutions to cure his drinking and drug use. He was in several private sanitaria in Minnesota and in New York. He remembers one in White Plains, New York. "The same name as that department store," he said, trying to place it, ". . . Bloomingdale's. I remember it because there was a doctor up there who gave me the only good advice I got all that time. But I couldn't follow it. He told me to get as far away from my mother as I could. But she wouldn't let me go and I wasn't strong enough, I guess."

An old family friend I talked to in Minneapolis recalled one of the incidents that led to Sterling's going back to a sanitarium. "When Sterling was drunk and hard to handle his mother often asked me to come over and talk with him. One evening very late she phoned. Sterling was wild and threatened to harm his mother and her nurse, and they were frightened. The police came and that night Sterling went back to another private institution. That's the way it would go: he'd be in a few months and beg his mother to get him released, and finally she would and he'd start drinking again and there'd be trouble, and he'd go back in."

In 1941 Mrs. Williams suffered a back injury resulting in her confinement to a wheelchair and around-the-clock nurses. In 1947 she also became quite deaf, but as the court found later, "her mind remained keen for one her age and she retained the ability to understand details about her property and its management." In 1947 she created a living trust of her property, with the Northwestern National Bank of Minneapolis the trustee. She transferred to this trust various pieces of real estate in Minneapolis and some farm property in North Dakota. The trust provided that she get the income of $1,500 a month; upon her death the income was to go to her son.

The bank was doing this management for a fee, of course. It came to about $3,500 a year, and before long Mrs. Williams began wondering if she wasn't paying too much to have someone handle her money. Her fears were supported by Oscar A. Nordquist, a Minneapolis lawyer who was guardian of Sterling Williams. Nordquist is six feet one, erect, rather moon-faced and nearly bald. He was a Navy officer in World War II, and one man who knew him thought of him as "a good salesman . . . he instills confidence."

In 1947 Nordquist became the guardian for Sterling, to protect his interest in the $16,000 worth of farm property left him by his father, and the far greater interest he had in his mother's estate, since he was her sole heir.

Mrs. Williams had agreed to the appointment of Oscar Nordquist as her son's guardian, of both his person and his estate. The law makes the distinction carefully. The guardian of the person is supposed to look after the incompetent. As Sterling recalls it, "Nordquist would come over once a week or so and smell my breath and say, 'Sterling, you've been drinking beer again.' " As special guardian of Sterling's estate and interest in his mother's estate Nordquist had even less to do. The farm property was being well managed by a professional farm management firm which checked on the tenant farmer; and Mrs. Williams' estate was in the capable hands of the bank, which managed to increase its value while they supervised it. Even the bank didn't have too much to do. The biggest part of Mrs. Williams' estate was a two-story commercial building in downtown Minneapolis, worth about $575,000. It was managed by a real estate firm.

For centuries the annals of avarice document a simple, basic plot: A has a lot of money; B wants to get it. If A is an aged client and B is a lawyer guarding A's estate, there are some interesting variations. Of course, lawyer B can simply steal from the funds entrusted to his care. The trouble is that stealing is a felony and is generally punished fairly severely; worse, it isn't easy to conceal outright theft very long.

Or lawyer B can loot the estate "legally" by making gross and repeated charges for legal and personal services he claims he provided his client. If he can continue this long enough, undetected, the estate will be his in time. There are hazards, of course. For one thing there may be relatives around. Since they look upon themselves as heirs to the estate, naturally they are terribly nosy if they suspect their inheritance is being attenuated by unnecessary legal fees. If there are no known relatives? That leaves the client, who *might* get wind of the charges levied against her estate. But if your client is adjudged an incompetent by the court, naturally she is not in an ideal position to dispute your charges. That leaves you with the last hazard: the probate judge who has to approve the legal fees and charges you assess against your incompetent client's funds. An alert, upright judge would quickly sense the inflated outrageous fees and put an end to *that;* but if the judge is a complaisant friend, or if you've done considerable favors for the judge or his relatives? Well, then, things might be different. Everyone knows that the shine of gold glazes the eyes.

Even without the blinding glare of gold there are other ways in which probate judges can incur considerable obligations to lawyers. Judges have to be elected. Campaign managers are invariably lawyers, and other lawyers serve on the committee. Campaign funds have to be raised and the major contributors, again, are lawyers.

Probate Judge James G. Kehoe of Minneapolis had been in probate nearly all his adult life. He started as a probate court clerk in 1921. In 1930 he was made a probate court referee, which meant that he was designated by the probate judge to determine fees in some cases and hold hearings just like a judge. Lawyers liked him. A tall, heavy-set, good-looking Irishman, he was never niggardly about attorney fees. Then in 1947 he became the probate judge of Hennepin County. In addition to the thousands of estates that went through in court every year there were also some 800–900 applications for guardianship of incompetents filed. In many cases lawyer friends of the judge would be appointed attorney for the guardian or even special guardian to watch over the incompetent's property.

There were other favors Probate Judge Kehoe could dispense. In Minnesota, as in many other states, probated estates require appraisers who receive percentage fees of the total value of the estate.* Their work is not only routine but unnecessary and is, of course, paid for by the estate. One of Judge Kehoe's favorite appraisers was his son-in-law, William J. Richard, a chemist. (An appraiser doesn't have to be a lawyer.) The judge appointed him appraiser for at least thirty-five estates.

In many ways, then, Judge Kehoe was a *reasonable and generous man.* No attorney handling the estate of a wealthy incompetent need fear that his requests for payments of legal and other services would undergo nit-picking examination.

That took care of the problem of the probate judge. How about nearby, nosy relatives who might raise a hue and cry just because hard-working attorneys were asking fair fees for themselves? No problem there, either. As far as anyone could tell, the Williamses, mother and son, had no immediate relatives anywhere, let alone in Minneapolis.

That left, finally, Mrs. Williams and her son. She was eighty and confined to a wheelchair. He was an alcoholic and if you regularly gave him "cigarette" money, why, he might well be so happy that he wouldn't even think of asking embarrassing questions—even if he could find out what was happening to the assets of his and his mother's estates.

There was the problem of another trustworthy attorney. Not

* See Chapter 11.

only could this other reputable attorney reduce suspicion about the size of the fees, but he could serve another useful purpose. Managed skillfully, two attorneys could put on a marvelous display of legal battling over issues involved in the many aspects of the guardianships. Such a display would, of course, offer instant verification that a great deal of legal work was being done in behalf of the wards of the guardian.

The other attorney Nordquist found as a useful ally was Frank Durham, who was fifty-nine years old in 1949 when he first entered the case. He was gray-haired, of medium height, and clearly had been quite handsome when younger. He wore brown suits that clashed with the purplish cast of his drinker's complexion. "A fine, reputable lawyer," one attorney commented. "I could never figure out how he got mixed up in this."

Durham came into the case through a St. Paul attorney, Hugo Hendricks, who had been hired by Mrs. Williams to get her son's incompetency removed legally. Somehow the matter aborted, and Sterling remained a ward of lawyer Nordquist. The fact that Nordquist got a court order calling for the payment of $1,000 a month out of guardianship funds to Sterling may have served to quiet his worries about being an incompetent. But only two such payments were made. During one of the hearings on the matter, lawyer Hendricks said, while Sterling was close by, "Now we are going to revoke that trust."

He was, of course, referring to the trust Sterling's mother had established. As long as the bank was in control of her estate there was little leeway for fancy legal fees. Naturally, the bank had to be removed. Mrs. Williams' willingness to revoke the trust was based on not only her desire to save the $3,500 the bank was charging her for its yearly services but her belief that Sterling had recovered and, as a good businessman, would help her in managing her money. But Nordquist, as guardian of Mrs. Williams' son, Sterling, thought that *she* needed a guardian. And on November 1, 1949, he applied to the court for the appointment of a guardian for her, too, on the ground that she was incompetent to manage her estate, that she was old and physically and mentally infirm.

At this point Mrs. Williams said she wanted a Minneapolis attorney rather than Mr. Hendricks of nearby St. Paul. Hendricks made an arrangement with Frank Durham to replace him on what lawyers delicately call "a referral" arrangement or "a forwarding fee." The matter is delicate because Canon 34 of the lawyers' Canons of Ethics flatly prohibits a division of fees where there is no division of service or responsibility. Nevertheless the practice of dividing fees with another lawyer who has done no more than refer a client is widely used. In theory such practice can lead to disbarment, but in fact it almost never does. It is the most widely violated of all the ethical canons. Hendricks turned over Mrs. Williams to lawyer Durham for a "forwarding fee" of a third. It was, in time, to mean a neat $15,300 for Hendricks.

Durham's first job was to oppose Nordquist's attempt to establish a guardianship over Mrs. Williams and her property. He was remarkably unsuccessful, neglecting even to bring Mrs. Williams into court to show that she was, in spite of her age and physical disability, alert and quite as capable of handling her affairs as she had been since 1916. So, early in 1950 Nordquist became guardian of Mrs. Williams, too. Durham did appeal the decision but never brought it to trial. Thus by 1950 Nordquist was in full charge of the Williamses and their money. Mrs. Williams had revoked the trust with the bank less than a month before Nordquist had claimed she was incompetent.

As the District Court was to comment much later:

At no time did Hendricks, Nordquist or Durham attempt to dissuade Mrs. Williams from revoking the trust, or advise her that it had been well and economically administered and that her objections to its management were without foundation and were unwarranted, or advise her that the return of control and management of her estate to her personally was extremely improbable, and that the continuance of the trust was for her own best interest and that of her son, Sterling C. Williams.

It was, economically, a terribly unreasonable expectation. Why on earth should they have given such sensible advice when it could have cost them a chance to make $250,000 in legal fees?

The rest was fairly easy. Nordquist and his ally, Durham, would meet beforehand in probate court to decide what fees they were going to ask the probate judge to approve. Naturally, it was vital that neither Mrs. Williams nor her son get wind of what was up. Ordinarily when a petition is given the probate court for payment of legal and guardianship fees, the parties who will have to pay the fees must be notified, and a hearing is held. The way to avoid notifying the Williamses was quite simple. As the District Court judge was to comment later, Durham and Nordquist

would either meet and go together to the Probate Court, or would meet there. Durham would waive notice of hearing and would consent to the granting of Nordquist's petition, and Nordquist would waive notice of hearing and would consent to the granting of Durham's petition.

They were very chummy and accommodating in other ways, too:

No information or notice was ever given to either of the wards [Mrs. Williams and her son] that the petitions for fees were to be presented. . . . No objections were ever made by Nordquist, as guardian of Mrs. Williams and of Sterling C. Williams, to any of the petitions for fees to Durham, nor was any endeavor made by him to have the petitions disallowed or the amounts reduced; and likewise, no objections were ever made by Durham. . . .

As long as Mrs. Williams was kept ignorant of what was going on in probate court, they were safe. As the District Court was to say later:

Both Nordquist and Durham . . . had personal deals and contacts with Mrs. Williams, and knew she had the mental capacity to understand ordinary business transactions . . . and that she would fight vigorously the allowance of the excessive fees sought. To avoid her opposition they willfully acted in concert to keep her in ignorance of the charges being made and the high costs of the various guardianships. . . .

Since they were asking large sums each time, you might think they would at least go through the formality of detailing the onerous work they had performed on behalf of their clients—Mr. Durham as attorney for Mrs. Williams, and Nordquist as special guardian for Mrs. Williams and her son, Sterling. But Durham and Nordquist were so confident of their invulnerability, so sure of the probate judge's amiable carelessness, they didn't bother:

> None of the petitions were accompanied by any statement of account, or contained any definite statement of the time spent on the services claimed to have been rendered, the nature of the services, the time they were performed, or their value.

Under law Nordquist was supposed to file annual statements on guardianship detailing income and expenditures of the moneys entrusted to his care. He didn't. The probate court didn't notice, perhaps because it was enveloped in an

atmosphere and condition that resulted in a relaxation of vigilance and careful scrutiny that is required if "vicarious generosity" is to be avoided in handling the property of helpless wards of the court.

Just how careless they were able to be in the Hennepin County Probate Court is illustrated by an order dated October 28, 1954, in which Judge Kehoe approved a payment of $5,000 to Nordquist, $3,000 to Durham and $1,000 to William M. Thomson, one of Nordquist's law partners. Yet Nordquist's petition for this $9,000 was unsigned, unsworn and didn't even make a request for the allowance of these fees. It is hard to imagine a more accommodating probate judge anywhere.

Generosity breeds generosity. When Nordquist became guardian of Mrs. Williams he asked Judge Kehoe to appoint appraisers. Since the personal property was principally in cash and negotiable securities, there was clearly nothing to do with them. But there was the Sterling Building Mrs. Williams owned. Judge Kehoe appointed two appraisers: O. J. Anderson and Romeo J. Riley. They weren't chosen casually. Mr. Anderson was better known as Probate Judge Anderson of nearby Wright County.

And Mr. Riley happened to be a Minneapolis alderman. Mr. Riley did the actual work: he spent an hour looking over the building, returned to Nordquist's office and signed the appraisal they had prepared. For this hour he received $1,000 and so did Judge Anderson. The appraisal was completely unnecessary, but since Mrs. Williams was paying the $2,000—even if she didn't know about it—it wasn't altogether "an extravagant expenditure," as another judge was to call it later.

Between 1949 and 1955 the Nordquist-Durham team applied for and got $203,395 in fees out of the Williams family—fees which the mother and son didn't know about.

It broke down this way:

Nordquist	$107,695
Durham	64,000
Tanner	27,700
Thomson	4,000

Both Tanner and Thomson were associates of Nordquist, and he shared in their fees, too.

Mrs. Williams died on March 16, 1955, aged eighty-five. This provided another fine opportunity to put in more requests for fees. Nordquist and Durham each put in for—and got—$20,000 for special and general administration of her estate. Thus bringing the legal take up to nearly $245,000.

Others should share in their good fortune. Surely more appraisers were needed to verify the value of the assets in the estate. This time Judge Kehoe turned again to his friend, Alderman Riley, and to a chemist named W. J. Richard, who by chance was Judge Kehoe's son-in-law. Each man this time got $1,750, so that the estate was burdened with another extravagant $3,500 expenditure.

More than a quarter of a million in legal expenses over a comparatively short period was bound to affect the estate. When Nordquist took over the estate everything was free and clear. In order to raise more money he sold the North Dakota farmlands and got a $188,000 mortgage on the Sterling Building in Minneapolis. The mortgage was necessary because as guardian he had neglected to make any provision for the payment of inheritance and estate taxes on Mrs. Williams' death.

With Mrs. Williams dead, the game continued as before—until a tiny cloud appeared in the shape of an unexpected relative who had come to Minneapolis for the funeral.

The relative was Mrs. Frances M. Purdy of New York, who is Sterling's cousin. Mrs. Purdy, a widow, is a well-to-do real estate operator in New York. She owns and manages a Madison Avenue building together with her daughter, Joan Purdy. When she was at the funeral Mrs. Purdy met an old friend of hers who was also a friend of the Williams family. The friend, a contemporary of Mrs. Purdy's, had worked as a confidential secretary for a prominent Minneapolis attorney. She had been hearing rumors of very large legal fees being taken by the guardians of Mrs. Williams and Sterling Williams.

Sterling was having one of his bad times. He had been hospitalized for delirium tremens and had not been able to attend his mother's funeral.

When Mrs. Williams died, Nordquist was holidaying in Florida with his wife and daughter. Nordquist came right home when he got news of the death of the woman who had, unknowingly, been the most generous of clients in the annals of the Minnesota Bar.

Now for the first time he heard that there was a Williams cousin around. Mrs. Purdy sought him out with a suggestion. Mrs. Purdy's Minneapolis friend, who has asked me not to mention her name, recalls the meeting:

Nordquist wouldn't listen to what Mrs. Purdy recommended and told her she had *nothing to say about anything*. Mrs. Purdy asked my help and we went to see Judge Kehoe in the Probate Court and asked him to appoint the Northwestern Bank as joint administrator of Mrs. Williams' estate. His answer was "why should the banks be brought in on these large estates?" He refused. We talked to several attorneys to see if the issue could be forced, but none wanted to be involved.

They didn't want to get involved because any sensible lawyer would quickly realize the case might mean economic suicide. Getting involved here, no matter how delicately it was put, meant saying a sitting probate judge had been too generous. Inevitably, when you came up before him with the estate of your future client there would be a certain degree of hostility, a chill that could slow the pace of the court to a glacial flow. And worse things, too.

But Mrs. Purdy persisted, and in time she interested attorneys Arthur D. Reynolds and George A. Lewis. They quickly sensed a long, drawn-out court trial—it was not the kind of matter on which Nordquist and Durham would yield gracefully, since it was like asking them to surrender a gold mine. If a long trial was involved they would need an experienced trial man. They approached Ray G. Moonan, a heavy-set Irishman with a great nose and square face who was then fifty-eight and had been specializing in trial work for thirty-five years.

Recently Moonan recalled his own doubts about getting involved. "It would be a long, drawn-out business. I could see that right away. It would have to be a contingent fee affair, which meant we might end up without a dime unless we got a substantial recovery for the estate. And it was going to arouse some hard feelings."

Reynolds had told him that shortly after Mrs. Purdy had approached him about taking on the case, another lawyer he knew slightly advised him to stay out: "You're asking for disbarment," he said. And soon after Moonan became interested, he also received a call from a prominent Minneapolis attorney who urged him, for his own good, "don't get involved."

But these implied threats and unasked-for-advice only served to make Moonan decide to take it on. He stayed in character. Although he is one of the ablest attorneys in the city and tries about 150 lawsuits a year, Moonan is still odd man out in the tight circle of the city's more successful lawyers.

He belongs to the local and state bar associations but is fairly irreverent about them: "What they do is meet once a year, get drunk and tell us how to reform ourselves." He also belongs to the International Trial Lawyers Academy and the American College of Trial Lawyers, the most prestigious associations of attorneys who specialize in trial work. "Oh, they have nice meetings in places like London and Mexico City, so the trips are good for tax deductions. And sometimes you learn things."

Learning things is a fetish with Moonan. His favorite expression is "We're all new at now; we have to adapt continuously." With a tonsured fringe of white hair, Moonan looks like an Irish Father Superior of some not-too-strict order. I asked him what he had learned from the thousands of cross-examinations he had conducted: "We all have a finite mind and we're weak.'"

What enabled Moonan to come to a quick decision about taking on the Williams case was that he is his own boss. He has two partners: a son and a son-in-law. In addition, three nephews are associates in the firm. "What's the word?" Moonan asked with a laugh after giving me the details. "Nepotism." The firm is still known simply as "Ray G. Moonan, Attorney At Law." For a prospering and prominent local firm, Moonan's office makes none of the expensive pretense of the corporate law factories. His desk is plain, battered oak, and the building is not new.

Moonan, aided by his nephew, John E. Castor, fired the first broadside on March 15, 1956, a full year after Mrs. Williams died. He filed a petition in probate court, on behalf of Sterling C. Williams and Frances M. Purdy, his cousin. In it he asked the court to set aside all its orders allowing fees to Nordquist and Durham, to reexamine all their accounts and orders and to remove guardian-administrator Nordquist and Durham as personal attorney for Sterling. It was a strong petition: it asked the court to do all this because it said Nordquist and Durham had engaged in a conspiracy to obtain their orders for fees through fraud upon the court.

Naturally, Probate Judge Kehoe had to remove himself from the matter since he, after all, had been the judge who had approved all those expensive fees and, if the allegation was correct, had been taken in by the fraudulent acts of the two lawyers.

Since another probate judge was needed in the matter, it meant that Judge Kehoe would exchange places and courts with another judge. He asked for the services of Probate Judge O. J. Anderson of nearby Wright County.

Ray Moonan politely pointed out informally that Judge Anderson did, after all, have a slight interest in the case. Some years before he had received an appointment as appraiser in the guardianship of Mrs. Williams and had profited thereby to the extent of $1,000. But Judge Anderson brushed this aside. He didn't think this disqualified him at all.

The case was heard on May 1, 1956. Judge Anderson first knocked out the petition of Sterling C. Williams to appear in the matter. He was, ruled the judge, incompetent and therefore could not present a petition to appear. But Judge Anderson ruled that Frances M. Purdy's petition was valid. Then on February 1, 1957, he said, nothing doing. More formally,

. . . upon due consideration of the evidence, including all the files and records herein, the Court finds that the evidence will not sustain a finding that said orders, or any of them, were procured through fraud or misrepresentation, and that said petition should be denied.

Moonan now carried the case to District Court where Judge Leslie Anderson—no relation—heard Nordquist and Durham move that Mrs. Purdy's appeal should be dismissed: not only did she have no connection with the case, but she had also failed to show any legal grounds on which her plea could be granted. Judge Leslie Anderson decided that he would not dismiss the Purdy action, that there were important matters in the case that the State Supreme Court should consider.

By now, February, 1959—nearly four years after Mrs. Williams' death—the State Supreme Court got the case.

In their brief before the State Supreme Court, Nordquist and Durham and their attorney, Horace Van Valkenburg, a prominent Minneapolis lawyer who had once been president of the State Bar, made a curious admission:

The only aspect of the situation which appears to be remotely capable of supporting the claim of . . . fraud relates to the manner of presenting the accounts and petitions to the probate court. . . . It must be admitted that the procedures here used could be adapted to a fraudulent use if the parties so intended.

Early in March the court handed down a decision written by Chief Justice Roger Dell, which held that Frances M. Purdy was a proper person to bring the actions against Nordquist and Durham; that there were important issues that should be tried in the case. Justice Dell spelled out just what issues:

In this case a large number of wrongful acts are alleged, among them that Nordquist and Durham "entered into an unlawful and illegal conspiracy . . . to raid" the estates "by abstracting therefrom . . . excessive, exorbitant, illegal and unconscionable fees" by surreptitious means. . . . If proved, the estate is entitled to recover. Whether or not a conspiracy actually existed and whether the fees were unreasonable present only questions of fact.

Justice Dell was not unmindful that a conspiracy—if one existed—would not have been possible without the "inaction of the Probate Court. . . . By this inaction they could dissipate the assets of the estate of these incompetents unhampered."

It was obviously going to take a long time to ascertain these facts, and it fell to a retired judge, James Montague of Crookston, Minnesota. In Minnesota, as elsewhere, retired judges are often called back to handle difficult and protracted cases that might easily clog up the regular district courts. The Montagues are prominent in the bar and courts of Minnesota. The judge's cousin, James E. Montague, was to become president of the State Bar.

Judge Montague, who would hear the case without a jury, opened it in the Hennepin County District Court on November 2, 1959. He was then nearly eighty, short and whitely fragile, but had an alert, precise mind. At the end of each day's session he would retire to chambers and type his notes on a rickety old portable while chain-smoking cigarettes. When he agreed to sit in the case he had asked one indulgence of the contestants: he wanted to continue his practice of taking a winter vacation in Arizona as he had been doing since his retirement from the bench.

Since it was going to be an extended case, the two local dailies simply had their reporters look in from time to time. "Nordquist and Durham weren't happy to see me in the courtroom," recalls Timothy Blodgett who had covered the case for the Minneapolis *Star,* the afternoon daily. "I remember trying once to talk to them during a recess. . . . Both brushed me off, which didn't surprise me."

Alan McConagha who looked in on the trial for the *Tribune,* Minneapolis' morning daily, recalls:

The testimony itself wasn't very thrilling, usually the painstaking process of getting figures in evidence. But I loved to watch Ray Moonan work. He would plod up and down in front of the courtroom, patiently, quietly, like a big bear getting his points in evidence. He seemed to suggest a great reserve of strength, but the manner of his examination was always understated.

I had heard rumors that attempts had been made to give the trial no publicity, or the barest minimum. I asked McConagha:

I think maybe there were some efforts somewhere to get the whole thing played down. Just as a guess, maybe someone talked to the paper's lawyers or something of the sort. This didn't have any bearing on the way the story was handled. . . . Nordquist may have made some efforts on a more removed and elevated level. For some reason, I rather suspect he did. But the newsroom staff at the *Tribune,* thank God, has always been well protected from this kind of pressure.

In the trial before Judge Montague, Ray Moonan had Nordquist on the witness stand for thirty days. "He wasn't very responsive to questions," Moonan recalls. "I'd have to ask him five to get one answer."

When the trial concluded on October 5, 1960, at 3:25 P.M., the transcript of testimony and argument ran to 4,438 pages bound in 27 volumes. In his concluding arguments Moonan asked the judge not only to remove Nordquist and Durham from any relationships to the estate of the Sterling Williams but for them to repay in full the $248,498 which he had estimated they had taken in fees. There was another $100,000 they had paid out in fees to others—appraisers and other lawyers—but this, he knew, could not be recovered.

On March 21, 1961, Judge Montague was ready with his decision. In a 75-page decision he set out 31 "findings." One of them was that in the five years and two months Nordquist and Durham were in control of the Williams estate they spent $406,935 "for an average of about $80,000 per year. . . . Almost 60 percent of the total estate was spent for the fees of Nordquist as guardian and of Durham, Tanner and Thomson."

Then Judge Montague came to his "Conclusions of Law."

1. That failing to fully inform and advise Mrs. Williams and her son, Sterling, had been a breach of the duty of Nordquist and Durham to them in their roles of guardian and attorney, and "in conjunction with their methods and conduct in the procurement of grossly excessive fees for their services . . . constituted a fraud upon Mary Edith Williams and Sterling C. Williams."

2. That the routine practices and methods used by Nordquist and Durham in presenting petitions for allowance of fees and the manner in which they procured the approval of the probate judge "constituted a fraud upon the Probate Court."

3. That Nordquist's "careless and unbusinesslike administration of each of the trusts, his failure to make reports as required by law, his failure to keep accurate and correct records of the financial transactions involved, . . . his subordination of the interests of his wards to his own interests and those of others to whom he paid excessive fees, make his removal as guardian of the Estate of Sterling C. Williams and as administrator of the Estate of Mary Edith Williams necessary for the interest of each of said estates."

Still, Judge Montague didn't think "the fraud involved here is of a nature that requires" *all* the fees to be repaid. He thought Nordquist had made a sincere effort to rehabilitate Sterling Williams; that everything possible was done for Mrs. Williams even though there was extravagance; "but nothing that was done could justify the extraction of such excessive fees by officers of the court."

He had estimated that Nordquist and Durham and associates had taken $245,493 in legal fees.* He now ordered them to repay $139,000, which meant that in spite of the fraud on their wards and on the probate court they were still entitled to keep $106,000 in fees.

It was a notable victory for Ray Moonan and a disaster for Nordquist and Durham. The one-column headlines the next morning in the *Tribune* didn't help: FRAUD FINDING IS FILED IN ESTATE CASE. Nor the more explicit one that afternoon in the *Star:* 2 LAWYERS CHARGED WITH FRAUD.

Nordquist and Durham indicated they would appeal Judge Montague's decision. This could mean more legal expense and delay, and finally on May 25, 1963, a settlement was reached: some $70,000 would be repaid to the estate. The repayment was made up this way:

Oscar A. Nordquist	$44,415
Frank H. Durham	16,695
George W. Tanner	7,700
William M. Thomson	1,190
	$70,000

In the "stipulations" which ended the case, the explanation given for the settlement was that

there has been considerable acrimony between the parties hereto, the persons connected herewith, and their attorneys with reference made to the commencement of certain lawsuits as between the aforesaid; and

*Moonan's own estimate was slightly higher: $248,498.

. . . it is desired that all litigation arising out of the above captioned matters be terminated.

The money was paid over to the Midland National Bank of Minneapolis, which since 1961 had been the new special guardian of Sterling Williams and special administrator of his mother's estate. Since the case had been undertaken on a contingent fee basis, Ray Moonan and his associates were allowed a one-third fee of $23,333 plus some $1,500 in expenses, so that Sterling actually recovered a net of some $45,000.

The *final* settlement of the case didn't make the Minneapolis dailies for some reason that Ray Moonan still doesn't understand. "A big strange case that had been in and out of the papers for more than seven years and the public never did find out what finally happened. It's like a long novel published without the concluding chapter." *

The Sterling Williams estate now has about $441,000, yielding a conservative $15,000 a year. It costs about $10,000 a year to run the house Sterling lives in, including $6,000 a year for his nurse-housekeeper. In addition the estate has to pay out $3,600 a year to former District Judge Levi M. Hall, who is the court-appointed special guardian for Sterling and special administrator of his mother's estate; another $3,600 a year goes to Ray Moonan, who is counsel to the special guardian. Capital will have to be dipped into.

For a comparatively modest annual fee of $7,200 the estate is looked after carefully, and Judge Hall checks on his ward, Sterling, at least once or twice a week. When I visited Sterling recently in the red brick corner house his family has owned since 1929, he told me he "was pretty contented now." He had just had a seventieth birthday party, to which some of his friends came.

"I read a lot," Sterling explained. "I watch color TV. I go to

---

*One of the reasons the final settlement received no publicity was that it was deliberately not filed with the Clerk of the District Court, Gerald R. Nelson. As far as he and his records are concerned, Judge Montague's 75-page ruling in 1961 was the final one in the matter. Not filing the stipulation meant the press had no easy way of finding out what was in it.

the movies and the Tyrone Guthrie Theater and once every few weeks go to the Minneapolis Athletic Club for luncheon." Mrs. Hansen, his nurse, chauffeurs him on these outings.

Sometimes he thinks back on the lengthy legal battle to save his family's estate, and he gets what he calls "dark thoughts" about lawyer Nordquist. "I don't like him . . . somebody you shouldn't have in your house. I call him . . . No, don't put that down. Just say he's not a nice person." His trifocal glasses shook slightly on his nose and his fingers twitched.

Between the time of Judge Montague's ruling in 1961 and the final settlement of the case in 1963, a curiously related offstage drama was taking place in Hollywood and Chicago, headquarters of the American Bar Association. On April 20, 1962, ABC televised a show called "The Blind Goddess" in its series, *Target: The Corruptors,* which was very loosely based on the investigative adventures of a colleague of mine, Lester Velie. In this episode a corrupt judge conspired with a political henchman to defraud the estate of a fifteen-year-old deaf-mute girl out of property worth $100,000. As the ABA's terribly unhappy Standing Committee on Public Relations put it, the episode

left with the viewing public the impression that the probate courts generally are shot through with graft and corruption. Upon the recommendation of this Committee [ABA] President John C. Satterfield lodged a strong protest with . . . ABC Television Network, with the producers . . . and with the advertising sponsors of the series. . . . Mr. Satterfield requested that "The Blind Goddess" be withdrawn from any later rebroadcasts. ABC agreed to so withdraw the film as far as its network was concerned. . . .

Obviously, poor old Sterling Williams isn't nearly as attractive and appealing a victim as a teen-age deaf-mute girl, but his story, if ever told on TV, has certain advantages. The ABA's vigilant public relations committee could not accuse it of being fictional or of giving the public the wrong impression.

The wrong impression *I* worried about was the one the Hennepin County Bar Association might be giving the public by not doing anything in the matter of lawyer Nordquist and Judge Montague's findings of "fraud." I wrote the association's Ethics Committee and was told that "all Proceedings of the Hennepin County Ethics Committee are confidential."

I phoned Ralph S. Parker, an aging lawyer who is secretary of the Ethics Committee. He was rather voluble and spent most of the time warning me against writing about the case. "You're flirting with libel, you know. There's something about the case you don't know about. Better check the court records."

What he meant, of course, was that the case was finally settled out of court and that Nordquist and the other lawyers had to pay back only $70,000 instead of $139,000. Meanwhile he told Oscar Nordquist I had been making inquiries about the case. Nordquist wrote me that "by subsequent order of the District Court the case against Mr. Durham and myself was dismissed with prejudice." In law the last two words generally mean that a case cannot be reinstituted, that it has been settled finally. But to lay eyes "with prejudice" has an ominous sound, almost as if the case had been thrown out totally, which it had not been. That it had been settled for a lesser sum didn't erase the ruling about fraud being practiced on the Williamses and on the probate court itself. Nordquist's letter to me concluded ominously: "I am transmitting this information to you in order that you may avoid making any actionable errors in your contemplated article." Having been duly warned to watch out by Ralph Parker of the Ethics Committee and Oscar Nordquist, who presumably had come before that committee, I was naturally more curious than ever about what the Ethics Committee did about Nordquist and Durham.

In July, 1967, during a visit to Minneapolis I told Harry H. MacLaughlin, co-chairman of the Ethics Committee, of my great interest in the case. He promised to take it up with the full committee. Two weeks later he wrote me that the "Committee has a rule which prohibits the disclosure of its actions to anyone without the consent of the persons involved." Obviously, attorneys Nordquist and Durham would not give such permission.

Since I was in Minneapolis I thought it worth a call, anyway.

Mr. Nordquist, who is now a partner in the law firm of Berg, Nordquist and Degen, was a little surprised that I had managed to get a copy of the final stipulation in the case and that I knew the matter had been settled with the repayment of $70,000. He did not care to discuss the matter, and he would not tell me what the Ethics Committee had done about it. I said that obviously they hadn't done anything about disbarring him because he was still in practice, so I assumed that possibly he had been censured. Nordquist wouldn't confirm this: "You can draw your own conclusions." And hung up.

If he did get a letter of censure it would be a purely private matter between himself and the Ethics Committee. In a recent one-year period the committee sent letters of censure to six attorneys.

Still trying, I approached Sidney S. Feinberg, a Minneapolis lawyer who was president of the Minnesota State Bar. Feinberg was a speaker on bar discipline at the 1967 ABA convention. I told him of my great interest in the Nordquist case, and he promised to try to find out for what, if anything, the Hennepin County Bar had done about it. As of July, 1968, I hadn't heard from Mr. Feinberg.

Judge Montague had not only used the word "fraud" several times but hinted to the bar association that this was a matter worth their attention. Near the end of his 1961 judgment in the case he said:

A matter of this kind can undo much of what the Bar Associations and the profession generally has done in recent years to improve public relations, and to maintain the high standing of the profession in the eyes of the public.

As far as the eyes of the public were concerned, nothing visible had been done about disciplining Nordquist. After a time you start rethinking basic premises. Perhaps I was thinking too harshly about Nordquist's conduct in this case. I discussed the case in fairly full detail with a lawyer I know who spends all his time on grievance work in a large metropolitan area. What would his alert grievance committee have done in the matter? "We'd have bounced him."

Judge Montague was already dead when I became interested in the case, so there was no way to get his off-the-bench comments. I already knew Ray Moonan's views, but then, of course, he was an involved party and perhaps prejudiced. At this point I wrote to the two Minneapolis reporters who had covered the case in District Court. Alan McConagha, who had been the Minneapolis *Tribune*'s court reporter at the time, is now the paper's European correspondent based in London. He wrote me that he was "frankly shocked that Nordquist is still practicing law. I'm dumbfounded . . . I just don't understand it." He felt that the fact that Nordquist wasn't disbarred after all the harsh things Judge Montague said about him "says as much about the Minneapolis Bar Association, I think, as it does about Nordquist." It was, he concluded, "one of the worst cases of legal fraud" he knew of. He suggested that I get in touch with Tim Blodgett who had covered the case for the Minneapolis *Star*. Blodgett, now Associate Editor of the *Harvard Business Review*, wrote me he was

shocked to read that Oscar Nordquist is still practicing law. I had thought that the Minnesota Bar Association brought disbarment proceedings against him and his co-defendant, Frank Durham, and the State judiciary ruled against Nordquist. . . .

I talked to a Minneapolis attorney I knew who had been active in Bar Association affairs. "It was a hell of an embarrassing business for the bar," he said. "Judge Montague called it fraud but still there was no felony trial. Disbarment is a serious business. Don't forget everything Nordquist did as guardian got the approval of the Probate Judge. And the Judge was dead. He could have stopped the whole fraud in its tracks right away, but he must have felt well-disposed to Nordquist, who had given the Judge's son-in-law a nice appraiser fee of $1,750 for doing almost nothing. Then you have to remember that when Nordquist was called before the Ethics Committee in 1966 he was represented by Horace Van Valkenburg who had been his attorney during the trial before Judge Montague. I'm sure the fact that Van Valkenburg had been president of the Minnesota State Bar didn't hurt Nordquist any before the Ethics Committee. The State Bar president commands a lot of respect in Minnesota, you know." *

He spoke to one of his law partners on the intercom, asking for a date when someone had died. He turned to me and nodded:

"Another thing I just remembered. The Nordquist hearing at the Bar came up a short while after we had a terrible shock here. The Johnny Dorsey mess in February, 1966. He was one of the best corporation lawyers in town, ex-president of the Legal Aid Society, the County Bar Association and what-not. A very nice guy. Maybe forty-seven, forty-eight. He took his wife to an ABA meeting in Chicago and vanished suddenly from the Palmer House. A few days later his body is found off Highway 66 near Flagstaff, Arizona. Shot himself. The State Tax Department had been after him to pay taxes due on an income of $215,000 he earned between 1962 and 1964. Crazy. His firm, Dorsey, Owen, et cetera, is one of the biggest around here, and he could have rounded up whatever payments were called for out of their petty cash, practically. He left a note for his wife: 'I've made a mess of everything, especially taxes. I still love you.'

"Everyone knows lawyers aren't supposed to be sentimental. You know the bit: 'How did you get that broken toe? I kicked my lawyer in the heart,' and so on. But Dorsey's suicide was a real shocker here. Naturally, a few lawyers felt it was the fault of the State Tax Department for hounding him or something. From there it's a short hop to: 'Everyone's against lawyers, we gotta close ranks.' You know, it's not too far-fetched to think that maybe Nordquist got off with only a wrist slap in 1966 because of Dorsey's suicide. It could be. You never knew the Bar could be sentimental, eh?"

*Elsewhere, too. When Paul Alfonsi, the Republican floor leader in the 1965 Wisconsin Legislature, was convicted in July, 1966, of accepting a bribe to promote passage of a highway construction bill, he hired Ray McCann, president of the State Bar, and Donald O'Melia, immediate past president of the Bar. The State Supreme Court reversed his conviction.

Piecemeal they win this acre first, then that,
Glean on, and gather up the whole estate;
Then strongly fencing ill-got wealth by law,
Indentures, cov'nants, articles, they draw,
Large as the fields themselves, and larger far
Than civil codes, with all their glosses are.
—ALEXANDER POPE, *Satires of Dr. Donne*

In 1966 about 1,200,000 Americans lived in varying limbos as patients in mental institutions of all kinds—federal, state, county and private. No one knows how much patient money or property had to be managed by court-appointed guardians or lawyers in the United States. One of the few useful clues is that in 1966, just in Manhattan and the Bronx, court-appointed guardians and lawyers administered assets worth $75 million for the 3,105 incompetents who had property worth $2,500 or more. These two New York counties have about 3.1 million people, or roughly 1.5 percent of the total U.S. population. If this ratio of hospitalized mental patients-to-population held for the rest of the country, we would come up with a national total of some $5 billion belonging to our 1.2 million patients. But if the New York $23,000 average of patient property were extended to the 1.2 million patients we would have an awesome $22.5 billion worth of patient property around the country.

Nobody knows how close either of these extrapolations is. Do Manhattan and Bronx counties have more incompetents, proportionately? Do they have more money than incompetents in the rest of the country? The two counties do have much higher ratios of nonwhite residents—Puerto Ricans and Negroes—who usually have less of everything than do whites, competent or not.

Still, we have attained a stage where nearly everyone has some money *rights,* and there are few incompetents who are not entitled to some kind of pension, Social Security or Veterans Administration money. In our society the *totally* propertyless adult is vanishing like the freight-riding hobo.

There are nearly 100,000 "incompetent" veterans in the United States with court-appointed legal guardians. In a recent twelve-month period—from July 1, 1966, to June 30, 1967—the Veterans Administration paid out $6.2 million in guardian commissions and $2.4 million in attorney fees to lawyers who represented the guardians. Because the VA naturally takes special interest in veterans under guardianship, it has managed, often by vigorous legal action, to keep these fees as reasonable as it can under law. Another group of "incompetents" who have gotten recent, if belated, federal attention are the 130 Agua Caliente Indians of Palm Springs, California, whose land holdings are worth more than $50 million. In 1959 some sixty-nine guardianships and conservatorships were set up by court order to protect these Indians and their property. A recent and continuing investigation shows that the guardians and conservators, mostly local lawyers and judges, have been able to get fantastic and apparently quite legal fees.*

But Indians and veterans are only small parts of the millions of Americans who now have court-appointed guardians and court-appointed lawyers for guardians. There are no *national* statistics on how badly incompetents have been nicked and tricked by the men appointed to protect their savings.

Our newspapers are the recorders of our joyous moments—engagements, weddings, births—and some of our sorrowful times—deaths, bankruptcies and divorces. But the appointments of legal guardians are almost never part of the daily news parcel. Consequently, the fees granted these guardians and attorneys are also not newsworthy—even though the data is on file at the local courts and generally available for inspection.

Recently Samuel S. Backlar, a friendly, earnest lawyer, retired

*See Chapter 14.

as an assistant attorney general of New York State. He had been in charge of the Mental Hygiene Bureau work of the office for many years. Because he was interested in the problem and knew of the many abuses in the area, he asked for and got a small grant from the National Institute of Mental Health to make "a comprehensive study of the administration of the property of the mentally ill and to recommend state legislation to improve existing conditions." One of the aims of his project was to "eliminate the possibility of misappropriating the property of the mentally disabled."

First he combed the law reports of several states and found 100 scattered cases where the property of the mentally ill was mismanaged. These had become court cases only because the mismanagement was so gross and the size of fees so large that some member of the family got a lawyer to file a case and pursue it—at considerable cost. As a result, many of the fees charged by the guardians and lawyers were reduced. But it took a lot of time and effort, which may be why Sam Backlar was able to find only 100 cases.

He also talked to probate and surrogate judges in several states and to lawyers familiar with guardianship cases. In a summary of his findings that appeared in the *New York Law Journal* for June 8–9, 1967, Sam Backlar wrote:

My investigation has revealed a state of affairs . . . which gives cause for deep concern and which I believe would cause great public indignation were the facts known to the public. . . .

. . . the person who goes into a mental hospital and has some property is relegated to an expensive, archaic system as a result of which he is pauperized . . . if a patient is discharged from a hospital and finds out that his meager savings are gone, he may have another mental breakdown.

He recommended that the New York State Judicial Conference appoint a conservator to have jurisdiction over the management of the property of the mentally disabled.

Under this system fees for attorneys, for guardians, for special guardians and for referees, as well as premiums for bonds, would be eliminated. These expenses are a burden upon the estates of the mentally ill. This simplified system would also reduce the expenditure of time, effort and money by the estates of the mentally ill. The operation of a state-wide system for the benefit of the mentally disabled is justified. These patients need special protection because they are a special class of help-less people.

Sam Backlar is fairly realistic. He knows the present system is a source of many fees for lawyers who receive patronage appointments as special guardians, referees and as attorney for the guardians. The fees are extraordinarily generous, the money is certain, and the work almost always is negligible.

Recently I discussed Backlar's idea with a friend who once had a responsible administrative post in the New York State courts. "Not new," he said. "Every few years some intelligent judge, disgusted by the smelly patronage of the whole operation, says to his other judges, privately, of course: 'Let's get some paid staff people to do the work for nominal fees that would be paid by the incompetent's estate. After all, the work is almost routine, a job for a good $150-a-week bookkeeper.' The last judge who suggested it was Botein, but the other justices in the Appellate Division just didn't want the Division to take on the added burdens, so nothing happened."

In the years I've known Presiding Justice Bernard Botein certain ground rules have governed our talks. Quite properly, of course, he never discusses pending cases or the content of matters he and his fellow justices consider. Knowing this, I didn't ask if he had made such a proposal. But he was willing to discuss the general workings of the patronage aspect of the court's handling of incompetents' estates.

In New York State the property of an incompetent, if worth more than $2,500, is managed by a committee which is often not a group but a single person. Often it is a member of the incompetent's family; if there isn't a family or a suitable member available to handle the matter, the court will assign an attorney. The committee—in other states the preferred designation is guardian or conservator—must file with the clerk of the court that appoints him a list of the property he has taken over and the fact that he has taken out a suitable bond.

Every year, the committee handling property of an incompetent must file in January an inventory, account and affidavit with the court clerk. In February of each year these accounts and inventories are examined by one of the official referees appointed by the Presiding Justice of the Appellate Division. For Manhattan and the Bronx, the Appellate Division's Presiding Justice is Bernard Botein.

When he became Presiding Justice in 1958 he found "too much laissez faire" in the handling of these annual accounts by the referees, all of whom were patronage appointments. "A lot of little estates hadn't been checked out in fifteen to twenty years. The four referees at the time were simply skimming the cream, taking only the big cases," he told me.

Some of the referees might handle only fifteen cases a year and make $50,000, more than the governor or mayor of New York. And they were getting these court-approved fees for very part-time and quite undemanding work.

In 1962 Judge Botein modified the patronage aspects. First, he decided that the fees should be spread around more: nine referees would handle Manhattan and another three for the Bronx. In effect, he tripled the number of referees. They were to be limited to $20,000 a year for their part-time work. And he appointed Supreme Court Justice William C. Hecht, Jr., to supervise the entire operation.

Justice Hecht is an anomaly in normally Democratic New York City: he is the only Republican judge sitting on the Supreme Court there. Although he is now seventy-seven and past retirement age he has been called back twice—"I'm a second retread" —to help out in the New York Supreme Court's busy calendar.

"In the old days," Judge Hecht recalled, "there were a lot of fat pickings for the referees. In theory you don't have to be an attorney to be appointed to the job, but in practice all are. And they're permitted to practice law regularly. Since they get an expense allowance of $20 for stenographic help for each case, this is an added sweetener. All of them use their regular law offices, and since they average about 100 examinations a year, this gives them another $2,000 income to help pay their regular stenographer."

The cases come in first to Joseph M. Ficco, a thin, good-humored civil servant who is officially the Clerk of the Additional Special Term of the Supreme Court, but as he likes to joke, "They always call me the Incompetent Clerk." Ficco makes a rough estimate of the size of the estate involved, and Judge Hecht then assigns the cases to the referees so that none of them gets only big ones or just small ones.

New York City itself pays the referees' fees in cases where the estates are $5,000 or less. For this the maximum fee is $60. There were 385 of these small estates in 1966, but there were also 105 cases in which the estates were over $100,000. Naturally, the larger the estate, the bigger the referee's fee. These estates get examined every year, unlike the ones under $100,000, which need to be examined only once every two years.

The referee plums are handed out for political reasons—referee Edmund Dollinger of the Bronx, is the son of the Bronx District Attorney. Or as consolation prizes: two of the referees are former municipal court judges who were unbenched for political reasons. Or as a reward: Seymour M. Klein, a successful attorney, got a refereeship because of a particularly difficult unpaid investigation he undertook for the Bar Association. Another referee is a former Chief Clerk of the Supreme Court. The youngest referee is Timothy M. Taylor, a Negro who made $12,265 from this part-time post in 1966. The highest earner in the bunch was referee Harold Lazar, an attorney and former Republican district leader in upper Manhattan, who got fees of $19,160 for his work in 1966.

The referee's job essentially is to audit the report of the committee, but since many of the committees are banks and trust companies, it often makes Justice Hecht wonder if the whole setup "makes any sense."

In addition to the referee patronage, which is at least controlled and has upward limits on the earnings of the appointees, there are other and even more profitable forms which are much harder to supervise.

The case of Helen M. Rivas, millionairess—her father founded the Jell-O fortune—is a splendid illustration of how profitable it is to be a minor, invisible part of the tragedy of becoming a nonperson, an incompetent.

Mrs. Rivas, who came from upstate New York, had been married three times and had noted philanthropic impulses. Before she became incompetent she gave $5,000,000 to the Strong Memorial Hospital of Rochester for a psychiatric wing, $50,000 for the building of the Rosary Church of Niagara Falls, and $2,000,000 to establish the Medical Foundation of Buffalo.

In May, 1958, she had a stroke and was admitted to the Westchester Division of the New York Hospital. Her condition deteriorated, and in December, 1958, her only child, Mrs. Constance W. Stafford, who was her mother's main beneficiary and executrix of her will, went into New York Supreme Court for an adjudication of her mother's competency. These adjudications are heard in Special Term, Part I, of the Supreme Court, called by lawyers "plum Part." The first plum emerged when Judge Francis X. Conlon appointed a special guardian, Edward V. Loughlin, a former leader of Tammany Hall, to the post of protecting Mrs. Rivas' interests during the adjudication of whether or not she was competent. For his remarkably brief work he asked for and got $20,000 in March, 1959, the day she was adjudged incompetent after medical testimony.

Judge Conlon also named a commissioner to preside over the determination of her incompetency. On December 23, 1958, this Christmas present went to lawyer Fred. J. Carusona. On March 4, 1959, Carusona asked for and got $4,000 for his endeavors.

The following year another special guardian seemed called for, and this time Judge Vincent Lupiano appointed Irving Smith, a Brooklyn lawyer, in December, 1959. Smith asked for and got $22,500 for his chores in March, 1960.

Now that Mrs. Rivas was incompetent, she had a committee

consisting of her daughter and George Spohr, an attorney, and the Morgan Guaranty Trust Company. When the committee presented its first annual report on the way her property had been handled, Justice Lupiano appointed an attorney, Irving Mendelson, as referee. He checked the accounting of the committee's report and asked for $25,000, which he got.

Naturally the interests of some of the other beneficiaries named in Mrs. Rivas' will had to be protected. In February, 1960, Judge Lupiano had some post-Christmas gifts for deserving attorneys. He appointed Salvatore J. Iannucci as special guardian for Diane Reid Woodward and Lawyer Henry Shuman as special guardian for Walter Fleming Stafford III, Reid Stafford, and Constance H. Stafford. Their work was brief, and on March 3, 1960, Iannucci got $7,500 and Shuman $15,000. That same date lawyer George Spohr received $60,000 for acting as attorney for the committee.

In 1963 attorney Seymour M. Klein, as referee, got $8,500 for checking the committee's accounting. In 1965 it was the turn of Bernard N. Newman, Republican leader of Manhattan, to get in on the action. He received $7,500. In 1965 Mrs. Rivas died after being in a coma for three years. Just before she died another lawyer, Stanley M. Katz, was appointed special guardian on February 5 to protect the interests of her heirs. He asked for $40,000 for work that apparently lasted barely a month. But on March, 6, 1965, Judge Loreto introduced the first niggardly note into the generous fee structure and reduced lawyer Katz's request to $30,000.

After her death George Spohr's law firm, attorneys for the committee, asked for a neat $300,000 for their work, and again Judge Loreto felt this was a bit too much. He gave them only $250,000.

But neither Judge Loreto nor any other of the judges in the Supreme Court thought any of the other fat fees they had already allowed during and just after Mrs. Rivas' incompetency were "unwarranted and scandalous" even though these added up to a very legal $450,000.

Mrs. Rivas' estate while she was alive was worth about $12,000,000, and about 4 percent of it—$450,000—wouldn't be missed too much. None of the referees or special guardians had, of course, anything to do with the care or treatment of Mrs. Rivas at the hospital nor even the actual management of her property.

Admittedly, the Rivas matter was a rare lip-smacking plum. But even on much smaller estates of incompetents there are comparatively bountiful fees for the lucky lawyers who are appointed. For example, Helena Butler was adjudged incompetent in 1957 and admitted to the Harlem Valley State Hospital in New York. Attorney Rhea Z. White was appointed both her committee and attorney for the committee. Miss Butler had about $16,000 in savings accounts and received $90,000 on the death of a sister. She was in the hospital four years and died there in 1961. During that period attorney White asked for and got $2,801 for her services as the committee for the incompetent and $10,300 for her services as attorney to herself as committee, for a total of $13,101. Since the patient was at the hospital all that time, there were no problems of providing care and guidance for the patient, Helena Butler. The official court referee, Hugo Pollock, who checked the annual accounts of attorney White, got $398. The bonding company, which said, in effect, they would make good if Miss White took any of the money entrusted to her care, was given $1,190. So among these parties the estate of Helena Butler was hit for $14,689 on an estate of some $106,000.

When Mary E. Coleman was adjudged incompetent in 1957 she had $62,677 in bank accounts, stocks and U.S. bonds. She was sixty-nine. Here the attorney got $3,500, the special guardian $1,500, the committee $1,125 and the referee $770 for a total of nearly $7,000.

The percentage was increased considerably in the case of Delia O'Hara, sent to Central Islip State Hospital in 1957. She had $16,000 in bank accounts and Social Security payments of $61 a month. Here the committee got $551, the attorney $2,500 and the referee $118, for a total of $3,169, or about 20 percent of her total estate. She died in 1964.

The names of certain lawyers and committees occur repeatedly in the incompetency court records I examined. For example, Alfred and Jenny Brainard, I noticed, were frequently appointed committees for the incompetent by various Supreme Court judges when the hospitalized person had no next of kin. Mr. Brainard is a real estate broker in Manhattan. When I asked to interview him he said he was too busy. He admitted that he got his appointments "through personal friendships with Supreme Court judges." He knew, he said, "a lot of them," Supreme Court Justices Thomas A. Aurelio and Vincent Lupiano in particular. The Brainards grew up in the same East Side neighborhood with Aurelio, who retired from the bench in December, 1967. They live in a four-story apartment house owned by the Aurelio family, and they belong to the Manhattan Democratic Club, of which Judge Aurelio was once a member.

In a typical recent year, 1963, Mr. Brainard was appointed the committee in twelve cases by Judge Lupiano. Nearly always Mr. Brainard chose as attorney for the committee of the incompetent either Robert Mitchell or Edward Pious, both of Manhattan.

Recently, I went through the court records of the cases of twelve incompetents in which these attorneys and Mr. Brainard had worked together. The total value of the estates was $126,000. For their legal services attorneys Pious and Mitchell received $9,772 and Mr. Brainard about $4,600. Their combined services represented a take of nearly 12 percent of the value of the estates. Sometimes the percentage was considerably higher. When Edith Patterson was hospitalized in June, 1960, she was worth about $1,290, mostly in a tiny savings account and a pension of $50 a month from the New York Dress Industry's Retirement Fund. Of her estate Mr. Mitchell got $450 in legal fees and Mr. Brainard $52 in committee fees. She died less than six months after she entered the hospital. The legal and committee fees in this case amount to about 40 percent of all she had in the world.

I discussed these cases with a former New York court official. Perhaps after all, there had been lengthy and weighty legal issues involved here that merited high fees, even considering the modest sizes of the estates. He laughed. "Any lawyer learns how to make a little work seem like a lot if necessary. But in these cases it's almost impossible. Better than 99 percent of it is pure bookkeeping routine. There's next to nothing to do, and what little there is is done by the lawyer's secretary, who fills out the forms routinely. Believe me, if the work was badly paid you'd have trouble getting lawyers to do it. How come they're so anxious to get these assignments?"

He went on to point out other attractions of incompetency cases for lawyers. "You never see the incompetent so there are absolutely no conscience tugs which you might have if, say, you had to go visit him once or twice a year. You'd go out to say hello to Incompetent #148765, and now he'd be a sad, hopeless fellow human. It might be a little harder when you were next making out your final legal fees. Now this way he's just a number and you can tell your conscience: 'What the hell, the hospital will get it or some miserable relatives or the Public Administrator if he doesn't have any relatives.' So you take and take quietly and you're not a self-accused son-of-a-bitch. You will gather from this impassioned defense," he concluded with a sad smile, "that I've succumbed. Judge _____ has just thrown me a few incompetents."

One day I was phoned by a lawyer in a large Eastern state. He had worked twenty-five years in the office of the attorney general of his state, mostly handling incompetency cases. He retired and was toying with the idea of doing "a hot exposé book." He heard that I was working on the subject.

We met in New York for luncheon and he outlined his exposé. It would, indeed, make an explosive story, affecting several prominent state officials. Without question, a major statewide scandal.

The racket worked this way. An incompetent was sent to the state hospital. The hospital representative, checking on possible assets, discovers the patient has, say $3,000 in a savings account. This means the state hospital has the right to fix a monthly rate for the patient's care, since he wasn't completely indigent.

An assistant attorney general, in charge of the mental health cases in the state, handled all these matters through his old law firm, which still carried his name. First, a committee would be appointed for the incompetent. Who was the committee? The son of a woman who worked as a secretary in the office of this assistant attorney general. He would phone the hospital administrator, and they would agree on a monthly care rate for the incompetent. Say, $65 a month. Now the exact amount of the patient's existing indebtedness to the hospital would be worked out. Then a luxury fund of $5–$10 a month was set aside and a burial allowance of $350. Now a special guardian has to be appointed to check on these expenditures from the patient's funds. This is patronage for the court. Legally the committee has to have an attorney. The assistant attorney general's old firm would be appointed attorney in these cases, and their minimum fee was $300. The young man, the perpetual committee? He'd get 5 percent of the incompetent's assets.

In the time my informant worked for the attorney general, hundreds of such cases went through this profitable routine. He estimated that the assistant attorney general's old law firm made at least $75,000 out of it annually.

"Probably more," he said. "If the estate was over $5,000 they could duplicate the legal charges easily. First there'd be an intermediate accounting of the way the committee handled the incompetent's assets, and then when the patient died a final accounting. So that even for a pitiful little $6,000 estate the phony 'legal' fees could run $600–$700.

"According to the court records nice, steady fees went to his old law firm. But you don't give away that kind of money just for old times' sake. This state official *had* to be getting a big piece of it back, in one form or another. Not only was it unethical, it was downright illegal. Once in 1957 I thought the whole thing would break wide open. A schoolteacher had a breakdown and had been hospitalized. A committee managed her $12,800 in savings. She recovered after four years, and when she came out she found there was only $4,100 left. They showed her the list of charges and everything, legal and proper, but she was going to the papers and raise a stink. Someone down there must be looking after the crooks. A day before she was going to talk to a newspaper editor she was killed in a bus accident."

After he learned of the racket and of the connection of the assistant attorney general with it, my informant took his evidence to his boss, the attorney general. This was late in 1949. The official was disturbed and then asked my informant to keep quiet. Why? Well, the assistant attorney general was an old friend of his, in fact had been his campaign manager. There was no need to raise a fuss. He'd talk to his old friend.

The talk didn't change matters. The racket continued.

"What really galled me," my informant went on, "was that this louse became a big expert in the law of incompetency. All kinds of social work groups called on him to talk about the great legal problems in the handling of incompetents' estates. And about the great protection the law now provided—a 'powerful shield' he used to call it."

The racket continued until quite recently when the assistant attorney general died. "I threatened to quit four, five times, but I always let the attorney general talk me out of it. No guts. I was in my late fifties. What was I going to do? Start a law practice?"

When he finished I said the story could make a great exposé—if he could provide the evidence. He nodded slowly. "Yeah. I figured. You'd have to have names and stuff wouldn't you? Let me think it over a little first. I'll talk it over with the wife."

He phoned a week later. "Ahhh, I'm too old to get involved in this. I figure I got a few good years left, why should I get everybody in the office mad at me. Let's forget it. So I won't be a hero."

•   •   •

"A lot of lawyers around here are pretty mad at me," says Jack A. Roper, a former World War II Air Force navigator, who is now chief counsel of the New York Veterans Administration office. "I'm the son-of-a-bitch taking away their bread and butter."

Roper is one of the VA's 475 lawyers around the country who spend part of their time trying to keep the estates of incompetent veterans from court-sanctioned legal raids. These estates receive about $300 million a year from the VA. The VA is authorized to prevent excessive legal charges from being levied by court-appointed lawyers and special guardians in any court in the country. According to one estimate some $9,000,000 a year is saved incompetent veterans on lawyers' fees through the VA's vigilance. (There are nearly 150,000 veterans—or their children—for whom court appointed fiduciaries act.)

The appearance of a VA attorney in a case where the judge has granted outsize fees in an incompetent veteran's estate is not a cause for rejoicing in the courtroom. As Roper tells it:

"The judge looks down his nose at us and says, 'What the hell are you VA guys doing here?' The clerks of the court, who often have a cozy relationship with some of these lawyers who get these patronage appointments, also give us the evil eye. If the judge doesn't know by now, I explain that in all fifty states the VA is considered a party of interest by state and local courts in veterans guardianship and commitment matters. Otherwise they'd be able to throw us out if they wanted to."

Roper, who had been an attorney before he entered the Air Force, has the New Yorker's traditional tolerance for the invisible balances of politics. "Sure, I know the judge was once a practicing lawyer, and he likes being a judge and wants to be reelected. So he rewards helpful lawyer friends with these assignments. But there's no reason why some poor incompetent veteran off in some VA hospital has to become an involuntary contributor to the judge's reelection campaign. So we go into court and fight these fees."

The effectiveness of the VA lawyers in some cases was illustrated in 1966 in the case of Henry Becan, a World War I veteran who has been an incompetent since 1936. Becan, a bachelor, is now seventy. He gets $50 a month from the VA, and there was only $1,430 in the "estate" for which his brother, Edward, was the committee. Becan is one of 3,042 incompetent veterans in the New York area who have committees caring for their savings. Another 1,078 have trust companies or banks handling their money.

His brother chose as lawyer for the committee Harold V. Dempsey. Then Supreme Court Justice Hyman Korn appointed another attorney, I. Saul Fleischman, as special guardian to check all that the committee had done in the previous nine years. For their services Dempsey asked for and was granted $750 and Fleischman $250, or $1,000 in attorney fees for an estate worth $1,430; roughly 70 percent of its value.

As the Appellate Division was to say later when the VA protested the fees, Fleischman's fee was too much for what he did:

His examination of the committee's bankbook and records embraced only a small portion of the accounting period. He neither visited the veteran at the hospital nor did he make any proper inquiry to ascertain his present physical or mental condition or needs.

Accordingly, the court cut both fees down to $300 for Dempsey and $100 to Fleischman, so that the fees now represented only 28 percent of the estate's value. Since then the Appellate Division has ruled that no special guardians, or guardians *ad litem*, as they've been renamed, are needed in VA estates of less than $2,500. On all estates the VA itself does the final auditing of all accounts.

"In all these patronage appointments the fee is almost all gravy for the lawyer. The girl in his office does all the paperwork," says Roper.

Besides trying to keep down court-approved raids on dwindling estates of veterans, the VA attorneys also keep an eye on lawyers who aren't satisfied with the sizable fees for unnecessary paperwork. Some of them are nakedly larcenous.

"The great trouble in all this," sayd Philip H. Thomas, director of the VA's Guardianship Service, and a former St. Louis lawyer, "is that in most local courts no one is really looking into these guardianship matters. Oh, some courts have accounting clerks, but if no one calls abuses to their attention they're just not going to see them." To help the courts spot jiggery-pokery with incompetent veterans' estates, Thomas' division has field attorneys who actually check once a year on the assets supposedly in the veteran's estate.

"Everybody likes to think veterans are one of those sacred

American subjects like motherhood and apple pie," he says. "I wish they were. Instead we often find that an incompetent veteran's estate is just a great temptation for some lawyers. The veteran is off in some hospital, the money is in the lawyer's hands and no one is really looking, so who's to know?"

Thomas and his asistant director, Abraham Friedman, a bald, bow-tied ex-Brooklyn lawyer, used to be surprised at the caliber of the attorneys who would get tempted. "These aren't the local shysters, desperately trying to keep head above water," Friedman says. "The top men in the bar sometimes."

During World War II a new VA field attorney assigned to upstate New York visited a prominent local attorney who was handling the estates of three incompetent veterans. The VA lawyer called him and asked if he could come in to make an assets check. The attorney-guardian suggested five P.M. When the VA man appeared, the lawyer was in a great hurry. For each of the estates he trotted out a group of government bonds and tried to distract the VA man by muttering what a great hurry he was in. When he finished the VA lawyer went back to his hotel and was unhappy: something about the bonds bothered him. Then he realized what it was. He suspected that at least two of the bonds bore the same serial number. Since that was terribly unlikely, the only possibility was that the local lawyer had shown him the same bonds for each of the three estates. When the VA man appeared unannounced at the lawyer's office the next morning the attorney refused to show all three sets of bonds at the same time. The VA attorney turned to the nearest federal judge with his suspicions: "He doesn't have the bonds, judge." The VA, properly irate, discussed prosecution with the federal attorney, but by then the matter had become very delicate: the attorney who had "borrowed" from the estates of the veterans had just been elected a local judge. The U.S. attorney decided not to prosecute.

In a more recent case in New York City, a local attorney who was guardian of a veteran's estate had "borrowed" $900 from it and couldn't replace it. Over a period of four years he finally managed to get it repaid with $25 and $50 repayments. Just when

the VA decided that perhaps this called for prosecution, the lawyer was appointed a city magistrate by Mayor Wagner. He died
not long ago.

Still, the VA is on the job—looking, checking and preventing
where possible any judge-lawyer combinations from getting away
with too much for very long. The rest of us haven't had such
constant protection for our incompetent citizens or relatives.

But things could be worse: you could be an Indian incompetent, theoretically rich but practically defenseless from the on-
slaughts of the men appointed to protect you by the courts.

Their story is in the following chapter.

14 THE SWINGER AND
HIS INDIANS

By our Apostolic authority we define and proclaim that the Indians, or any other peoples who may be hereafter discovered by Catholics, although they be not Christian, must in no way be deprived of their liberty or their possessions.

—POPE PAUL III
Letter to the Archbishop of Toledo, 1537

A lawyer is a learned gentleman who rescues your estate from your enemies and keeps it himself.

—LORD BROUGHAM

Many bar associations conduct programs to interest high school and college students in law as a career. They have lawyer-conducted courthouse tours and essay contests and other dreary, ineffective ploys. What they *should* be using are lots of reprints of a five-page color spread in the April, 1966, issue of *Playboy* on the $100,000 Palm Springs, California, bachelor pad of thirty-seven-year-old James McNider Hollowell. For the millions of high school and college readers of *Playboy* it was a new look at the modern, with-it lawyer. From the opening caption onward, anyone could see that twice-divorced lawyer Hollowell really had it made.

At the start of the day, James Hollowell pauses outside his mountain-girt Palm Springs pad to scan the morning headlines before hopping into his Jaguar for the five-minute spin to his downtown office.

There were gorgeous semidraped chicks all over the pad. The fireplace revolves and so does the television. "So I can watch it in the bathtub—because I'm lazy," Hollowell told George Ringwald of the *Riverside Daily Enterprise*. His account went:

It is a house where the Japanese shoji screen doors can be pulled shut to close the master bedroom from the living room but seldom are because it makes for openness, and because . . . well, it is that kind of a pad, too. Like there is a neatly-lettered sign that says: "No one under 21 admitted."

"Even 18 is risky," says owner-bachelor Hollowell, who happens also to be an attorney and ought to know. "It's 'contributing' to delinquency of your minor—anything under 21, buddy."

And there are the paintings on the wall, like nudes, and . . . well distinctive. Hollowell indicated the one hanging on the wall of a den-library off the living room, identified the artist as a man from San Diego, and said: "This was something new for him—his nudes were always ones in pink shoes." On this one you didn't notice the shoes. Even in the bathroom—identified by a sign over the door as the "Ladies Locker Room"—there are paintings of nudes.

Hollowell recalled the team from *Playboy*, the photographer and two beautiful models: "I did a good job of chasing this one brunette around for the photographer, so they brought her back a second time for a cocktail party. . . ." Hollowell did worry about the picture spread, whether it was "going to hurt his lawyer image."

"That got me worried," he said, not looking too worried. "I don't know . . . my ego says, 'Do it!' But it was a concern. The fact that I'm a bachelor . . . well, I'm still a cold fish with my clients—I don't make overtures and I don't date clients." He said, "I hope when the article comes out, they don't get the idea that I'm a lecherous old man. . . ."

As far as Palm Springs went, lawyer Hollowell didn't have to add the bit about not dating clients. His most important clients are a group of thirty dark, heavy-faced Agua Caliente Mission Indians for whom Hollowell is guardian, conservator or attorney. The land-rich Indians helped make possible the great bachelor pad in the Deep Well area of Palm Springs. Hollowell is only one of several lawyers, judges and state officials who have found that the desert can produce millions—if you can only find the right Indian guide.

The great desert legal boom started in 1959 when Congress decided to end the government's trusteeship of the Agua Caliente Indians and their assets. Some 25,144 acres of Palm Springs, worth about $50 million, were distributed to the 104 Indians in such a way that each got land allotments worth $333,000. An additional 2,000 acres was set aside for tribal purposes and maintenance of the tribal council.

Naturally the Indians under twenty-one needed guardians to help them take care of all that money, and some of the adults, too. Under the jurisdiction of the California Superior Court in Riverside, some sixty-nine guardianships were created for minors and fourteen conservatorships for adults. Only twenty-two members of the tribe were deemed competent to handle their own affairs.

"When this thing got rolling," recalls Edmund "Pete" Siva, a member of the tribal council, "everybody was grabbing himself an Indian." Another Agua Caliente Indian, Anthony Andreas, Jr., remembered "there was a mad rush to my house—everybody wanted to be appointed conservator."

But McCabe had other ideas, and in Palm Springs, McCabe was the law.

Hilton H. McCabe, a native Californian born in 1907, was admitted to law practice in 1937. He came to Palm Springs in 1947 and became one of its most active local attorneys, serving on the school board and the Chamber of Commerce. In 1953 Governor Earl Warren appointed him to the Superior Court.

McCabe is a tall, long-faced, cold, prim judge, impeccably dressed. He is distant, has a limp-fish handshake and ran a very tight courtroom. He wasn't liked by most of his judicial colleagues. When he was promoted to a higher court in 1965 a huge portrait of him was presented for hanging in the Riverside court. A fellow judge irreverently called it, "McCabe walking the waters."

A locally printed book appeared called *The Golden Checkerboard*—the Indian land parcels are located checkerboard fashion across the desert—and it bore a foreword by Supreme Court Justice Tom Clark. He wrote that he was sure the Indians "would be the first to acknowledge the selfless contribution of the man they affectionately call 'The Little White Father of the Indians of Palm Springs.' " As it turned out the Agua Caliente Indians had rather less complimentary names for Little White Father McCabe, and the book was soon withdrawn from sale when the Indians threatened legal action.

Under California law the Indians could have selected their own guardians or conservators, but Judge McCabe knew the best man to make those appointments was Hilton McCabe. In fact when a Department of Interior official, Robert Cox, once raised the issue with the judge, he told Cox that he "would not appreciate" having Cox or anyone else advising the Indians "of their rights to nominate a person of their choice for guardian or conservator of their estate, as provided under California law."

The judge's magisterial manner, his almost autocratic airs, are not unique. In 1956 Professor James G. Holbrook, after analyzing the Los Angeles trial courts for the American Bar Association, described what happens to a lawyer who is suddenly elevated to a Superior Court judgeship:

He finds himself surrounded by an almost fawning group. It is "Yes, your Honor, this" and "Yes, your Honor, that" from morning until nightfall. Court attaches are dependent upon him for what at his whim can be a pleasant or unpleasant task. Lawyers are dependent upon his pleasure as to the time of trial, conduct of trial, and result of trial. Citizens can have their property, their independence and even their lives dependent upon his judgment. There is no real control over his hours, his industriousness, or his thoroughness. It must be a breathtaking sensation when all this finally dawns upon him, and it takes both humility and untold strength of character to emerge unscathed.

Obviously, not all judges emerge unscathed. It becomes infinitely more difficult if $50,000,000 worth of land is in the hands of a small group of Indians who have to be protected from the evils of firewater and white men with forked tongues.

Judge McCabe decided to allow his appointees a fee of three

quarters of one percent per year of the value of the Indian hold-ings—plus, of course, larger percentages for "extraordinary serv-ices." For the conservators and guardians he chose from among key local citizens, lawyers and nonlawyers, but the most favored was a local attorney named Eugene E. Therieau. At one time, Therieau, a former mayor of Palm Springs, represented as guard-ian or attorney thirty-three of the eighty-two Indians who were under court supervision. For his services he collected $231,232. In 1961 Therieau became the local municipal court judge and turned over his law practice to James Hollowell. Up until then, Hollowell hadn't been doing too well in private practice. He began to flourish very quickly, even though Therieau held on to most of his guardianships. But Hollowell did now handle eight estates.

In 1962 Judge McCabe, looking around at the condition of considerable prosperity he had engendered among local attor-neys, trust companies and prominent citizens who were guarding or conserving dutifully—and profitably—decided that there was one important step he had forgotten. Surely, these wealthy In-dians should have wills made out so that there would be a proper distribution of their estates when death came.

Recently, Raymond C. Simpson, who is attorney for the Agua Caliente tribal council, recalled just how Judge McCabe went about it. In an affidavit's stilted language he narrates how

said Hilton McCabe proceeded to explain that it was his opinion that all of the members of the Agua Caliente Band of Mission Indians who were eligible to make wills should proceed with the drafting and execu-tion thereof;

That said Hilton McCabe further explained that several people had inquired as to the propriety of having him serve as executor of their estate due to the fact that he was judge of the Superior Court [but] he had looked into the matter and wanted to let them know that it was perfectly all right for him to serve as executor should the Indian testator or testatrix so desire.

A surprising number of Indians under conservatorship sud-denly found that they so desired. Quite quickly wills were drawn, and Judge McCabe was appointed executor in ten wills, nine of which were prepared by attorney James Hollowell. Later the Indians involved were interviewed and it was found "that in most cases the designation of executor and waiver of bond requirement was accomplished with something less than complete disclosure and understanding to the Indian concerned."

Ordinarily a will calling for someone outside the family to serve as executor—at a percentage fee fixed by the state—almost always calls for the executor to be bonded for the full amount in the estate. But Judge McCabe, knowing of his own integrity, was able to suggest that the bonding requirement be waived. As to the propriety of a sitting judge who was in charge of the whole program of Indian guardianships and conservatorships getting fees from the estates, well, that was a little peculiar. According to Canon 23 of the Canons of Judicial Ethics of the state:

> While a judge is not disqualified from holding executorships . . . he should not accept . . . if the holding of it would interfere or seem to interfere with the proper performance of his judicial duties. . . .

Obviously, Judge McCabe could see no such interference, and before long the executorships began to pay off. Five Indians who had made out wills died of natural causes, and Judge McCabe collected $19,318 for his nominal duties as executor in those estates. A typical estate was that of Clara Segundo Bow, the first to go. She died on April 6, 1962, less than two months after she had drawn her will at the timely suggestion of attorney Hollowell. Her probated estate was about $56,000, mostly in cash. In October, 1962, when her estate was closed, the executor, Judge McCabe, put in his request for the allowed fee of $1,772, and lawyer Hollowell put in for a similar amount, since the percentages allowed in California are the same for attorneys and for executors.

But as time went on, both Judge McCabe and attorney Hollowell wondered if they weren't being too modest in their fee requests. When the next Indian will-maker to go, Celia P. Hopkins, died on April 20, 1965, the fees rose considerably. She left an estate of $83,000 and executor McCabe asked for the statutory $2,471 plus another $2,000 for "extraordinary" expenses. These, he claimed, consisted of

making necessary arrangements with funeral home for burial; considerable discussion with family and heirs . . . consummating sale of corporate securities . . . assistance in preparation and filing of state and federal income taxes . . .

What makes his list so extraordinary is that these are the very ordinary and commonplace services that an executor performs or are done for him by the attorney for the estate. But Judge McCabe received his requested $4,471. The attorney for the estate got $3,971, so that between them they took $8,442, or slightly more than 10 percent of the total estate. The other three estates followed similar patterns and, in all, Judge McCabe has received $19,318 in regular and extraordinary fees as executor of the estates of Agua Caliente Indians.

There are still another five wills in which he is named as executor. Since the judge is sixty-one at this writing (1968), he might not live to serve as executor for *all* five. But then, the Indian's life expectancy is not nearly as high as the white man's. Besides having physical and medical disadvantages, there are psychic factors, too. Possibly, worry and anger over the exactions of the white conservators and guardians might tend to cut short Indian lives even more. Judge McCabe also received a $25,000 fee for serving as conservator in a case related to the Indian guardianship program. In all, then, he has earned $44,000 in such fees while on the bench in the past five years.

In 1965 Judge McCabe was promoted by Governor Pat Brown to be an Appellate Judge in San Bernardino. When he left Riverside and the Indian program his place was filled by Judge Merrill Brown, who took his cues on Indian affairs from Judge McCabe and never signed any court order on Indian matters unless he knew it had McCabe's approval. In effect, then, even from San Bernardino and his lofty judicial perch, Judge McCabe remained the guiding genius of the guardianship and conservator program he had instituted in 1959. Ordinarily when the guarded Indian youths came to man's estate at twenty-one they asked to be relieved of their guardianships, but Judge McCabe in his wisdom decided that at twenty-one only the name would change: from guardianship to conservator. So the fees and exactions kept on going.

How they went is illustrated by the financial histories of some of the protected Indians. Wilford Bow became a ward of the Superior Court when he was five years old and died of a malignant tumor when he was thirteen. In that eight-year period his estate had income totaling $23,325—mostly rentals from land—but in that same period his guardians and their attorneys were awarded by Judge McCabe fees totaling $20,351. His guardians got $13,906 and their lawyers received $6,445, with most of it going to Jim Hollowell, the *Playboy* exemplar.

Ray Patencio, a bright, bespectacled twenty-one-year-old college student, has decided to become a lawyer. As an Agua Caliente Indian who has been under guardianship for the past nine years Ray realized the way to real wealth is not just getting land allotment as he and other Agua Caliente Indians did, but in being a lawyer—or even a judge—and having the supervision over those properties as guardian or conservator. In that period, Ray's lands were leased out to developers who paid his estate rentals of about $110,000. Of this, his guardians, conservators, attorneys and real estate brokers took about $58,000, or some 52 percent of the total. A big piece of it, $25,000, was taken by Judge Therieau as a fee for getting some of the land leased. Since he was not a real estate broker but merely Ray's guardian, there was some question of propriety in the judge's getting the fee. But he got it.

Ray seldom saw his guardian, the judge, or got any explanation of his business affairs. When taxed with this, Judge Therieau, a short, peppery jut-jawed fellow, said: "If the Indian was interested, he could find out whatever he wanted. It wasn't the guardian's duty to run him down and tell him why every T was crossed." In talking to reporter George Ringwald the judge said recently that the business of being guardian and conservator had been a "most interesting job." He added, with insouciant candor, "and very rewarding, as you know."

Attorney Hollowell, the swinger, also got some $8,000 out of Ray Patencio's income, as attorney for guardian Therieau. In addition Hollowell found other ways to increase his take. Real estate developer Roy Rey, who leased 40 acres owned by Ray Patencio and built condominium apartments on it, had to turn to lawyer Hollowell to get approval of every sublease. Hollowell charged him $250 to $350 for each order, which were merely routine duplicates. Only the tenant's name and description of the premises had to be changed. For getting Rey a master lease on the property and giving Patencio a 5 percent increase in rental, Hollowell asked an outsize $3,500, even though he had no part in the negotiation of the increase. When Rey stalled on paying this, Hollowell was pretty nasty. "This is not a typographical error," he made it clear to an incredulous builder, Roy Rey. "Until this is paid no further services will be rendered, nor will I argue my fee with you." Rey had to pay rather than let all leasing of apartments come to a halt.

On May 19, 1967, the great bonanza for the court-appointed guardians, conservators and attorneys of the Agua Caliente Indians petered out, when Secretary of the Interior Stewart L. Udall took over all operations pending an investigation. May 19 was fittingly ironic: it is the anniversary of the birth of Honest St. Ives, the thirteenth-century patron saint of lawyers.

In 1965 the Agua Caliente Indians had an income of $747,000 from land leases and other investments, while the fees of their protectors amounted to $280,000, or 37 percent of the income. These seemed, noted Secretary Udall drily, "unusually high."

A task force of investigators and attorneys was sent into Palm Springs and Riverside, California, by Udall. Their first report, on October 13, 1967, documented the following:

1. Guardians and conservators of Indian estates and their lawyers have collected payments from third persons doing business with the es-

tates in circumstances which suggest that they were actually serving the interests of third persons.

2. Those representing the Indians in trust capacities have claimed and been awarded fees from the Indian estates for which they were also compensated by others doing business with the estates.

At the very least the canons of legal ethics were violated wholesale.

The investigators had fully audited sixteen Indian estates for this preliminary report and found that the guardians, conservators and their attorneys had received "excessive" fees, for example:

—in 3 cases fees were between 18.5% and 26% of the gross receipts of the estates.

—in one case, 32.5%, in another 45.5%; and 51%; and in still another 61.6%. And a final, splendid one, 340.1%. (That is, the estate's guardians took out three and a half times more than the estate took in.)

Most of the Indian estates were removed totally from the guardians or conservators and turned over to the Indians themselves in April, 1968.

In San Bernardino, Judge McCabe, presiding justice of the State Court of Appeal, one of the highest ranking of all the judges in California, sits in what some envious lesser judges call "McCabe's new Taj Mahal courthouse." There he must surely wonder how the "Little White Father" of the Agua Caliente Indians was now being regarded with such grave suspicion by (1) those nosy investigators from the Department of the Interior and (2) the even graver snoops from the state's Commission on Judicial Qualifications, which can help get a judge unseated with notable dispatch.

In its final report, the Department of Interior's Task Force recommended in April, 1968 that the entire Agua Caliente Indian guardianship-conservatorship system be abolished. In his letter accompanying the final report Secretary of Interior Udall wrote:

Eugene E. Therieau, now Judge of the Municipal Court of Palm Springs, and Mr. James Hollowell have, between them, been awarded fees of approximately one-half million dollars over the last seven years. The conduct of each reveals instances of apparent conflicts of interest, double charging and fee-splitting.

In fact, the Judge got $257,000 and lawyer Hollowell $227,000. Judge Therieau's term of office expires in January, 1969 but he announced that he was going to retire. He said his decision was not influenced by the investigation and its disclosures.

Secretary Udall added his own judgment on the Palm Springs mess:

I am appalled that the state of affairs described in the report has not only existed under ostensible state and federal supervision; it has flourished. As a lawyer I find it particularly disturbing that much of the responsibility for the morally-shabby state of affairs revealed must be laid at the door of some members of the local bar and court.

But as of July, 1968, no attorneys have been disbarred, no judges disrobed and none of the "excessive" fees dislodged.

15 *WHY DON'T WE LIKE LAWYERS?*

Lawyers, I suppose, were children once.
——CHARLES LAMB

Why don't we like lawyers?

I don't mean *professional* lawyer-haters such as Charles Mc-Cabe, an acidulous columnist for the San Francisco *Chronicle,* who began a 1966 diatribe thus:

> I am one of that vast body of loyal, devoted, red-blooded American cynics who despise lawyers as they despise no other class of fauna. . . . The three times I was most deceived and most poorly served, were when I allowed my affairs to go into the hands of officers of the court, sworn to protect my interests. . . . My experience led me to the belief, doubtless mistaken, that most lawyers are swine. And not even nice swine. . . .

Mr. McCabe wasn't around when I visited San Francisco, and I couldn't get the details on his three deceptions and poor service at the hands of lawyers.* But while talking to an old friend in the *Chronicle* city room I did get an idea of what might be behind some of the bad press our lawyers often get.

Maybe we have a lot of writers, editors, reporters and newscasters who have been done dirt—or *think* they have—by lawyers.

*John Crosby, another columnist who delights in going after lawyers, has since moved to London where he does a weekly column for *The Observer.* Still he manages to keep his down-with-lawyers franchise. In a November, 1967, column he alluded to the high cost of "real necessities" in America. "Law, for instance. Well one needs a lawyer in England now and then, but nothing like the extent Americans need them. . . . In England a solicitor can be persuaded to look over a lease for as little as $1.40: in America a lawyer won't even start drumming his fingers on his desk for less than $50 and to get him to look properly portentous costs another $100."

Understandably these men and women would from time to time get in unkind comments about lawyers in their writings and broadcasts. Just a theory, but I thought it worth checking in my several cross-country trips while researching this book.

In Chicago I started with Mike Royko, the free-wheeling columnist of the Chicago *Daily News* who often takes out after lawyers. Royko couldn't think of any personal involvement that may have soured him on them. He hired a lawyer once to check his contract with the newspaper. Royko was satisfied the man did a good job and was glad to pay him. But, he went on, "The Bar here calls me a crab. I needle lawyers in the hope they'll straighten things out. They don't, but I keep trying. We have a lot of lawyers in town who do have integrity, who know of the dirty things a lot of other lawyers get away with, but there isn't much they can do about it. I get a lot of leads for the stuff I use from things these lawyers tell me."

He thinks that the three years he spent covering Chicago courts for his paper may have given him a permanent warp on the bar. "Every day you saw something wrong in the courts. We've had guys on the bench here who should've stood in front with their hands cuffed. I got pretty disgusted at the things some lawyers would do to get publicity, especially in divorce and negligence cases. Some of them used to pay one reporter—not on *my* paper —two hundred bucks every time he got their picture in the paper in connection with a divorce case he was handling."

In 1965 Royko did a column headed: "Bar Associations Always Charitable—Toward Lawyers":

The St. Louis Bar Assn. went into court recently and tried to convince a jury it was a charitable organization. It did so because someone had died and left it a fortune. It could save $135,000 in taxes by suddenly becoming a charitable organization. The association's lawyers tried to convince the jury it existed primarily to do good things. They related how it furnishes free legal wisdom for people who can't afford to buy it, how it keeps an eye on the integrity of judges, and how it promotes the dignity of the law.

The other position was taken by the Internal Revenue people. They told the jury the main function of the bar association was to look out for the best interests of lawyers. The jury listened to both sides, then ruled that if the bar association commits acts of charity, it doesn't do so often enough to duck out of any taxes. This was an unfortunate decision. Bar associations being the same in most cities, it could leave the widespread impression they are not involved in charitable works. . . .

In Milwaukee, Edward S. Kerstein, who has been keeping an eye on lawyers and courts for the past thirty-three years, told me he, personally, had never been harmed by a lawyer. But there were at least two reporters he felt had been taken by having to pay much too high fees for having simple wills drawn. "Those reporters aren't going to like lawyers for a long time."

Leonard Downie, Jr., a splendid investigative reporter for the *Washington Post,* told me that "I and my relatives have little contact with lawyers that has made an impression on me. That is, as far as personal matters are concerned." But as a *reporter:*

I first came in close contact with lawyers when I began covering the local courts and did the research for my series on the lowest court here, the Court of General Sessions. . . . Some of the lawyers handling the most criminal cases were public drunks and worked in the court drunk. Others specialized in extorting money from their appointed clients by asking for "bond fees" and pocketing the money along with their own fee. . . . They often could not remember the name of their client when going before a judge with him.

. . . the Bar Association refused to acknowledge the conditions in the court or do anything about them even after the series appeared. . . . Instead, *an Association committee was assigned to investigate me and my reasons for writing the series.* [Emphasis added.]

In December, 1966, he did a long Sunday piece on probate costs in and around the District of Columbia.

I found that the costs of probate, including lawyers' and executors' fees, seemed too high and were being assessed on an all-that-the-freight-will-bear basis. . . . The Bar Association complained most vociferously about the piece. . . . The lawyers did not dispute my facts, merely the

had gotten a $2,900 settlement in an accident case and two others felt "neutral" about lawyers. One felt positively happy about lawyers. His wife was one; so was his father. Five were more or less neutral on the lawyers.

I don't think my little survey *proved* anything. Dare I extrapolate my eleven reporters and newscasters who had adverse experience, to the American people as a whole? In that case of course we have a real problem for the bar's public relations people to handle. In 1966 we had about 115 million Americans who were twenty-one and over. If nearly half of them had some adverse experience with the bar—about 57 million adults—where do you begin persuading them they have the wrong slant on lawyers?

Complicating the problem, of course, is the presence of novelists in our midst who from time to time make lawyers characters in their tales.

Our first antilawyer novelist was George Watterston, who lived from 1783 to 1854. Since he was also a lawyer who had practiced in Maryland and later in the District of Columbia, lawyer Watterston came by his bias fairly. As a later biographer was to say of him, "he never missed an opportunity in any of his books to make a derogatory remark about lawyers." But Watterston wasn't a bias-blinded crank. He was happily married, had eight children, became the first Librarian of Congress in 1833 and began the movement to build the Washington Monument in the District.

He called one novel *The Lawyer,* with a subtitle, "Man As He Ought Not to Be." It appeared in 1808 in Pittsburgh. The book is told in the first person by the villainous hero, a lawyer named Morcell. He makes our contemporary skunk-hero, Sammy Glick, sound like a good boy who just fell in with bad company.

Morcell learned law from his tutor, a disbarred lawyer. He was brought up, comments a critic, to "disregard the rights of everyone. Justice means nothing to him but he is proficient in the technicalities of the law." He is thrashed, with good reason, by a fine fellow named Ansley. To get even, Morcell seduces Ansley's sister, Matilda, and flees when he learns she is pregnant. He drinks and lechers freely. He forces a poor widow with six chil-

dren, who owes him a legal fee, to sell the bed she is lying on. As
he tells it:

I was, however, inexorable and illegally commanded the constable to
arrest her. Unwilling to lie in prison she promised to dispose of her bed,
the only moveable chattel of any value in her miserable hut. . . . I had
the inhumanity to accompany the constable to the wretched hovel on
the day of the sale and to stand calmly by and behold him drag the bed
from beneath her—for she was actually ill—and expose it for sale.

He's a wretch, all right. In Baltimore he's hired by the husband
of a woman who was seduced by their landlord. Instead of pursuing the case righteously, Morcell takes a bribe from the landlord
and sells out his client. In another town where he sets up practice
his activities become so villainous he is forcefully expelled by the
townspeople for "my heinous practices."

Finally, penniless, socially and professionally discredited, Morcell reforms. He goes to a "remote and distant part of Maryland,
endeavoring by charity and benevolence to expatiate in some degree, the crimes of which I have been guilty."

Watterston started a long line of antilawyer novels and essays.
As one commentator pointed out in 1887,

to represent lawyers in a newspaper article, or in a novel, in an odious
or ludicrous light, is often as pleasant to the author as it is to a junior
boy to get the chance of throwing a stone with impunity at one of the
tyrants of the school.

This is all well and good, says Edward J. Bander, a lawyer who
is now the librarian of the New York University Law School, except that " 'junior boy' gets a spanking for expressing himself,
while 'writer boy' gets royalties. Not since the heyday of progressive education has abnormal conduct been so well rewarded."

Bander got back at lawyer-denigrating novelists in an amusing
piece he did in September, 1959, for the *Journal of the American
Bar Association.* It was called: "Some Legal Fiction: Woe Unto
You, Novelists!" He wrote: "Rabelais, Fielding, Thackeray,

Kafka, Balzac, Trollope and Dickens, some of these men trained in the law themselves, have found the lawyer an easy mark." These memorable but fictional lawyers

are treacherous and lecherous machines to entangle even the wary in the spidery webs of the law. . . . It's quite a game and there is this to be said for it—some great novelists have succeeded in using the law as a stepping-stone to their success and current writers may be excused for recognizing a good thing when they see it. They cannot, however, be so easily pardoned for the arbitrary, pretentious, impossible manner in which they portray the law and its servants.

One of the counts Bander lists against the novelists is that their lawyer characters spend too much time in bed. "It's getting so that a female who takes her novel reading seriously will consider it ill-advised to be examined by a lawyer without a nurse being present."

But what really hurts, Bander admits, is that "these lawyer novels are so successful . . . novelists do much better with the law than lawyers do."

("Well, maybe I am a *little* jealous," Bander told me recently. "I'm writing a novel myself.")

·   ·   ·

When satirists travel in their imaginations, why on earth do they have to visit a land with a vicious breed of lawyers—and then write one of the great classics that nearly everybody looks into in their impressionable teens? How much can the ABA and state bars spend on public relations gimmicks such as "Law Day" and Gavel Awards to media to offset those lines in *Gulliver's Travels:*

Very many among us were bred from their youth in the art of proving by words multiplied for the purpose that "white" is "black" and "black" is "white," according as they are paid.

This fine bunch of "pettifoggers," as Jonathan Swift termed them, were vicious but pretty stupid. Many were of so great ignorance and stupidity that it was hard to pick out of any profession a generation of men more despicable in common conversation, or who were so much looked upon as avowed enemies to all knowledge and learning. . . .

If you were impressionable enough back then, you might even think that the decline and fall of the Roman Empire—as seen by Gibbon—was due in part to a bunch of Roman lawyers:

Some of them procured admittance into families for the purpose of fomenting differences, of encouraging suits, and of preparing a harvest of gain for themselves or their brethren. . . . Careless of fame and of justice, they are described for the most part as ignorant and rapacious guides, who conducted their clients through a maze of expense, of delay and of disappointment; from whence, after a tedious series of years, they were at length dismissed, when their practice and fortune were almost exhausted.

Then the poets have to get into the act, too, and what are you going to do if hundreds of high school English teachers suggest that the class memorize that little Sandburg sandbagging:

In the heels of the higgling lawyers,
Too many slippery ifs and buts and howevers,
Too much hereinbefore provided whereas,
Too many doors to go in and out of.
  When the lawyers are through
  What is there left, Bob?
  Can a mouse nibble at it
  And find enough to fasten a tooth in?

And sometimes even cantankerous school texts get into the act of knocking the lawyers. There is a widely used text on career guidance for high school students, *Occupations Today*. It is written by two guidance experts, Brewer and Landy, and published by Ginn and Company, a huge textbook publishing firm. When it came to the law as an occupation, the authors had certain cautions for their teen-age readers:

. . . yet the profession as a whole has far to go before it can be said to live up to its ideals and possibilities. Perhaps the reason for this is the temptation which comes into the work of the lawyer. . . . Before you choose a vocation in which thousands of young men are not succeeding, you should ask yourself, "Am I especially well equipped to push past those men and make good in law?" This means, for one thing, are you able to resist temptations and keep your record honest.

A mite gloomy, perhaps, about the thousands not succeeding, and maybe a bit too frank on the lawyer's temptations, but still an honest and rather mature discussion of some of the difficulties lying in wait for those youngsters thinking of going to law school eventually.

Not to the ABA's ever watchful Public Relations Committee. It might not be able to do anything about Swift, Gibbon or even Sandburg, but guidance experts Brewer and Landy should be a whole lot easier. The ABA's committee wrote Ginn and Company that the offending material was " 'comic' in its weirdly inaccurate and misleading portrayal of the legal profession." It was no joke to the alarmed publisher who, according to the proud ABA Public Relations Committee,

responded with notable promptness and vigor. Wherever possible the books were withdrawn from circulation or sale, and the authors instructed to re-write the offending section on The Occupation of Lawyer so as to conform with the facts. . . . At least one other textbook is now under consideration for a similar reason. It should be understood and emphasized that what is being done is in no sense an attempt at censorship nor does it contemplate any so-called "book burning" nonsense.

It couldn't be "censorship" because whatever the ABA's Public Relations Committee says often enough, like Alice's Red Queen, must be true.* In any case, in the text's 1956 edition, drily points

---

*Charles L. Dodgson, the English mathematician who wrote *Alice in Wonderland* under the pseudonym of Lewis Carroll, may have had a glimpse of future textbook tampering when he wrote: "That's the reason they're called lessons, because they lessen from day to day."

out professor Vern Countryman of the Harvard Law School, "there is no critical word of the legal profession and no suggestion of dangerous temptations in practice."

The lawyers' public relations watchdogs have had a harder time with the randomly spoken word on radio and TV. When Pamela Mason, a blithely outspoken resident of Beverly Hills, was interviewed on the *Merv Griffin Show* on the evening of October 23, 1967, over the stations of the Group W (Westinghouse) network, the dialogue went this way:

PAMELA: I think the reason for bitterness is there's an awful lot of legality attached to divorce. That's why it's such a rotten business. You see, because in comes a lawyer who expects to make a mint out of it. And he stirs up the anger so as to get a bigger fee because if it's a little simple divorce . . .

MERV: So now you're going after lawyers.

PAMELA: Oh, well, lawyers, you know what they are!

MERV: Male lawyers?

PAMELA: Well, there are one or two women lawyers but they wear silly hats. . . . It's mostly a male profession and it's a cruel, hardhearted profession that only a man could follow. Because, what they do—they go to school . . . at their parents' expense and they come out and put a label on the door—says they're a lawyer and then proceed to cut up everybody else's lives—and take a fee for it and they don't care whether you're right or wrong. . . . Well, they are dishonest, aren't they, among everything else?

Naturally, there were many calls of protest to the station—and lots of letters by lawyers to the public relations chairmen of their local bar associations. For example, a Queens, New York, attorney, wrote:

If ever the lawyer's image was degraded and our professional repution irreparably harmed it was last evening when this show was televised . . . once we allow ourselves to become complacent and falter in our efforts to protect this reputation we are lost.

Nothing much came of the bar protests to Group W. Mainly the network's own legal counsel stressed the fact that the stations had won awards in the past for the good things they had said about lawyers and the profession.

Lawyers with a higher boiling point than the ABA watchdog have long dismissed the modern denigration of the lawyer merely as a perpetuation of "The Ancient Grudge," as law professor Max Radin once did in a masterful article in the *Virginia Law Review*. But for many modern lawyers, what makes the old grudge harder than ever to endure is that it is kept alive and current mostly by *lawyers and judges.*

There's just too much "kidding" by lawyers says Henry Latimer Jordan, a director of the State Bar of Texas, writing in 1966. Lawyers have been their own worst enemies by "kidding" among themselves about the

integrity of the profession or any member. . . . The integrity of the legal profession is too sacred and vital to the profession for lawyers to "kid" about it. . . .

If lawyers really want to help their public relations they could do it by each vowing never to say anything other than complimentary about another lawyer except when necessary to discipline the lawyer, and to broadcast steadily to the world the truth that as far as integrity is concerned, we have a truly great group of gentlemen.

The only difficulty with Mr. Jordan's prescription is that lawyers are too far behind on most public opinion polls regarding professional integrity and public regard. Under the Jordan formula—a curious marriage of Coué and Carnegie—our 300,000 attorneys could spend all their time on this pursuit. By becoming full-time broadcasters of the integrity of this "great group of gentlemen," they just wouldn't have any time for clients. In turn, this would help solve some of the problems that give rise to the dangerous "kidding" Mr. Jordan deplores.

Judges also are responsible, says Denver Probate Judge David Brofman, who used to be chairman of the Colorado Bar Association's Public Relations Committee: "Too often the bad public

image emanates from people on the bench." And R. Leland
Hamilton, Executive Director of the St. Louis Bar Association,
provides a horrible example of the loose-lipped judge:

A judge from a small county . . . blasted some of the lawyers . . .
and also some of the judges in other courts. He said we had a great
many judges who should be digging ditches or put away in some ladies
home. The headline on the article used was "prostitute"; the judge had
referred to "legal prostitutes." So this article, in my estimation, tore
down much of the work that we've tried to build and some of the other
work we are trying to carry on.

Well, maybe we're trying *too* hard, says Harvey O. Payne,
public relations director for the State Bar of Texas:

Is it possible for the Texas Bar ever to create a totally sympathetic
public image of the lawyer? No . . . not even if we spent as much as the
50 largest banks spent on public relations . . . $31 million. . . .
If 4,000 Texas lawyers each win their case on a given day, it follows
that 4,000 lawyers must lose; and it follows also, that the clients of the
latter group of lawyers are not going to be happy, even though justice is
done. . . .
We must assume, then . . . that lawyers will continue to make enemies every day they practice. By its very nature, the legal profession is
the most abused and least understood profession in the world.

The way for lawyers to do their best public relations, he added,
would be if each followed five basic precepts. (1) Keep his client
informed currently, (2) itemize his billings, (3) "quit giving free
legal advice . . . , (4) stop cheapening himself by cutting fees;
and follow the minimum fee schedule. (5) Quit cussing his
brother-lawyers. How can the lawyers expect the public to think
more highly of them than they think of themselves. We must
never lose sight of the fact that when one single lawyer is vilified,
all lawyers are hurt."
After that Mr. Payne could only conclude with the inevitable
lines about a tolling bell—which he attributed to one John Dunn,

possibly a Texan. The original bell-tolls-for-thee John Donne was a contemporary of the French essayist Montaigne, an avid lawyer-hater who once wrote: "King Ferdinand wisely provided that no lawyers could join in the new colonies sent to America, lest law suits should get a footing in the new world."

Now that they have obtained substantial footing in the new world, lawyers are yearning for another boon:

"We want to be loved. But our profession is, by its nature, not very lovable," warned John H. Holloway, executive director of the Oregon State Bar, to a National Institute on Bar Public Relations in 1965. "The most we can ask for, generally speaking, is to be understood, to be respected and to be needed."

Holloway didn't think that it was *all* the public's fault for not understanding. A lot of lawyers made the job infinitely more difficult:

Each lawyer must realize that high ethical standards are absolutely required and not a matter of choice—high ethical standards not only in his professional life, but at least equally in his personal life. *It appears that, even more than in the past, young lawyers regard their licenses to practice as hunting licenses.* [Emphasis added.]

Besides out-of-season hunting, he saw lawyers guilty of other faults that would prevent people from understanding them: a lot of them are almost illiterate, not too coherent, and expansively verbose:

The majority of lawyers are, in my opinion, unable to express themselves properly or even passably. Too many letters and reports I see are not even intelligible. Some lawyers seem to feel that it's impressive and justifies a fee if they talk in high-sounding phrases, managing to convey in fifty words what could have been said in seven.

He didn't say how many of the verbose lawyers charged seven times more as a result. But lawyers have a precedent for that, too. Right into the nineteenth century, British solicitors used to charge their clients *by the word* in their briefs. A pithy solicitor who eschewed unnecessary verbiage could die of malnutrition.

In their further search for love and understanding, our lawyers have inevitably turned to psychiatrists. A few years ago the New York County Lawyers Association asked Dr. Herbert G. Modlin to do an informal psychoanalysis. He talked to some of his colleagues who had lawyer patients. All agreed on one point: ". . . probably the most strongly and frequently influencing motivation to the lawyer's choice of career is his unconscious preoccupation with rules and procedures. . . ." But Dr. Modlin hunched deeper: "Perhaps bending the rules is the paramount objective. Possibly he needs . . . to discover by his own testing *how much he can get away with while still staying just within the law.*" [Emphasis added.] Well, you can't build a public relations program on *that.*

Other psychiatrists have had their crack at the hard law of lawyer life: hardly anybody loves a lawyer. Dr. Andrew S. Watson of the University of Michigan, who has treated many an ailing or neurotic law student, finds most would-be lawyers are extremely shy. He thinks a law student is really looking to a highly personal and confidential relationship with his clientele who are, in effect, *relegated to dependency.*

In a recent book, *The Personality of Lawyers,* Professor Walter Weyrauch of the University of Florida Law School comments on Dr. Watson's findings: "Often the professional man may be motivated by the powerful belief that by assuming responsibilities he may gain something he does not have—emotional stability."

Professor Weyrauch talked to several psychiatrists. One mentioned that some of his "queerest" patients happened to be lawyers. Another psychiatrist related that lawyers are often difficult patients because of their well-developed and rigid defense mechanism.

He also found a 1960 survey of college students and their image of lawyers. A frequent comment was that the lawyer is apt to have a pretty wife but that his home life is not particularly happy.

Summarizing his findings about lawyers in general, Weyrauch finds they tend to be tense in their relationships with others, and lack human warmth and affection. . . . They are often gloomy, lack confidence in the future, and worry about their health and questions of security and old age. They [prefer] power and authority to persuasion.

With those qualities present in a lot of lawyers you can see the job the public relations experts have in making lawyers lovable.

Just how difficult a job it will be has been shown by polls conducted in Iowa, California, Texas and Michigan since the end of World War II. They were not flattering to the bar. Gallup and Roper polls in 1949 and 1950 showed the legal profession was not popular with the general public as a recommended pursuit for young people or even as a source of government leaders.

But you know *polls:* where are the names of Alf Landon and Tom Dewey in the list of U. S. Presidents, and so on? In 1959 Robert V. Wills, a curious and energetic lawyer of Long Beach, California, decided to find out for himself.

He chose, at regular intervals, 600 names from the pages of the Los Angeles and Orange County phonebooks. Attorneys and CPAs were eliminated, as were business addresses. He got 102 replies.

Most of those who answered felt that the work done by doctors, teachers and engineers was more important than the lawyer's work; that the average lawyer is more interested in winning his case than in getting at truth or the good of society. Most of them thought that lawyers are more interested in their fee than their client's welfare; that these fees were generally too high for the services rendered. Most thought lawyers who defend criminals commonly distort the truth and produce false evidence to help their clients.

The most comprehensive American poll of the public's attitude toward lawyers was undertaken in 1960 by the Missouri Bar, backed by funds from the Prentice-Hall Publishing Company, which turns out many books and newsletter services for attorneys. Some 300 laymen and 300 lawyers all over the state were interviewed personally in depth—about 90 minutes per interview—

and an additional 2,500 laymen and 2,500 lawyers answered an extensive mail questionnaire. The results:

- Most people rated lawyers below bankers, clergy, doctors, dentists and teachers in "general reputation." People who used a lawyer thought less highly of them than did people who never used one.
- Only 35 percent of the people thought lawyers were honest and truly dedicated to their profession.
- About 40 percent of the public believed lawyers' bills were too high.
- Most people—nearly 70 percent—believed that the basis for a lawyer's fee should be the "effort expended." (Obviously, this means that the public is against bar minimum fee schedules that provide a percentage fee for legal work in probate, personal injury, real estate, divorce or sale of a business. But the survey analysts delicately didn't go into the public opposition to percentage fees.)
- Most of the public and the lawyers themselves believed contingent fees in personal injury cases were much too high. Many of the complaints about lawyers overcharging came from people in the Kansas City area where the prevailing contingent fee in personal injury cases is 50 percent. Most people thought 25 percent or less would be fair.
- Nearly 57 percent of the people who used lawyers thought lawyers created lawsuits unnecessarily, that they didn't make enough effort to settle cases out of court as they should.
- Most shocking to the survey's conductors was the finding that almost 12 percent of the people who used lawyers were solicited for their cases, mainly in personal injury matters. Since soliciting is an ethical violation that could—but seldom does—lead to disbarment, a lot of Missouri lawyers are practicing who shouldn't be.

But the conclusion that really worried the Missouri lawyers as well as many others was the one pointed to by Billie R. Bethel, a pretty lady-lawyer who is director of bar economics for the Illinois State Bar:

Time and again, as an overwhelming theme of this survey, we have seen that the User of legal services is less impressed with lawyers, their integrity, their capabilities and their obedience to their Code of Ethics than are Non-Users. *This we have and can attribute to something that happens to that User once he arrives at your office and begins to conduct business with you.* [Emphasis added.]

At the 1965 Institute on Bar Public Relations one speaker, who obviously didn't believe the findings of the Missouri survey, insisted that the best way to solve the problem of the public's fear and distrust of the profession was personal contact with the lawyer. E. Donald Shapiro, the young hyperkinetic director of Continuing Legal Education for Michigan's lawyers, disagreed strongly:

Unfortunately, I can name examples, as we all can, of contact after contact and then fear and distrust began. And this is like smallpox, one person gets burned and it spreads and spreads and spreads—and all the Law Days in the world aren't as effective as the neighbor telling what happened when she dealt with the lawyer.

The logical conclusion is, clearly: *the fewer of us who have anything to do with lawyers the better we'll think of them.* The trouble with this is that if a lot of us stop seeing lawyers, just to keep a favorable image of them, the resulting drop in law business will make lawyers hungrier, even less ethical and far more rapacious.Then another survey, twenty years hence, will show a corresponding drop in the public's regard for lawyers, and that will lead to still fewer of us having anything to do with the profession, and so on. Eventually, of course, when none of us have anything to do with lawyers, the profession will enjoy our high regard and even admiration.

* * *

Having written—and enjoyed—my little ironical solution for the bar's public relations problem I'm reminded of Jessamyn West's caution: "A taste for irony has kept more hearts from breaking than a sense of humor for it takes irony to appreciate the joke which is on oneself."

Obviously the joke is on all of us. It may be hard to live with lawyers but in our increasingly complex world it's impossible to do without them—not this side of a millennium in which all men will be law abiding, just and reasonable.

All the past and future surveys on why we dislike lawyers or what we distrust about them won't change matters one writ. Two thousand years of irony, insult, satire and rolling condemnation haven't changed lawyers or modified their gross advantages over clients. In the following chapter, however, I have a few modest beginnings that could effect *some* change.

16 WHAT CAN WE DO?

The Thurians [an ancient people of southern Italy] ordained that whosoever would go about to abolish an old law, or establish a new one, should present himself with a halter around his neck, to the end that, if his proposal were not approved, he might be hanged at once.
—MONTAIGNE, *Essays*

We no longer hang reformers when their proposals are voted down. We merely disregard them—or reelect them. Occasionally they are paid heed, a law is passed, and some of us assume all is well. Not *all*. "One of the greatest delusions in the world is the hope that the evils of this world can be cured by legislation," complained Tom Reed, a noted Speaker of the U. S. House of Representatives early in the century.

Still, delusion or not, change via legislation is particularly unlikely for some suggested legal reforms. Everyone knows lawyers form the biggest single occupational bloc in our state legislatures and Congress. In New Jersey, for example, 47 of 83 legislators are lawyers, or about 56 percent. In the U. S. Senate, 68 of the 100 members are lawyers, and in the House some 314 of the 435 Representatives were admitted to the bar. In all, 71 percent of our congressmen are lawyers.

We got this top-heavy representation by lawyers in spite of several historical warnings. "That 150 lawyers should do business together is not to be expected," wrote Thomas Jefferson, referring to the first U. S. Congress. And earlier, in 1730, Rhode Island enacted a law excluding lawyers from membership in the legislature.

Just how much the lawyers have recovered from *that* law was indicated in 1956 by John Ben Sheppard, then president of the

National Association of Attorneys General, speaking at an ABA convention. He said the time seems to be coming when this county will pass under the virtual control of lawyers as a distinct group. "Lawyers have always been the real, ultimate custodians of our form of government."

Since the control is still not complete, nearly all our lawyer-legislators retain membership in their law firms. We haven't the faintest idea of the kind of fees they and their partners get from clients—many of whom have a special interest in state or federal legislation. How many of the 68 lawyers in the U. S. Senate, asks Tom Wicker of *The New York Times,* "could stand investigation of their political fund-raising, or of possible conflicts of interest between private income and Senate responsibility?"

Lawyers who are congressmen are barred from pleading cases to federal agencies for a fee. But there's no reason why their law partner can't. Nor is there any bar to their partner giving them a percentage of the firm's profits.

Jack Anderson, the Washington columnist, recently made spot checks into

the clientele of 60 or so congressional firms. With few exceptions they represent banks, real-estate firms and other companies that have a vital interest in legislation. Sen. Everett Dirksen (R.-Ill.) persuaded the late President Kennedy to appoint his friend Harold Woodward to the Federal Power Commission, which makes billion-dollar decisions affecting the oil and gas industry. Subsequently, Dirksen wheedled President Johnson into naming still another friend, Carl Bagge, to the same body . . . in Peoria, Ill., Dirksen's law firm represents Panhandle Eastern Pipe Line, one of the giant gas wholesalers, whose well-being depends upon the decisions of the Federal Power Commission.

Even so elementary a concession to ordinary ethics—preventing lawyer-legislators from practicing before state agencies—is almost impossible to secure in most states.

The appearance of lawyer-legislators as "paid counsel before boards and bureaus whose budgets and salary schedules they control and, in the case of senators, before officials whose appointments they confirm, presents a flagrant conflict of interest" editorialized the *Newark Evening News* in April, 1967. "If legislative ethics is the sole responsibility of the Legislature, it is a responsibility that has been ignored." The *Evening News* suggested that "real improvement in the Legislature's ethical standards . . . can come only through judicial intervention."

This, in turn, raised some other interesting questions for the Madison (Wisconsin) *Capital-Times* about lawyer-legislators:

. . . the resolution to amend the State constitution to allow the salary of judges to be raised during the terms for which they are elected is being pushed primarily by lawyers.

If it doesn't occur to these lawyers, who are enthusiastically and unanimously for this proposal, it does occur to many non-lawyers, that judges are important to the welfare of lawyers. How many of these lawyers support this measure because they realize they will be making appearances before judges whose welfare is affected by the proposal voted on? . . . there is a conflict here that works well for the lawyers and the judges. But it doesn't work well for the taxpayers.

California had a similar problem recently. A San Francisco *Chronicle* columnist wrote of "the exceedingly generous pension system which judges have lobbied throught the Legislature, where there are so many lawyers who hope someday to be judges."

In theory, lawyers seem particularly logical choices as our legislators. After all, the prime function of legislatures would seem to be the consideration and writing of laws. But even this is an illusion. Legislators suggest what they want, but the proposed laws are written by professional, salaried staff members of Congress and by special employes of various state legislatures.

Not long ago two political scientists—Heinz Eulau of Stanford and John D. Sprague of Washington University—interviewed several nonlawyer legislators in four states about their lawyer-colleagues. Some of the assessments they got included:

• There are too many lawyers. They represent clients, try to win lawsuits in the legislature that they can't win in the courts.

- Lawyers draw up laws so nobody including themselves can understand them. It makes business for them.
- Lawyers are lousy legislators. . . . They can't look at it as laymen can . . . he's not good enough to represent all the people. The average layman is better equipped to be a legislator.
- We shouldn't ever send an attorney to the legislature. They get so many laws to suit their own individual jobs that a wayfarin' man can't understand.

The latter comment was once given in a different form by the late Governor Herbert Lehman of New York, a nonlawyer. He complained of "the conspiracy of lawyer-legislators to perpetrate for their profession the obstructions to justice by which it prospers."

In many states lawyer-legislators can and do literally obstruct, or at least impede, justice through a curious device known as "legislative continuance." If the criminal hires an attorney who is a member of the state legislature, he can automatically secure a delay until the end of the legislative session, which can be several months away. "The higher echelon of hoodlums frequently hire members of the state legislature to represent them," Curtis T. Thatcher, managing director of the Kansas City Crime Commission, told me.

In Texas, the *Dallas News* described the local operation of the "legislative continuance":

Some attorneys in the Legislature have received fees in postponed cases and never actually participated in the preparation or trial. They served only to delay the litigation. . . . Informed sources say that the fees ran as high as $2,500 for attorneys in well-publicized cases of automatic postponement. A more common legislator retainer is said to be $500.

A move to end the device in Texas was proposed by a legislator-lawyer, Willis J. Whatley of Houston, who admitted that he had used it for clients occasionally. "I think the law is being abused now, and always has been. It makes the Legislature look bad, and it makes attorneys look bad."

The bill didn't pass.

Nor is there much chance that any other bills trying to outlaw some of the practices mentioned in this book would have much better luck.

There is a way of *bypassing* the legislature. In thirteen states the people can institute a constitutional amendment. Generally, in order to get the amendment on the regular ballot, 5 to 15 percent of the voters have to sign the initiative petition. Then if a majority of the voters support the amendment, it would become law. This was done by the Arizona realtors in their classic battle with the lawyers in 1962. It was an expensive battle calling for the volunteer services of thousands, but it can also be done on a shoestring by a comparatively small number of enthusiasts.

In 1960 the state of Washington had to go through a heated initiative battle to beat their lawyers on joint tenancy. For many families, joint tenancy is a way of beating the high cost of probate and the paralyzing delays in passing on property. Stocks, mutual funds, savings accounts and homes are some of the properties most commonly held in joint tenancy by husband and wife, or parent and child. Jointly held property goes to the survivor with a minimum of fuss and cost, and almost always reduces the size of the estate that passes through probate. Since legal costs in probate are fixed on percentages of the total estate, the more that passes by joint tenancy the more the probated estate is reduced, and, accordingly, the smaller the lawyer's fee.

Joint tenancy's popularity is a comparatively recent phenomenon. GI's in World War II commonly put their war bond purchases in joint ownership with their brides or parents. Yet, a century ago, joint tenancy was quite rare because there were many state laws against it, and women had limited property rights. Today the only state that bars joint tenancy is Louisiana.

In 1960 joint tenancy was permitted in Washington State for husband and wife but not for father and son, mother and daughter. The battle began after State Senator Albert L. Rasmussen, a Tacoma labor leader, gave up trying to get a joint tenancy bill through the legislature. "The lawyers," he told me, "wouldn't let it get out of committee. I knew unnecessary probate was costing

Washington millions of dollars each year in legal and court costs, a great hardship on those least able to afford it."

Together with some like-minded union leaders and a few public-spirited lawyers, a committee was formed to get joint tenancy into law by way of an initiative measure. Spending only $1,300 for petitions and pamphlets, the group succeeded in getting 187,000 signatures so that the voters would have a chance to decide whether or not joint tenancy should be permitted. Supporters of Initiative 208 included the State Federation of Business and Professional Women's Clubs, the State Grange, and the State Labor Council.

Opposed was the State Bar Association, which campaigned actively. But a few lawyers spoke out for the measure, including Thomas E. Grady, former State Supreme Court Justice. "Lawyers will put forth a lot of 'scare heads' supposedly for the protection of the public," he said, "but the real reason for opposition with many will be the loss of probate business." Another attorney, Willard Hedlund of Tacoma, was even blunter when asked to help the Bar Association fight the initiative measure:

If our Bar had exercised more leadership in the field of streamlining and cheapening probate procedures . . . we would not be faced with Number 208. . . . For us now to fight this actively will tend to create an image of a fat, vested interest trying to preserve our "take" and further damage our poor public relations.

Initiative measure 208 passed overwhelmingly. It was done for remarkably little cost, but still, it did have powerful supporters. It is not the kind of thing that can be done every year because a lawyer-dominated legislature refuses to act on some reform. (An earlier Washington State attempt at an initiative measure that would have limited legal probate fees to one percent of the estate didn't get sufficient signatures.)

If reform legislation is difficult to achieve and initiative measures are even tougher to get through, what's left?

There is always the possibility of self-reform—in spite of Henry Adams' dismal conclusion that "no priesthood ever reforms itself." As I wrote earlier, the ABA's committee on discipline is now evaluating the state of bar discipline throughout the country. Admittedly its chairman, former Supreme Court Justice Tom Clark, is having difficulty in even getting basic statistics from most local bar associations, so we should not be too hopeful of the effectiveness of the committee's ultimate recommendations—let alone the chances of their adoption by local bars. In addition, another ABA committee is preparing a modern version of the Canons of Ethics U.S. lawyers have supposedly been guided by since 1908.

The proposed new code, which will be introduced to the ABA meeting in 1969, will have a new set of disciplinary rules which, says the committee chairman Edward L. Wright of Arkansas, "if widely adopted, should result in increased observance of professional responsibility. . . . They will contain no toothless platitudes."

With legislative reform almost impossible and effective self-reform unlikely, there is a temptation to fall back on the cynical deliverance once suggested by Dr. Samuel Johnson: "Combinations of wickedness would overwhelm the world did not those who have long practiced perfidy grow faithless to each other."

This isn't much consolation, for most lawyers are not evil men and, even worse, few of them think that what they do in the name of the organized bar is wrong. On the contrary, most lawyers think they and their bar associations are unduly abused and vilified by the press and public.

• • •

Still, much can be done even without the assistance of lawyer-dominated legislatures. My suggestions depend on the cooperation of the press, the governors and the highest-ranking state and federal judges. More specifically:

What can the press do?

In traveling around the country I was most impressed with the ingenuity and digging efforts of some key investigative reporters who have paid attention to local shortcomings in the courts, the bar and the law. In various parts of this book I've already mentioned the admirable work of reporters such as Leonard Downie, Jr., of the *Washington Post;* Edward S. Kerstein of the *Milwaukee Journal;* Paul Hoffman and Marvin Smilon of the *New York Post;* George Ringwald of the *Riverside* (California) *Daily Enterprise;* Paul Dean of the *Arizona Republic;* and Howard James of the *Christian Science Monitor.* There are a number of others, too; but generally they labor alone in their own backyards, and there is little or no contact among them. Yet, the conditions they expose locally are often duplicated elsewhere; are, indeed, often national in scope.

The kind of digging they do is arduous, takes time and almost always brings down the wrath of influential sections of the local bar. Not all editors are ready to take on such opponents. I think some foundation could make quite a useful contribution by funding a small organization that would serve to give a sense of national importance to the work of these reporters. I think these men could be made even more effective if they could meet once a year, informally, to exchange experiences and discuss series they have done or would like to do in their areas. They would find often that what they think of as purely local conditions are far more widespread, far more entrenched. A monthly newsletter for these investigative reporters would help them keep in touch and exchange experiences. Inevitably, such a growing organization would encourage more editors to let reporters develop into investigative specialists.

Newspapers could also put more pressure on bar associations to make them publicize disciplinary actions taken against lawyers. Some might even follow the lead of Adam A. Smyser, editor of the Honolulu *Star Bulletin,* who recently told an ABA disciplinary panel that "not only do you lawyers need more publicity in this area, but I think it might be a good idea if you allowed us laymen to participate in the proceedings of bar disciplinary groups."

What can the governors do?

Some bold governor could institute this innovation: let him appoint a small group whose sole function would be to make semiannual surveys of the workings of the civil law and the courts on the public. The small staff might consist of one of the new breed of sociologist-lawyers, and an experienced newspaper-man-investigator. Every six months they might issue a cogent, readable report of the particular abuses they found in some specific area: probate courts, incompetency hearings, the workings of sheriff's sales for debt, garnishee abuses, the inadequacies of bar discipline. The possibilities are many. Properly publicized in each of the state's counties, such semiannual or annual surveys could not only highlight the evils of some malfunctioning part of the law or the courts, but could easily become the basis of gubernatorial recommendations to the legislature. Once the situation had been effectively publicized *on a statewide basis,* there would be considerable pressure on the legislators—both lawyer and non-lawyer—to pay heed.

I asked an old friend, a high-ranking Eastern judge who has run a large judicial system, about the possible political pitfalls of this suggestion. He didn't think there were any. "The governor could only gain votes by showing he was on the right side of these obscure but important areas affecting the middle class. Sure, he might get some lawyers and bar associations mad at him, but I suspect that would only give him more public support than he'd lose. Some smart governor ought to try it for a few years."

What can high-ranking state and federal judges do?

Increasingly, our state court systems are getting administrators who help the courts run more smoothly. In the process the state's chief justice or the chief appellate judge is getting considerable powers over all the judges in the state. What I propose is fairly revolutionary, so perhaps the initiative had best come from the federal court system, which exercises an increasing degree of supervision over all federal judges.

For openers, perhaps a requirement that all federal district judges who appoint lawyers as trustees in commercial bankruptcy cases be required to make public each year a full list of all the trustees they appointed—and how much the trustee received as a fee from the bankrupted business. Bankruptcy trusteeships for lawyers are a notorious source of patronage. In New York City in one recent year, Federal Judge Matthew T. Abruzzo appointed his former law partner, Joseph F. Ruggieri, to a series of corporate bankruptcy and receivership cases that were good for more than $100,000 in fees. Once federal judges were required to make these lists public, the way would be prepared for state judicial systems to do the same.

The patronage fees lawyers now get out of probate and surrogate courts on estates, guardianships and incompetencies obviously call for public listing. If every Supreme Court justice in New York were required to list all his patronage appointees—and *how much* they earned totally—the annual list would become vilely embarrassing in a few years. The public has no idea of how much a few special lawyer-friends get from each judge in patronage. The concentration of favors—and the size of them—might well lead at least to legislative correction to cut down the size of the take.

Once court patronage appointees were publicized by *name and amount every year,* the obvious next step would be the legislators themselves. Every lawyer-legislator required to list all his legal income for the year—and the clients who paid him—would either become terribly embarrassed or a lot more circumspect. Ideally, it might even, in time, lead to the gradual elimination of the practice of legislative persuasion by means of legal fees to the lawmaker's law firm, the most accepted form of upper-level bribery in our society.

Whenever this is proposed there is a cry from the full-throated legislative warblers, such as Senator Dirksen of Illinois, that this would serve to make legislators "second-class citizens," since the rest of us don't have to make such disclosures. But then, of course, the rest of us don't have the opportunities that present themselves to many lawyer-legislators.

Senator Dirksen's hypocritical outcries were properly answered by former Senator Paul Douglas, an ex-economics professor. He said disclosure of a legislator's stockholdings, law contracts or other interests "is hardly a sanction and certainly not a penalty. Yet it would sharpen men's own judgment of right and wrong, since they would be less likely to do wrong things if they knew these acts would be challenged."

In a sense Paul Douglas' words apply to much that has appeared in this book. Essentially, what is called for on the abuses by lawyers and bar associations is the certain knowledge that their present and future acts *will be challenged*. At present there is little danger. The suggestions I've presented, if used, could help make the public more aware of the dangers, more ready to help the right challengers—the press, the governors, or the chief justices.

Toward the end of their successful campaign against the lawyers of Arizona, the realtors used the stark, brutally vague slogan: *Stop the Lawyers*. It seemed to strike a responsive chord.

Possibly we have to do just that in order to bring some balance to the one-sided relationship between the American middle class and our lawyers. If a balance is achieved with the help of wiser and fairer lawyers the needed changes can be taken on gradually and in comparative calm. But if the reforms come without the bar's help, the lawyers will undergo a loss of public confidence that will put them back even beyond Shakespeare's older outcry: "The first thing we do, let's kill all the lawyers."

We won't, of course. We need our lawyers and, in an increasingly complex world, will need them more and more. But we need them on fairer terms.

NOTES ON SOURCES

INTRODUCTION

p. 10: Footnote: Motion filed by the NAACP in the United Mine Workers case against the Illinois State Bar, October Term, 1967, No. 33, p. 20.

p. 11: The Choate speech is given in full in Charles Hurd's *A Treasury of Great American Speeches,* pp. 133–135.

p. 13: Justice Douglas' conversation: in *National Geographic Magazine,* July, 1958: "West from the Khyber Pass," pp. 1–44.

CHAPTER 1

p. 24: Sherpick speech: in *Bar Bulletin,* New York County Lawyers Association, May–June, 1962, pp. 9–10, and in *The New York Times,* May 18, 1962.

p. 26: ABA Client Security Fund Report, August, 1967, p. 3.

p. 30: Epton quotations: from a letter sent me.

pp. 31–33: Quotations from the Fund's opponents: in "Minority Report of the State Bar Committee of 1959–60 on Client Security Funds," signed by Galen Knight, James Petrini, John A. Young and William Zeff.

p. 35: Voorhees describes these cases in *Journal of the American Judicature Society,* February, 1959, p. 155.

pp. 40–42: Most of the Houlihan material is from talks with D. Lowell Jensen and from the 29-page Probation Officer's Report on John C.

Houlihan, Superior Court, State of California, County of Alameda (ACSO-66-4597).

p. 42: San Francisco *Call* editorial, October 12, 1966.

p. 44: Johnson and Hopson, *Lawyers and Their Work* (1967), pp. 505–508.

p. 44: The Eicholz case is described in detail in the *New York Law Journal,* May 1, 1967, p. 17.

p. 49: Abel: in *Florida Bar Journal,* September, 1964, p. 466.

CHAPTER 2

pp. 52–53: Most of the statistics in this chapter are taken from the report of the California Assembly Interim Committee on Judiciary Relating to Domestic Relations, January 11, 1965, and from the U.S. Statistical Abstract for 1967.

p. 56: O'Gorman, *Lawyers and Matrimonial Cases* (1963), p. 71.

p. 56: Carlin, *Lawyers on Their Own* (1962), p. 98.

pp. 56–57: Report of the California State Assembly Committee on Domestic Relations, p. 83.

p. 58: The recommended San Francisco fees are reported in the *Chronicle,* December 8, 1966: "How Much a Lawyer Costs."

p. 59: Judicare statistics: from the *Wisconsin Bar Bulletin,* June, 1967, pp. 11–15.

p. 60: Philadelphia divorce quotation: in Circular No. 1 of Community Legal Services (undated), p. 4.

p. 60: The Bar Association's luncheon gambit is detailed in the *Philadelphia Bulletin,* June 24, 1962, p. 18.

p. 61: Blackburn quotation: in *Parade,* June 4, 1967, pp. 34–35.

p. 62: Quotation on adversary procedure: in the California Assembly report, p. 67.

p. 63: Ploscowe, *The Truth About Divorce,* p. 187.

p. 64: Quotation on unethical practices in divorce: in the California Assembly report, p. 166.

CHAPTER 3

p. 69: Meehan: in 28 *Brooklyn Law Review* 99 (1961).

p. 72: Buckley vs. Gray, 110 Cal. 339, 42 P. 900, 31 LRA 862, 52 Am. St. Rep. 88 (1895).

p. 73: Lucas vs. Hamm, 15 Cal. Rprtr. 821 (September 5, 1961).

p. 74: Lahy: in 2 *University of Richmond Law Notes* 203 (1966).

p. 74: Goldberg vs. Bosworth, 215 NYS (2d) 849 (1961).

p. 75: Rothstein quotations: from a talk he gave on March 2, 1967, at a forum on lawyers' malpractice conducted by the Association of Trial Lawyers of the City of New York.

p. 77: Dorf vs. Relles, 355 F2d 488 (1966).

p. 78: Sitton vs. Clements, 257 FSupp 63 (1966).

CHAPTER 4

pp. 83–84: The Jackson case aftermath is described in the *Arizona Republic,* September 22, 1967: "Jackson Footnote," p. 21.

p. 92: Time letters: September 22, 1967, p. 12.

CHAPTER 6

p. 110: Major Hopkins item: in the Boston *Post,* October 13, 1964.

pp. 111–112: Rutledge: in *University of Cincinnati Law Review,* Vol. 15, 1941, pp. 237–238.

p. 112: Otterbourg: in "Study of Unauthorized Practice of Law," September, 1951, supplement to *Unauthorized Practice News,* pp. 2–5.

p. 112: Johnstone: in *Lawyers and Their Work,* p. 194.

p. 113: Riggs: in *Arizona Government Studies,* No. 2: "Vox Populi: The Battle of 103," p. 15.

p. 114: Tucson *Daily Citizen,* November 15, 1961, p. 2.

pp. 114–115: These newspaper reactions are reprinted in an Arizona Association of Realtors booklet, "The Story of Arizona's Proposition 103."

pp. 117–118: Arizona News, July 6, 1962.

p. 119: Arizona News, September 21, 1962.

p. 120: Southern California Law Review, Vol. 37, No. 1, 1964, p. 1.

pp. 121–122: The Creekmore case is in 367 SW Rep 2d 419 (1963).

p. 124: The Minnesota case is 207 Minn 642, 646; 290 NW 795–797.

p. 124: Stirling: in *California State Bar Journal,* November–December, 1966, p. 870.

CHAPTER 7

pp. 126–130: Gatner material: from *Law and Contemporary Problems,* October, 1936: "The Liability Claim Racket."

p. 130: Chicago's American, June 16, 1966.

p. 133: Insurance Management Review, July 3, 1965, p. 25.

pp. 133–134: The fee study appears in *Insurance Counsel Journal,* April, 1966: "A Study of Contingent Fees in the Prosecution of Personal Injury Claims."

p. 134: LaBrum: in *Federation of Insurance Counsel Quarterly,* Summer, 1965 (Vol. 15, No. 4), p. 34. The Rosenberg quotation is on p. 30.

p. 135: Ryan: in *Insurance Counsel Journal,* October, 1958, p. 500.

pp. 135–137: The New Jersey Bar meeting is reported in the *Newark Evening News,* December 1 and 2, 1967.

p. 137: Dukakis: from a talk he gave on October 3, 1967, at the Auto Claims National Conference at the University of Illinois College of Law.

p. 139: The Social Security material is from Roy L. Swift, information officer of the U.S. Department of Health, Education and Welfare, and from a May 23, 1965, *Minneapolis Tribune* report, "Many Applicants Called Lawyers' Victims."

pp. 140–141: *Ohio State Law Journal,* Vol. 20, pp. 329–345.

p. 144: The Strickland case is reported in the *Miami News* and the *Miami Herald,* February 21, 1961.

p. 148: Phelan talk: in *Federation of Insurance Counsel Quarterly,* Summer, 1965, p. 58.

pp. *150–151: The New York Times,* March 23, 1960.

p. 151: Richardson: quoted in a booklet, "Contingent Fees," by Professor William F. Willier, Boston College Law School, p. 59.

pp. 151–153: The case Judge Weber ruled on is Civil Action No. 65–669, U.S. Dist. Ct. for the Western District of Pennsylvania: Ora Williams vs. Baltimore & Ohio Railroad vs. Erie-Lackawanna Railroad.

p. 153: The Gary, Indiana, case is reported in *The* (Gary) *Post-Tribune,* April 25, 1956: "$25,000 Won, Gets $4,166." The Miami case is in the *Miami News,* November 7, 1958: "Limit on Attorneys' Fees Is Sought in Court Action."

p. 153: The Los Angeles case is reported in the *Los Angeles Herald-Examiner,* November 6, 1963: "Contingency Fees—How Lawyers Profit from Accidents."

p. 156: Radin: in 28 *California Law Review* 587 (1939).

CHAPTER 8

pp. 157–158: Hallinan interview: in the San Francisco *Chronicle,* November 1, 1965.

p. 158: Article on Soviet Lawyers: in *Current Digest of the Soviet Press,* May, 1961, pp. 8–9.

p. 158: Lundberg: in *Harper's,* December, 1938, p. 11.

p. 159: Goldsmith, *The Citizen of the World* (1762).

p. 165: Judge Austin: quoted in *Chicago's American,* June 16, 1966: "Lawyers Tripped Up in Fake Injury Claims."

pp. 165–166: Gilb, *Hidden Hierarchies: The Professions and Government* (1966), p. 242.

CHAPTER 9

p. 194: Johnstone and Hopson, *Lawyers and Their Work,* pp. 62–63.

p. 195: Gleick: letter in *Journal of the American Bar Association,* June, 1962, pp. 516–517.

pp. 196–197: Habermann talk: in